The Reading Intervention Toolkit

Author

Laura Robb, M.S.Ed.

Foreword

Mary Howard, Ed.D.

SHELL EDUCATION

Publishing Credits

Corinne Burton, M.A.Ed., *Publisher*;
Kimberly Stockton, M.S.Ed., *Vice President of Education*;
Conni Medina, M.A.Ed., *Managing Editor*;
Sara Johnson M.S.Ed., *Content Director*;
Kristy Stark, M.A.Ed., *Editor*;
Kyleena Harper, *Assistant Editor*;
Lee Aucoin, *Multimedia Designer*;
Grace Alba Le, *Production Artist*

Shell Education

5301 Oceanus Drive
Huntington Beach, CA 92649-1030
http://www.tcmpub.com/teachers

ISBN 978-1-4258-1513-4

© 2016 Shell Educational Publishing, Inc.

Table of Contents

Foreword

I still vividly recall my elation the first time I heard about Response to Intervention (RTI). I was filled with a sense of hope that an RTI design could embrace every learner. Sadly my hope soon dissipated as I saw RTI unfold in the trenches and I was reminded that *what* we do is inconsequential without a clear vision for *why* we do it and *how* to do it in the most effective ways. Questionable interpretations and implementations spurred by books, websites, seminars, and a virtual flood of programs made me fear that the promise I saw in RTI had become lost in the marketplace shuffle. As my hope had faded from view, I wrote a book titled *RTI from All Sides: What Every Teacher Needs to Know* in response to time-wasting non-solutions far removed from the students they purported to support.

Thankfully, Laura Robb's powerhouse book has reawakened my sense of hope. *The Reading Intervention Toolkit* brings the RTI promise back into focus as quick fixes and silver bullets are transformed into the authentic differentiated practices and targeted supports worthy of the lives RTI is intended to enrich. Each strategy is based on high-engagement instruction and interventions grounded in reading and writing that is repositioned in the hands of knowledgeable teachers. No fluff. No stuff. No silliness. No spreadsheets that reduce students to numbers. No one-size-fits-all recommendations that suck the very heart and soul from RTI. Laura redefines RTI as instructional excellence with students at the center of our efforts through flexible practices that put teachers face-to-face with children.

Why is *The Reading Intervention Toolkit* needed now more than ever? Based on a study exploring the negative impact of RTI, the research suggests that this is the result of three possible missteps: 1) incorrect selection of students, 2) mismatch between student needs and the interventions provided, and 3) misalignment between core instruction (Tier 1) and the interventions offered. The study illustrates that well meaning but misinformed applications of RTI may have led to its demise. In short, RTI did not fail us; we failed RTI (Sparks 2015).

Two things set Laura's book apart so that we can reclaim the RTI potential. First, she reminds us that nothing we do in the name of RTI will be adequate without active engagement in reading and writing with interventions to address specific needs of students based on daily assessment in the heat of learning moments. This lofty but achievable goal is reiterated by Richard Allington (2006). He states:

> "Struggling readers need larger amounts of more expert, more personalized, and more intensive reading instruction. In the end, the quality of that instruction is critical, and high-quality instruction for struggling readers cannot simply be boxed up and shipped to a site" (20).

Laura broadens our canvas beyond isolated skill and drill that has plagued RTI. Strategy ideas focus on differentiated practices at increasing levels of intensity that can be embedded across the school day, regardless of time constraints. Flexible support options in a context of daily learning range from five to 40 minutes, affording varied layers of instructional intensity from "making the rounds" to teach, reteach, reinforce, and assess in on-the-spot learning to the increasingly intensive interventions designed to accelerate progress in small-group and side-by-side settings. Read-aloud, shared, guided, and independent practice form an overarching support umbrella of powerful, intentional, open-ended options.

Foreword *(cont.)*

The second thing that sets Laura's book apart from others is illustrated in Pernille Ripp's cautionary advice: "If we focus more on the intervention than the child that needs it, we have lost our way" (1). Laura repositions our efforts on students in a myriad of ways. *The Reading Intervention Toolkit* is a love note to teachers from her first words in the introduction, "Classroom Teachers Can Reach and Support All Readers." These eight words represent the spirit of this book and Laura's deep belief that the foundation of RTI resides in maintaining Tier 1 teachers as decision makers. Each suggestion revolves around high-interest texts within meaningful literacy events through teacher-supported oral reading, one-to-one conferring, small-group instruction, peer supported partner work, and independent application. She acknowledges the role of motivation with choice, interest, and engaging talk, demonstrating her commitment to increasing the volume of reading and writing, rather than dancing around it.

Throughout this book, Laura shows us how to accomplish a renewed RTI purpose. She demonstrates that immersion in active and joyful literacy is the work of RTI, citing three key oft-missing intervention ingredients: instruction using engaging books, discussion of self-selected books for independent reading, and listening to teachers read aloud. She offers classroom snapshots to give strategy ideas a face with teacher tips and suggestions to continue the conversation at the end of each chapter. Page after page, Laura whispers words of wisdom in our ears to help us elevate conferences and initiate interventions based on the needs of students. Laura's words are a testament to expert, personalized, and intensive reading instruction focused squarely on the child that needs it. In Laura's own words:

"The goal of all intervention in grades 4 to 8 is to help students comprehend, interpret, and analyze reading materials, as well as improve their motivation to read, write, think, and discuss. Targeted interventions are focused lessons designed for students who need extra support in reading and writing" (15).

The time has come to demonstrate a sense of urgency that will change the direction of RTI. For too long, tiers have been relegated to real estate over shared responsibility. For too long, targeted support has been removed from the first line of defense where moment-to-moment daily support can be offered. For too long, interventions have been trivialized with the "stuff" far removed from our vision of best practices. For too long, we have ignored the serious, thoughtful, informed, responsible state of the "art of teaching" (Zemelman, Daniels and Hyde) that comes from meaningful, authentic, purposeful, and intentional teaching in the hands of teachers with a deep knowledge of literacy instruction. For too long, we have viewed RTI as the end goal when the success of students is our first priority.

As I have savored each word in Laura's masterful book, I imagine a bridge from where we have been to where we need to be. *The Reading Intervention Toolkit* reignites the promise that has always resided within RTI—a promise that can only become a reality when we keep students at the center with practices that allow them to read, write, and talk their way across the day. This is the RTI that I envisioned—Responsive Thoughtful Instruction our students deserve. There is no doubt in my mind that this book can change the RTI success trajectory.

And my hope is at last renewed.

—Mary Howard, Ed.D.
author and literacy consultant
RTI from All Sides: What Every Teacher Needs to Know

Dedication

With love for my son, Evan, an outstanding principal.

My thanks to the students I have worked with because they made this book possible. Sincere thanks to the third and fourth grade teachers at Quarles Elementary in Winchester, Virginia, and to Katy Schain and Katherine McHale, who let me work with English language learners at Daniel Morgan Middle School in Winchester, Virginia.

My deep appreciation and thanks go to my editors, Sara Johnson and Kristy Stark, whose great organizational vision shaped this into a book that teachers can easily navigate and use.

Introduction

Classroom Teachers Can Reach and Support All Readers

Recently, I taught reading to a group of seventh-grade English language learners who were reading at a third-grade instructional level. During 10 weeks, the students and I met daily for 50 minutes. I divided the time into 25 minutes for a teacher read-aloud and guided reading, and 25 minutes of independent reading. The students had never read an entire book. Instead, they had only read short texts and answered multiple-choice or fill-in-the-blank questions for each one. They were not purposefully talking or writing about what they read, nor was their ESOL teacher (English for Speakers of Other Languages) reading outstanding fiction and nonfiction to them. So, I changed the focus of their instruction.

For guided reading, I gave students three nonfiction books to choose from, and they agreed on a biography about Roberto Clemente. For independent reading, I started with graphic novels, brought about 20 to class, and had students choose. Gradually, independent reading choices included biography and informational texts. Over the 10 weeks, the students and I read and discussed two nonfiction books; students also wrote short responses in their readers' notebooks. Moreover, all but two of the students read from 10 to 15 books during independent reading, and that's when I had short five-minute scaffolding conferences with individuals or pairs.

Many of the schools I work in around the country have adopted reading intervention programs similar to the one those seventh-grade students used—programs that focus on skills. Why? Skills such as phonemic awareness, phonics, decoding, and fluency are easy to assess and enable teachers to collect measurable data. However, there are three key ingredients that are often missing in these intervention curricula: instruction using engaging books, discussion of self-selected books for independent reading, and listening to teachers read aloud every day. Educators such as Stephanie Harvey, Ann Goudvis, Harvey Daniels, Linda Dorn, Ellin Keene, and Regie Routman agree that students who listen to teachers read aloud and have meaningful conversations about these texts also build their listening capacity, background knowledge, and understanding of literary language. Actually, according to Richard Allington, Mary Howard, Linda Hoyt, Donalyn Miller, and Steve Krashen, students who practice skills daily without reading self-selected whole books don't improve their reading skill. Moreover, because students don't read books, they slide backwards, and this backward slide can result in low scores on state tests, frustrating teachers and administrators.

I wrote this book for fourth to eighth grade teachers to address the instructional challenges that they face. Educators agree that high quality core reading curricula can support about 80 percent of the student population, enabling them to show solid, annual growth. But, to move all students from a frustration zone into their learning zone and ultimately to independent reading learning, lessons need to respond to the needs of every student.

To assist teachers with strategies in this area, **Chapters 1 and 2** discuss responsive teaching and differentiation. The heart and soul of this book is introduced in Chapter 2 where I discuss, in great depth, four kinds of interventions that can support students' reading. The first three can be readily integrated in the core reading curriculum. The last type of intervention is meant for students reading significantly below grade level and often needs to be conducted in addition to regular classroom instruction.

➤ 2- to 3-Minute Interventions: These occur while you "make the rounds" and continually circulate among students while they read and write about reading during guided practice and independent work. By providing short, on-the-spot scaffolds, you can support students and prevent small confusions from becoming large obstacles to learning. During this time, you'll also identify students who need more time to practice a strategy in their learning zone. To help them, you can schedule one or a series of 5-minute interventions while other students work on their own.

➤ 5-Minute Interventions: Sometimes, as a result of what you learned during a 2- to 3-minute intervention, you need to schedule an investigatory 5-minute intervention to get a better handle on a student's needs. Then, with the student, you can estimate how many times you'll meet during a week. Other times, a 5-minute intervention might be all a student needs to correct a misconception or provide the necessary scaffold to get back to speed with grade-level expectations.

➤ 10- to 15-Minute Interventions: There will be times when one student or a small group of students with a common problem will need more than five minutes of instruction that you scaffold. In the book, I suggest that you schedule longer interventions to help students make the necessary gains.

➤ 30- to 40-Minute Interventions: This type of intervention is for students who are reading far below grade level and would benefit from 30 to 40 minutes of additional instruction at least three to five times a week. Usually, instruction for these students is scheduled outside of core reading classes. Frequently, a reading specialist or special education teacher teaches these classes. However, this book points out that extra classes should be a combination of teacher-led instruction, student practice, and independent reading of self-selected books. In the book, I offer schedules with suggestions that enable you to work with students who struggle because not all schools have the resources for scheduling separate classes. The intervention examples in this book feature different grade levels and include lessons that address the four kinds of interventions.

Chapter 3 shares intervention tools and strategies for teachers and students. It is important to have a variety of methods to use to support your students during intervention. Models for think-alouds, reteaching lessons, one-on-one conferences, and word study are included as well as supporting forms and checklists to help keep you organized. Additionally resources for students are included to help them track their own reading progress, self-monitor their comprehension, and set goals.

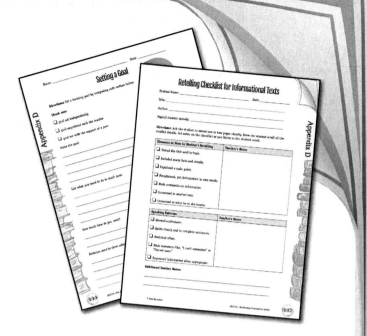

Chapters 4 and 5 use focus standards to discuss key reading strategies, such as inferring, finding main ideas and themes, and using context to determine a word's meaning. The texts for interventions in both chapters are available for you to use with your students. In both chapters, lessons for each type of intervention offer reasons for why I selected a specific intervention, my planning process, a list of several scaffolding possibilities, and often a classroom snapshot that shows the intervention in action. To help you respond to students who need more than the interventions you've offered, both chapters end with five reteaching lessons and the texts that go with each one.

Chapter 6 examines the importance of getting students to write about their reading. When students write about what they read, it provides a window into their understanding. Can they supply text evidence to support their ideas? Do they understand literary elements or the text structure? A variety of student resources are provided to support students' writing, such as graphic organizers and rubrics. Additionally, this chapter includes key interventions to use with students who struggle in writing about their reading.

Finally, **Chapter 7** concludes the book with key reminders and big ideas about reading intervention and the instructional practices that make the most impact with struggling readers.

In the **Appendices**, you'll also find conference forms for documenting interventions and student resource sheets that provide students with tips for reading literary and informational text deeply as well as guidelines for using context clues to figure out the meanings of unfamiliar words. I've shared the research on writing to improve reading and provided suggestions for you to try. Writing about reading is crucial as it's your ticket for getting into a student's head to observe his or her reading and thinking processes.

The **Digital Resource CD** is full of student and teacher resources, including templates, student reference pages, and engaging texts to use with the intervention lessons.

Each chapter closes with prompts and/or questions for discussing the information with a colleague or with a small group of teachers on your grade-level team or in your department. It's my hope that conversation will deepen your knowledge of the chapter's information and raise your comfort level with the information so that you will be able to try some lessons with your students or use the tools provided to create your own intervention lessons. In addition, I invite you to bring to a second meeting these intervention artifacts: students' assessments, goal-setting write-ups, and/or an intervention lesson that worked and one that didn't work so you can share ideas and offer feedback to support one another and your students.

As you read, reflect on, and discuss this book with colleagues, you will deepen your knowledge of the intervention tools and suggestions that can help you improve the reading of every student in your classroom.

—Laura Robb

Chapter 1

Setting the Stage for Reading Interventions

Responsive Teaching

Responsive teachers know what each student in a class does well and when a student requires extra support because they watch, listen, and have short but meaningful conversations with their students. Teachers who respond to students' needs intervene with scaffolds and guided practice to help struggling students with tasks, and then they gradually move those students to independence.

Russian psychologist Lev Vygotsky, who identified the zone of proximal development, also called students' learning zone, recognized the need for responsive teaching and scaffolding to help students become independent (1978). There are students who can master a strategy that they can't complete independently when they have the support of an adult or peer expert. For example, Mara, a fifth-grader, struggles with using dialogue to infer personality traits. Her teacher, Ms. Keller, watches and recognizes that Mara can master this type of inferring with teacher modeling and time to practice. Ms. Keller schedules a series of five-minute conferences, one each day, while other students read or write independently. During two of the scaffolding conferences, Ms. Keller thinks aloud and discusses the inferring process with Mara and watches Mara practice. At the third meeting, Ms. Keller decides to turn over part of the responsibility for inferring personality traits to Mara. By the fifth conference, Ms. Keller has moved Mara to independence with this reading skill. To ensure that Mara maintains independence, Ms. Keller partners Mara with Tanisha, and the pair work together until the teacher, by observing the pair's discussions and by reading Mara's notebook entries, feels Mara will be successful on her own.

Responsive teaching practices also consider students' culture. This intervention illustrates that a responsive teacher is a careful observer of students, watching them work when students practice independently, with a partner, or in a small group. The goal always is to meet individual needs and help each child improve his or her reading (Allington 2011; Owocki and Goodman 2002; Robb 2010; Routman 2014).

Research indicates that when teachers understand students' cultures, students become more engaged and motivated in their learning, and they progress and build trusting relationships with their teachers (Gay 2000; Hawkins 2012; Zubrzycki 2012).

According to Douglas Magrath (2016), culture is an integral part of language and language patterns; the meanings of words that name the same item and concepts in different languages have connotations that differ. For example, Magrath explains that American culture often considers time a concept that is future-oriented, while Hispanic culture often considers time as the present moment.

Culturally responsive teachers communicate frequently with students to understand their needs and frustrations and also to encourage students to communicate with each other (Delpit 2006; Gay 2000). Continual communication builds trust and shows students that their culture and individual learning needs are valued.

When teachers respond to the cultural and literacy diversity of their students, they meet students where they are and adjust tasks so students can succeed. For example, a district requires seventh-grade students to read a grade-level anthology, but there are several students reading three to four years below grade level. Here are some things teachers can do:

➢ Use the anthology selection to think aloud and model applying a skill or strategy (Hoyt 2013a and 2013b; Fountas and Pinnell 2013; Robb 2010 and 2013).

➢ Ask students to apply grade-level skills to texts at their own instructional reading level (Allington 2011; Bomer 2011; Routman 2014).

➢ Encourage independent reading of self-selected books. The more students read, the faster the rate of progress (Allington 2009; Allington and McGill-Franzen 2003; Krashen 2004; Miller 2009 and 2013; Robb 2013).

In order to know the types of reading interventions required for each student, responsive teachers reflect on the importance of four teaching practices and weave them into daily literacy lessons.

1. **The teacher models and thinks aloud.** Modeling and thinking aloud are two strategies that enable the teacher to help students learn how to apply a strategy or solve a problem (Burke 2010; Howard 2009; Keene 2008; Robb 2010 and 2014; Routman 2014; Wilhelm 2013). In a 10- to 15-minute mini-lesson, a type of explicit instruction developed by Donald Graves (1983) and popularized by Lucy Calkins (1994), the teacher can show the entire class, small groups, or individuals how strategies work. During the mini-lesson, the teacher can also scaffold a process such as identifying themes by explaining how this task can be organized into small steps.

   While modeling, teachers make their thinking visible to students and build students' mental model of a process. For example, when teaching students to make a logical prediction about what a character will decide, students first need to mentally review everything they learned about the character, including any decisions the character made. Then, students can use that information to make a logical prediction because it is based on evidence from the text.

2. **The teacher provides time to practice.** Students improve when they have time to practice (Howard 2009; Robb 2010; Routman 2014; Wilhelm 2013). Practice can be with a short text at a student's instructional reading level or with a passage or a few pages from a student's instructional reading book. The teacher can monitor and assess a student's application of a strategy from the student's writing about the reading or while watching the student's process during a conference (Allison 2009; Graham and Hebert 2010; Robb 2010). If the student's writing reveals an inability to cite text evidence to support an inference or to compare/contrast, then the teacher responds by planning an intervention.

3. **The teacher makes learning social and interactive.** Research suggests that engagement with tasks and motivation to learn increase when teachers shift the focus to student-centered learning. A student-centered approach uses methods such as collaboration through paired and small-group

discussions and inquiry to solve problems, interpret texts, and actively engage in meaningful reading, writing, and speaking (Adler and Rougle 2005; Keene 2008; Robb 2010; Routman 2014; Wilhelm 2002).

Teachers who use student-centered learning methods have multiple opportunities to be responsive to students who arrive at school with a variety of cultural backgrounds as well as a wide range of literacy experience and prior knowledge (Delpit 2006; Gay 2000; Tomlinson 2014; Smith and Wilhelm 2007; Wormeli 2007).

The teacher plans and targets interventions to meet students' needs. The goal of all intervention in grades 4 to 8 is to help students comprehend, interpret, and analyze reading materials, as well as improve their motivation to read, write, think, and discuss. Targeted interventions are focused lessons designed for students who need extra support in reading and writing.

The individualized focus of targeted interventions can make a difference in the progress of readers far below grade level because scaffolding and reteaching can move students to independence with a task (Adler and Rougle 2005; Allington 2011; Buffum, Mattos, and Weber 2009 and 2010; Duke and Pearson 2002; Howard 2009). It's important to view interventions through a positive lens and to see students who struggle or "don't get it" as capable of learning and making progress when you find ways to meet their needs.

The following are some ways that teachers can provide interventions for students:

➤ Pre-teach explicit vocabulary, such as three to four challenging words, prior to reading a text. In addition, you can teach word roots, prefixes, and suffixes so students have the tools for determining word meanings.

➤ Teach explicit comprehension strategy lessons that show students how to identify themes, big ideas, point of view, literary elements, and informational text structures, and how to infer and link these to themes, big ideas, and inferences about characters, topics, and people.

➤ Conduct extended discussions of text meaning that start with retellings to check basic comprehension and move to higher-order thinking, such as comparing and contrasting characters, analyzing the role of the setting, determining cause and effect, and identifying and analyzing multiple themes.

Teacher TIP

There is no one, correct fix for building students' reading and writing capacity. I suggest that when you plan interventions, you target them on a specific need and find two to three strategies that might work. That way if one isn't supporting the students, you have another strategy at your fingertips.

➤ Emphasize the importance of text evidence to support interpretations. This can be difficult for students who often resist returning to the text to nail evidence. Help students understand that their ideas are valid only when they support them with text details.

➤ Provide individual and small-group lessons, which offer opportunities to intervene by scaffolding a process. One-on-one and small-group interventions can occur while the rest of the class is reading and writing independently. Sitting side-by-side with a student or close to a small group can lower students' anxiety levels and make the lesson more accessible (Atwell 1991; Fountas and Pinnell 2000; Howard 2009; Scanlon, Anderson, and Sweeney 2010).

If frequent assessments reveal that scaffolds aren't improving students' reading skill(s), you can consider reteaching using materials that differ from the original lesson and scaffold practice.

Roadblocks to Responsive Teaching

Many teachers are required to deliver content from a grade-level anthology or novel to every student. To meet this requirement for students reading two or more years below grade level, teachers often read the text aloud to the below-grade-level group and have students follow along in the text, while the rest of the class reads the anthology independently. However, teachers soon realize that students don't pass the grade-level unit tests because they can't read the material.

This kind of accommodation doesn't improve reading because the teacher is reading, not the students, and for students to improve, they need to read (Allington 2009 and 2011; Allison 2009; Ford and Opitz 2015; Robb 2013; Routman 2014).

Two myths surround this type of teaching:

➤ **Myth 1:** Exposing students to grade-level texts even though they can't read them will support their ability to pass state reading exams. Learning information can provide the background knowledge needed to comprehend grade-level materials.

Reality: Reading grade-level texts to students to hear the information does not improve students' reading skills or their ability to comprehend texts far above their instructional reading levels. Background knowledge is one prerequisite for comprehending grade-level texts, but it is not enough when students lack vocabulary and independent reading experiences. This strategy is not a ticket to passing state tests.

➤ **Myth 2:** Having students follow along in the text while the teacher reads aloud will build their vocabulary and reading skill.

Reality: There is no guarantee that students are following along when the teacher reads aloud. If the vocabulary and syntax are too difficult, students quickly figure out what to do to look as if they are following along. Moreover, following a text is not a form of instruction, and it won't move students forward.

Backward Slide

Although often done with good intentions, teachers who exclusively read aloud to students who can't read and comprehend grade-level texts or have students primarily listen to audio of the texts often contribute to students' backward slide. Similar to Richard Allington's "summer slide" (2009), backward slide (and summer slide) occurs when students aren't reading. Therefore, one of the primary goals of intervention is to have students read, read, and read to build vocabulary, fluency, background knowledge, and the stamina to move forward.

Teacher TIP

Reading stamina is the ability to concentrate and read a text for 20 minutes or more. When students lack stamina, teachers can build it by having students settle down and read for 10 minutes until you observe they have met this goal. Then, gradually increase the amount of silent reading time until students can concentrate on reading for at least 20 minutes.

Class Size and Time to Teach

Teachers who have a wide range of instructional reading levels in their classrooms need to know and respond to what their students can and can't do on a daily basis and intervene quickly to clear up small confusions before they become large obstacles. This can happen when teachers have longer class periods and smaller classes (Chingo and Grover 2011).

Being a responsive teacher can become a challenging task when you have classes of 30 to 40 students reading at six to eight different instructional levels. Such a wide range of reading abilities is indicative of the heterogeneous groupings in many schools. Class size and the range of instructional student levels directly affect a teacher's ability to respond to students' needs with planned interventions. Chingo and Grover cite studies that show that reducing classes with 35 to 40 students to class sizes of 20 to 24 increased students' achievement over time (2011). Smaller numbers allow teachers to keep abreast of students' progress and intervene to help every student move forward and improve their reading.

Defining Reading Skill Versus Strategy

Teachers and students frequently use the terms *skill* and *strategy* interchangeably. However, these terms differ, and explaining them will clarify why I use the term *strategy* throughout this book. Here's how Peter Afflerbach, P. David Pearson, and Scott G. Paris explain these terms (2008):

➢ A skill is a well-practiced strategy, such as inferring or identifying big ideas. The term *skill* means that learners have proficiency with a strategy and can use it automatically in all situations.

➢ A strategy builds reading comprehension and requires practice in different situations until the learner can apply the strategy effortlessly or with automaticity in diverse situations.

Most students in grades four to eight, especially those who require intervention, are at the strategy level. Students can progress when they practice and learn from reading strategies that use entire books at their instructional levels and self-selected books for independent reading.

Using Extra Time for Reading Instruction

To accelerate achievement for developing or struggling readers and improve their vocabulary and reading strategy use, schools often provide an additional 30–40 minutes a day of reading instruction in small groups. However, the 30–40 minutes need to be divided between strategy practice and reading entire short and long texts. Why? When students practice strategies out of the context of meaningful texts, it is rare that they will transfer those strategies to other genres and learning situations (Allington 2011; Scanlon, Anderson, and Sweeney 2010).

A New Approach to Ensure Measurable Gains

In a school where I coach teachers, a small group of fourth-grade special education students used to receive an additional 40-minute class every day. Students completed phonemic awareness exercises, phonics worksheets, and comprehension cards. They did not read books, and the teacher did not read aloud to them. At the end of the first semester, no measurable progress had occurred.

The teacher agreed to pilot a different approach and to start the class with a 10-minute interactive read-aloud to build students' mental model of how to apply reading strategies and think about text.

During the remaining time, students chose books to read and reread. Three days each week small groups of students read at their instructional level and discussed the books with their teacher. Twice a week, students read books at their independent reading level—95% to 100% accuracy and excellent or satisfactory comprehension (Fountas and Pinnell 2009). Then, students discussed these books with partners. The discussions centered on retelling, literary elements, or information learned in nonfiction. Students also used prompts that encouraged discussion. For homework, students reread instructional books and self-selected independent reading books. By the end of the second semester, based on informal reading inventories, students made one-half to one-year gains in instructional reading levels.

Prompts That Fostered Discussion

To further their reading work, the fourth-grade teacher typed and printed the discussion prompts that follow and had students tape them into their notebooks. The prompts can also be projected onto an interactive whiteboard or written on chart paper. When pairs or small groups discussed a book, they agreed on one or more prompts. Sometimes, the teacher asked students to choose a prompt they discussed, write it in their notebooks, and list key points they discussed. The teacher also emphasized the importance of including text evidence with their answers.

The following discussion questions and prompts apply to any book, and students from each of the three tiers will find some they can reflect on and discuss.

Questions and Prompts for Fiction

➤ Who is the protagonist (main character), and what is his or her problem?

➤ Discuss two important settings, and explain why you believe each is important.

➤ Use a decision a character made and a problem he or she solved to identify two to three personality traits.

➤ Show how a character changed by pointing out the change in his or her personality. Then, discuss the event, person, setting, or conflict that caused the change.

➤ Choose one minor character and explain how he or she affected the main character.

➤ Were there problems that characters couldn't solve? Identify one or two and explain why you think each one wasn't solved.

➤ How does the title relate to the story?

➤ Discuss, using text details, two points that the author made about family, friends, feelings, nature, or life experiences.

➤ Are there examples of literary techniques such as flashback, foreshadowing, or figurative language? Identify one example and explain how it connected to a theme, a conflict, or a problem.

➤ Identify two antagonistic forces and explain how each one worked against the protagonist (main character). Why were these important to the story?

➤ Did the author create different moods? Find a passage that reveals mood and point out the words, phrases, and actions that helped create that mood.

Questions and Prompts for Biography

➤ Why is this person famous or important? How is that significant for society?

➤ Discuss two personality traits that helped this person achieve his or her goal.

➤ Identify two obstacles the person overcame and explain how he or she accomplished this.

➤ What traits and beliefs did this person have that enabled him or her to realize his or her dream? Select two to three to discuss.

➤ Select one person and one event and show how each one influenced the person's choices and decisions.

➤ How did this person affect the lives of other people during his or her time?

➤ Does this person's ideas or inventions affect people today? Explain why or why not.

Questions and Prompts for Informational Texts

➤ Why did you choose this book?

➤ What new information did you learn?

➤ What questions did the book raise in your mind but not answer? What can you do to find the answers to your questions?

➤ What did you learn from photographs and captions? How did these text features support the information in the text?

➤ What information did you learn from charts and diagrams? How did those text features support the information in the text?

➤ How did this book change your thinking about this topic?

➤ Did the author weave opinions with facts? Give an example of this and explain why it was significant.

Responsive Teaching with Tiers 1, 2, and 3 Readers

In a regular classroom, there is a core instructional curriculum that all students experience—this is Tier 1 instruction. Responsive teachers adjust the core curriculum so that it is accessible to every student in their classrooms. An effective way to adjust curriculum and differentiate instruction is to develop reading units around a genre and/or theme. To do this, find books and materials in your classroom and school library that relate to the genre and/or theme and that each student can read, learn from, and discuss with peers. This way, you can improve students' application of reading strategies to different texts and build their reading stamina, the ability to concentrate on reading. You can read more about this type of differentiation in Chapter 2.

It's important to note that even proficient and advanced readers become dependent, developing readers when faced with a text that contains new information and challenging vocabulary. It's helpful to revisit the definition of (and learning needs common to) each tier of readers so you can more efficiently provide interventions and organize partners who can support one another. In addition, responsive teachers understand that the most effective interventions are timely, based on students' struggles with

a task, and target a student's specific learning needs (Howard 2009; Owocki 2010). To pinpoint students' needs, teachers try to identify students' reading difficulties early in the year; they monitor students' progress throughout the year by observing them, listening to discussions, conferring, and using writing about reading to assess students' use of text evidence to support thinking.

Tier 1 Instruction

All students in your class receive Tier 1 instruction. Instruction includes whole-class and small-group lessons and instruction from the teacher that meets the needs of the diversity of reading and writing levels. By teaching small groups of students with common needs, you can provide reading instruction that meets students where they are, offers appropriate challenges, and helps them improve. Instead of practicing isolated skills, students who read below grade level should practice reading with motivating texts, as well as reading and discussing self-selected books during independent reading (Allington 2009; Howard 2009; Owocki 2010). Though a core curriculum defines Tier 1 instruction, responsive teachers are flexible and make adjustments that meet each student's learning needs. Educators agree that high-quality Tier 1 instruction can support about 80 percent of the student population, enabling them to show solid growth during the year (Howard 2009; Owocki 2010; NASDSE 2006).

Tier 2 Instruction

Students who require Tier 2 instruction are those who aren't making enough progress in the Tier 1 curriculum and who require additional intervention. Students reading one to two years below grade level can fall into this group. You can identify these students by systematically monitoring formative assessments and observational notes as students listen, follow directions, discuss texts, read, and write. It is helpful to administer an individual reading inventory to determine a student's instructional and independent reading levels. To move these students forward, classroom teachers can supplement the Tier 1 core curriculum with longer interventions and reteaching lessons, intensify instruction by working with pairs and individuals, and inch these students closer to becoming grade-level readers.

Tier 3 Instruction

Students reading three or more years below grade-level benefit from instruction beyond the core curriculum because they are at a high risk for failure. In addition to the differentiated core curriculum, these students can improve their reading by having an additional 30 to 45 minutes of reading instruction three to five times a week. Finding time to meet with students at risk for failing a grade, as well as having the funds for reading specialists, is often a challenge for schools. Following, you can find two sample schedules for addressing the needs of the three tiers of students. Select or adapt the schedule that works best for you.

 ## Planning for a 45-Minute Class Schedule

To meet the needs of Tier 3 students, this schedule requires a reading specialist or special education teacher who helps while you work with Tier 1 and Tier 2 readers. If your school doesn't have a teacher who can help, adjust the schedule using the suggestions that follow:

➢ On Tuesday and Thursday, spend 10 minutes on word study and 25 minutes supporting Tier 3 students.

➢ On Monday and Wednesday, work with Tiers 1 and 2, and have Tier 3 students complete independent reading.

➢ On Friday, work with Tier 3 students and have Tiers 1 and 2 students complete independent reading.

Interventions that occur soon after you've identified a need have a better chance of moving students toward independence with a task because you are supporting students when they need the strategy to learn.

Figure 1.1 Sample 45-Minute Class Schedule

Monday	Tuesday	Wednesday	Thursday	Friday
Vocabulary: 10 min.	**Interactive Read-Aloud:** 10 min.	**Vocabulary:** 10 min.	**Interactive Read-Aloud:** 10 min.	**Vocabulary:** 10 min.
Instructional Reading: 30 min.; can be guided reading or differentiated via genre; classroom teacher works with tiers 1 and 2.	**Independent Reading and Conferences:** 20 min.; all 3 tiers	**Instructional Reading:** 30 min.; can be guided reading or differentiated via genre; classroom teacher works with Tiers 1 and 2.	**Independent Reading and Conferences:** 20 min.; all 3 tiers	**Instructional Reading:** 30 min.; can be guided reading or differentiated via genre; classroom teacher works with tiers 1 and 2.
Word Sorting and Study: 15 min.	**Word Sorting and Study:** 15 min.	**Word Sorting and Study:** 15 min.	**Word Sorting and Study:** 15 min.	**Word Sorting and Study:** 15 min.
Wrap-Up	**Wrap-Up**	**Wrap-Up**	**Wrap-Up**	**Wrap-Up**
30-min. Class: Specialist works with Tier 3 students while classroom teacher works with Tiers 1 and 2; focus is reading and writing about reading in a notebook.		**30-min. Class:** Specialist works with Tier 3 students while classroom teacher works with Tiers 1 and 2; focus is reading and writing about reading in a notebook.		**30-min. Class:** Specialist works with Tier 3 students while classroom teacher works with Tiers 1 and 2; focus is reading and writing about reading in a notebook.
Homework: Independent reading 20–30 min.; practice word sort	**Homework:** Independent reading 20–30 min.; practice word sort	**Homework:** Independent reading 20–30 min.; practice word sort	**Homework:** Independent reading 20–30 min.; study word sort words for quiz	**Homework:** Independent reading 30 min.

Chapter 1

Planning for a 60-Minute Class Schedule

Having more time allows the classroom teacher to work with all tiers as well as have two days a week for independent reading and scaffolding conferences.

Figure 1.2 Sample 60-Minute Class Schedule

Monday	Tuesday	Wednesday	Thursday	Friday
Vocabulary: 10 min. **Instructional Reading:** 45 min.; can be guided reading or differentiated via genre; classroom teacher works with all tiers. **Word Sorting and Study:** woven into reading lesson (Tiers not working with teacher read independently or write about reading.) **Wrap-Up**	**Interactive Read-Aloud:** 10 min. **Independent Reading and Conferences:** 30 min.; all tiers **Word Sorting and Study:** 15 min. **Wrap-Up**	**Vocabulary:** 10 min. **Instructional Reading:** 45 min.; can be guided reading or differentiated via genre; classroom teacher works with all tiers. **Word Sorting and Study:** woven into reading lesson (Tiers not working with teacher read independently or write about reading.) **Wrap-Up**	**Interactive Read-Aloud:** 10 min. **Independent Reading and Conferences:** 30 min.; All Tiers **Word Sorting and Study:** 15 min. **Wrap-Up**	**Vocabulary:** 10 min. **Instructional Reading:** 45 min.; can be guided reading or differentiated via genre; classroom teacher works with all tiers. **Word Sorting and Study:** woven into reading lesson (Tiers not working with teacher read independently or write about reading.) **Wrap-Up**
Homework: Independent reading 20–30 min.; practice word sort	**Homework:** Independent reading 20–30 min.; practice word sort	**Homework:** Independent reading 20–30 min.; practice word sort	**Homework:** Independent reading 20–30 min.; study word sort words for quiz	**Homework:** Independent reading 20–30 min.

In order for the classroom teacher to work with the three tiers, students need access to high-interest and motivating books they can read independently. The high-quality books can also be used for instruction.

Chapter 1

Motivating Texts for Students Reading Below Grade Level

Finding materials for developing readers two or more years below grade level can be challenging. Using literature that students in grades one to three read can destroy older students' self-confidence, increase feelings of hopelessness, and confirm the belief that they are unable to catch up to peers reading on grade level (Allington 2010, 2009, and 2011; Guthrie and Wigfield 2000; Miller 2010; Robb 2000b and 2010; Tankersley 2005; Wilhelm and Smith 2013). The following section contains a selection of 30 high-interest books for reluctant and developing readers.

Figure 1.3 High-Interest Books for Reluctant and Developing Readers

Literary Texts	Lexile® Level
Island Book I: Shipwreck by Gordon Korman	610L
Island Book II: Survival by Gordon Korman	600L
Island Book III: Escape by Gordon Korman	620L
Stone Fox by John Gardiner	550L
Shiloh by Phyllis Reynolds Naylor	780L
Holes by Louis Sachar	660L
Becoming Naomi Leon by Pam Munoz Ryan	830L
The Outsiders by S.E. Hinton	750L
Miracle's Boys by Jacqueline Woodson	660L
The Great Gilly Hopkins by Katherine Paterson	800L

Biographies	Lexile® Level
The Secret Soldier: The Story of Deborah Sampson by Ann McGovern	590L
Go Fly a Kite, Ben Franklin by Peter Roop and Connie Roop	680L
Adventures of Shark Lady: Eugenie Clark Around the World by Ann McGovern	890L
Roberto Clemente by Dona and William Rice	930L
Jane Goodall: The Early Years by William B. Rice	780L
Helen's Big World: The Life of Helen Keller by Doreen Rappaport	770L
Nelson Mandela: Leading the Way by Tamara Leigh Hollingsworth	640L
Sojourner Truth: Ain't I a Woman? by Patricia C. McKissack and Frederick McKissack	960L
I Am Harriet Tubman by Grace Norwich	1060L
Leonardo DaVinci by Kathleen Krull	1010L

Informational Texts	Lexile® Level
Rome: World Cultures Through Time by Christine Dugan	600L
Amazon Rainforest by William B. Rice	610L
The Crossing: How George Washington Saved the American Revolution by Jim Murphy	1080L
Egypt: World Cultures Though Time by Shirley Jordan	710L
United No More: Stories of the Civil War by Doreen Rappaport	780L
Bug Builders by Timothy J. Bradley	710L
The Time Machine and Other Cases (Einstein Anderson: Science Detective) by Seymour Simon	620L
Bones: Our Skeletal System by Seymour Simon	1000L
Summer of Fire: Yellowstone 1988 by Patricia Lauber	850L
Unforgettable Natural Disasters by Tamara Leigh Hollingsworth	760L

The Connection Between Motivation and Engagement

Motivation and engagement are two important ingredients for igniting students' learning engines and sparking their desire to work and achieve at school and in life. Success is a great motivator (Guthrie 2004; Guthrie and Wigfield 2000). However, the students who require intervention conferences and reteaching gingerly walk a tight rope because they repeatedly struggle to experience success at school (Allington 2010 and 2011; Robb 2000a; Beers 2002; Tankersley 2005).

During whole-class activities, students who struggle should be mixed with those who are proficient and advanced learners because one group informs the others by sharing their thinking and problem-solving process during discussions (Marzano, Pickering, and Pollock 2004).

The following seven suggestions can help build motivation for learning and engagement with reading for those students who require intervention strategies to move forward (Francois 2015; Guthrie 2004):

1. **Create a community of learners who work in a safe environment with a teacher they trust and know will support them** (Lent 2007). During the first week of school, get to know your students by asking them to complete interest surveys, and answer questions about their reading and writing lives. Also conduct informal conferences with students.

2. **Praise students' successes with a personal note that reminds them how much you recognize their efforts and progress.** Leave a note on a specific piece of work in a students' journal/notebook. A note is concrete evidence of progress, and a student can reread it whenever he or she needs a boost in self-confidence or a nudge to continue to work hard. The note I clipped to the last entry in Isef's journal says: "You have read eleven books in three months and have improved your reading! I am proud of your efforts and see how much you have begun to enjoy reading. Keep up the great work!"

3. **Negotiate goals that are reasonable and that students can reach and experience success getting there.** During a conference with Sylvie, I pointed out the solid progress she's made with inferring and offering text evidence as support. We discussed what her next goal for reading might be, and I encouraged Sylvie to suggest one. "Finding themes," she said. I told her that finding themes is similar to inferring because themes are unstated and that she's chosen an excellent goal. "Can I work with Talia?" Sylvie asks. "Talia's good at that." I praised Sylvie for making this suggestion and was pleased she felt confident enough to work with a peer instead of her teacher.

4. **Find reading materials students can learn from so they can participate in partner and group work and research.** About a week before students chose a book for a unit on natural and man-made disasters, I worked with our school librarian and collected books and magazines that were at students' instructional reading levels. Next, I organized the books into stacks and asked students to select a book from the stack of books that they can learn from and read.

5. **Be positive as you "make the rounds" and always point out to students what they do well in addition to discussing ways they can improve.** I paused at Jamal's desk, read his notebook entry and said, "You've identified the tone of this chapter and explained how it made you feel, and I appreciate your ideas. Can you support your thinking by telling me some words and phrases from the chapter that helped you identify the tone? Excellent! Now add these to your entry."

6. **Be a good listener and show by your actions that you honor and understand students' frustrations and anxieties.** Lelia explained why she wanted to abandon her instructional book. "I've read and reread chapters 1 and 2, and I don't remember a lot. I don't know about that time (middle ages) and the book's boring." I told Lelia that this is the ideal time to switch books and offered her three alternates to browse through. I reminded her to finish the first two chapters over the next two days during independent reading time so she could be ready to discuss these with her partner.

7. **Build relationships by interacting with students, by building self-esteem through positive feedback, and by always showing them what they can achieve and where they can go.** Supporting every student you teach can be a daunting task. As you build a positive learning community, trusting relationships with students, and intervene to improve students' reading, their tense feelings and worries about completing a task can melt away. "Your writing plan for that argument paragraph has an excellent claim and text evidence for one point that's clear and detailed, Lucas! Now let's discuss a second detail to support your argument. You've got it. Add it to your plan."

Instructional Needs of English Language Learners

English language learners in our classrooms cope with many challenges as they develop language skills appropriate for school and everyday English. However, it's important to understand and honor the strengths students have with their native languages (Brown-Chidsey, Bronaugh, and McGraw 2009). Many English language learners will benefit from scaffolding and reteaching lessons in order for them to make steady reading progress. Keep in mind the practices that enable you to remain sensitive to individual's needs and challenges.

➤ Determine students' instructional reading levels.

➤ Adjust the curriculum so students can experience success while learning.

➤ Monitor them carefully to ensure that they are moving forward with specific strategies.

➤ Give students the gift of time. Slow down the pace of lessons so they can understand and absorb information.

➤ Whenever possible, work with pairs and small groups to heighten opportunities for language interactions through discussions.

➤ Help students see progress by pointing out what they *can* do after scaffolding and reteaching.

➤ Work on helping students set achievable goals so they develop self-efficacy and continue to work hard.

Continue the Conversation

Discuss these prompts and questions with your grade-level team or a peer partner. Reflecting on what you learn, what you know, and your students' performance can support your decision-making process regarding the kind of intervention plan you will develop.

1. Discuss why responsive teaching leads to positive interventions for students.

2. Share ways that you target interventions for struggling readers.

3. Work with colleagues to adjust teaching schedules so you can support all three tiers of students. Use the schedules and suggestions from Figures 1.1 and 1.2.

4. Bring an intervention artifact (e.g., student work or an observation form) to a second meeting, discuss with colleagues, provide feedback, and learn more about helping developing readers.

Chapter 2

Differentiation and Intervention: An Integral Part of Responsive Teaching

Researchers know that in a class of diverse reading abilities, one book or a grade-level anthology will not meet the needs of all learners (Allington 2011; Allington and Gabriel 2012; Tomlinson 2014; Robb 2008; Wormeli 2007). So the question to ponder is, *How do I meet every student's instructional needs to help each student improve?*

Richard Allington points out that by the middle grades and middle school, decoding is usually not an impediment to reading (2010, 2011, and 2012). However, researchers agree that poor general academic vocabulary, lack of targeted interventions, and no independent practice reading are obstacles to comprehending grade-level materials (Beck, McKeown, and Kucan 2013; Baker, Simmons, and Kame'enui 1998; Brozo, Shiel, and Topping 2008; Howard 2009). Two powerful ways that teachers can gradually help their students overcome these obstacles to progress in reading are by: (1) differentiating reading instruction and (2) scaffolding students' learning with targeted interventions.

Differentiating Reading Instruction

In order to prevent backward slide among students, it's important to develop a reading curriculum that has every student reading and progressing. There are three elements to a differentiated reading curriculum:

➤ Interactive read-aloud

➤ Instructional reading

➤ Independent free-choice reading

Interactive Read-Aloud

An interactive read-aloud is a 10- to 15-minute lesson. The teacher reads a text passage to students and thinks out loud in order to model how to apply a reading strategy to improve comprehension. The interactive element is inviting students to ask questions and involving them in the thinking and sharing of ideas. Interactive read-alouds can be presented to the whole class, small groups, and woven into scaffolding or reteaching lessons. These read-alouds provide students with mental models of how to solve reading problems presented by an expert, the teacher (Fountas and Pinnell 2012; Robb 2008,

2010, 2013; Serravallo 2010). By presenting interactive read-alouds to the entire class, you provide opportunities for every student to learn more about reading and build their mental models of how readers make meaning and connections to other texts and media.

Instructional Reading

Students spend 20–30 minutes at least three times a week improving their skill, fluency, vocabulary, recall, and comprehension by reading texts at their instructional reading levels. When students work at their instructional reading levels, they bring a solid vocabulary and some background knowledge to texts and can learn from them with the support of the teacher (Fountas and Pinnell 2009; Woods and Moe 2015; Vygotsky 1978; Wilhelm 2013). By teaching the wide range of instructional reading levels among students in your classes, you are differentiating reading instruction. As much as possible, teachers should allow students to choose from a variety of texts at their instructional level because choice can lead to motivation to learn and engagement with the text.

Independent Free-Choice Reading

When students read 40–60 self-selected books a year in addition to books used for instruction, they experience the practice needed to accelerate reading achievement and read more complex texts. Students who self-select books take control of their reading and can gain self-confidence and an enthusiasm for reading (Krashen 2004; Miller 2010 and 2013; Robb 2010; Routman 2014).

With independent reading, students practice transferring the skills and strategies they learn during instructional reading to reading materials that more closely align with an individual student's independent reading level. It's this practice that enables students to score high on achievement tests and read more complex texts (Allington 2011; Bomer 2011; Krashen 2004; Robb 2010 and 2013). However, benefits extend beyond practice because students develop literary taste, enlarge their academic vocabulary, develop an awareness of the multiple meanings and forms of words in different contexts, build fluency and background knowledge, and deepen their understanding of the structure of diverse genres.

Differentiate with Instructional Reading

Differentiating instructional reading means teaching students at their instructional reading levels. One concern I have heard in the past is that if teachers instruct students where they are, students won't have opportunities to think like grade-level readers. When students read instructional texts that are below their grade level, it is important that they apply and practice grade-level skills and

---

Criteria for Instructional-level Reading

At levels A–K, students must demonstrate 90–94% accuracy with excellent or satisfactory comprehension or 95–100% accuracy with limited comprehension

At levels L–Z, students must demonstrate 95–97% accuracy with excellent or satisfactory comprehension or 98–100% accuracy with limited comprehension

Criteria based on Fountas and Pinnell *Benchmark Assessment System*, 2009.

Criteria for Independent Level Reading

At levels A–K, students must demonstrate

95–100% accuracy with excellent or satisfactory comprehension

At levels L–Z, students must demonstrate

98–100% accuracy with excellent or satisfactory comprehension

Criteria based on Fountas and Pinnell *Benchmark Assessment System* (2009).

strategies. Moreover, with expert instruction, continual scaffolding, and a rich independent reading life (40–60 books a year), students can make one or more years' progress in one school year (Allington 2011; Allington and Johnston 2000; Krashen 2004; Miller 2010). That's a goal we teachers should have for all our students. What follows are two ways to differentiate instructional reading: guided reading and genre-/theme-based instruction.

Guided Reading

Developed by Fountas and Pinnell, guided reading is a teaching approach that organizes students into small groups of four to six who instructionally have similar needs and can read the same text (Fountas and Pinnell 1996; Richardson 2009; Serravallo 2010). A primary goal of guided reading is to help individual students acquire the skills and strategies to learn from increasingly challenging texts over time. Much more than practicing a set of reading strategies, guided reading is research based and targets and scaffolds instruction to students' needs using high-quality literature and informational texts. The text offers challenges for students along with opportunities to think deeply and solve reading problems, such as figuring out the meaning of unfamiliar words, making logical inferences, or identifying themes (Fountas and Pinnell 1996 and 2000; Richardson 2009; Serravallo 2010). With the teacher's support, students can improve their reading and apply strategies to the text because they are working in their learning zone (Vygotsky 1978). Guided reading works well when teachers have 60 or more minutes for reading and no more than four reading groups.

Genre- and Theme-Based Instruction

This is an adaptation of Reader's Workshop. Organizing your class this way means that each student reads a book related to a genre and theme at his or her instructional level (Fountas and Pinnell 2000; Robb 2008). This type of instructional organization places students at their instructional reading level, allowing them to improve. Choice can also be part of instructional reading as long as you know students' reading levels.

Once you've selected a genre or theme, ask your school and public librarian to pull books and organize them into stacks by reading levels. If your school has a leveled reading room, you can choose books that meet the range of instructional reading levels needed. Next, organize books into stacks of similar reading levels and place stacks on the floor around the room. Try to collect enough books so that students can choose two.

Direct students to a specific stack and give them about 15 minutes to browse through books. Here's what I say: *Each one of you will read different books during our unit on biography and the theme of obstacles. I'm directing you to books at your instructional reading level where you can progress as a reader. Choose two books that you think you might enjoy. If one doesn't work out, you have a second book waiting.*

Have each student write his or her name on a sticky note and attach it to the book's cover. If you have multiple classes of students throughout the day, this set of books remains at school so students in other class periods can use them.

Teacher TIP

Have students complete all instructional reading at school so you can observe, monitor, and assess them. This also allows you to provide books from your community public library, which gives the possibility for a larger variety of texts to be shared with students.

Classroom Snapshot: Genre- and Theme-Based Differentiated Instruction

I am working with a fifth-grade class on understanding the features and structure of biography and the theme is Obstacles. Since I am modeling lessons for a teacher I'm coaching, I want to keep the unit short so each student reads a different picture book biography at their reading level. Their teacher will follow this up with a unit on biography using chapter books. (See Figure 2.3 for a list of picture book biographies.)

I am using the picture biography *Wilma Unlimited* by Kathleen Krull to model a series of interactive read-alouds about making inferences, finding themes, and using context clues for tough words (Hoyt 2013a; Fountas and Pinnell 2013; Robb 2010 and 2013). These interactive reading lessons are for the whole class; students practice applying a strategy I modeled using their own biography.

First, students pair-share to discuss what they know about biography. You can collect their ideas on chart paper or use an interactive whiteboard and then decide whether students know enough about this genre to start reading. If students know little about biography, read aloud two to three short biographies and think aloud about genre elements to build prior knowledge. Figure 2.2 has a list of short biographies to use. If a small group needs more prior knowledge about biography, work with them while other students complete independent reading. Next, pairs discuss the denotative and connotative meanings of obstacles, the theme of this unit. Figure 2.1 has examples of denotative and connotative meanings that students came up with for the unit.

Figure 2.1 Denotative and Connotative Meanings of "Obstacles"

Denotative Meaning: *obstacles*

➢ something that gets in the way of what you want to do

➢ an object you go over or around like in a race

➢ something that you have to overcome to reach your goal

Connotative Meanings: *obstacles*

➢ hurdles, overcome and get stronger, handicap, mental block, negative emotions

➢ anxiety, illness, poverty, lack of food and medical care, allergies, being different

➢ ethnicity

After students read the first chunk of text in their biographies, I make the rounds and check each student's recall. If recall is poor, I ask the student to read the first chunk again to see if rereading improves recall. If the student offers a detailed retelling, I remind him or her that rereading is a great strategy to use when they don't remember enough information. If recall is still sketchy, I negotiate changing books with the student, offering several different choices, and have him or her select one or two (Allison 2009).

Next, students select two to three connotative meanings of *obstacles* and connect each connotation to what they've read. Then, they discuss these with a partner. Students jot ideas from their partner discussion and add text evidence to support their thinking.

Having conversations with partners about a different book can introduce students to other biographies they would enjoy reading. Reading, discussing, and sharing ideas from 20-plus biographies results in richer paired discussions about comparing people and obstacles they faced. Equally important, when partners discuss different books, they often want to read one another's books. Let them do so because partner discussions provide students with the rich background knowledge needed to read a book that is challenging.

Partners remain together during the entire unit and are no more than one year apart in instructional reading levels so they have ideas to share. As partners discuss, the teacher and I continually make the rounds to support pairs that are not talking and writing and to offer positive feedback to students on task. For example, students have selected three challenging words in the first chunk of text and place a small sticky note next to the word. I've modeled how to look for clues in the sentence with the word, but I cautioned students that they might have to reread the sentences before or after the word. When I pause at Sarah's desk, I notice that she has not set up a T-chart in her notebook to write the unfamiliar word on the left-hand side and the definition and clues on the right-hand side. "I can't do this," she whispers.

"Let's work together," I say, and I reread the sentence with the word out loud, think aloud, and explain that perhaps I should read on for clues. That works, and Sarah completes the notebook entry for that word. Next, I have Sarah reread another sentence with a tough word. She is able to find clues in the sentence for the second word and also points out that the illustration had clues. "I know you can figure out the third word," I say. "But raise your hand for help if you need me." And I move on to the next student.

This fifth-grade class had 22 students, and Figure 2.3 contains the list of picture book biographies that students read. The genre and the theme *Obstacles* are what really bound this unit together.

Chunk a Book

Show students how to divide ("chunk") a chapter book and place a sticky note after every two to three chapters, which is about enough text for average readers to read in one setting. Have students write **Stop to Think** on each sticky note. Advanced readers can place a sticky note after four to six chapters, as they have the expertise/stamina to read longer chunks. As a modification, you might have to start the chunking process for several students or pair them with others who can complete the task on their own. At first, students will need you to model this process for each new unit. Eventually, students can complete this independently as you circulate and provide support when needed.

Figure 2.2 Collections of Short Biographies

Enemies of Slavery by David A. Adler, illustrated by Donald A. Smith

Girls Who Rocked the World: Heroines from Joan of Arc to Mother Teresa by Michelle Roehm McCann and Amelie Welden, illustrated by David Hahn

Hand in Hand: Ten Black Men Who Changed America by Andrea Davis Pinkney, illustrated by Brian Pinkney

Let It Shine: Stories of Black Women Freedom Fighters by Andrea Davis Pinkney, illustrated by Stephen Alcom

Rabble Rousers: Twenty Women Who Made a Difference by Cheryl Harness

Figure 2.3 Picture Book Biographies

A Home for Mr. Emerson by Barbara Kerley, illustrated by Edwin Fotheringham

Campy: The Story of Roy Campanella by David Adler, illustrated by Gordon C. James

Crazy Horse's Vision by Joseph Bruchac, illustrated by S.D. Nelson

Duke Ellington by Andrea Davis Pinkney, illustrated by Brian Pinkney

I, Matthew Henson, Polar Explorer by Carole Boston Weatherford, illustrated by Eric Velasquez

I've Seen the Promised Land: The Life of Dr. Martin Luther King, Jr. by Walter Dean Myers, illustrated by Leonard Jenkins

Malcolm X: A Fire Burning Brightly by Walter Dean Myers, illustrated by Leonard Jenkins

Molly Bannaky by Alice McGill, pictures by Chris K. Soentpiet

Muhammad Ali: The People's Champion by Walter Dean Myers, illustrated by Alix Delinois

Playing to Win: The Story of Althea Gibson by Karen Deans, illustrated by Elbrite Brown

Rachel: The Story of Rachel Carson by Amy Ehrlich, illustrated by Wendell Minor

Rosa by Nikki Giovanni, illustrated by Bryan Collier

Sawdust and Spangles: The Amazing Life of W. C. Coup by Ralph Covert and G. Riley Mills, illustrated by Giselle Potter

She Loved Baseball: The Effa Manley Story by Audrey Vernick, illustrated by Don Tate

Sixteen Years in Sixteen Seconds: The Story of Sammy Lee by Paula Yoo, illustrated by Dom Lee

There Goes Ted Williams: The Greatest Hitter That Ever Lived written and illustrated by Matt Tevares

Testing the Ice: A True Story About Jackie Robinson by Sharon Robinson, illustrated by Kadir Nelson

The Champion of CHILDREN: The Story of Januz Korczak, written and illustrated by Tomek Bogacki

The Real McCoy: The Life of an African-American Inventor by Wendy Towle, paintings by Wil Clay

The Story of Ruby Bridges by Robert Coles, illustrated by George Ford

To Go Singing through the World: The Childhood of Pablo Neruda, written and illustrated by Deborah Kofan Ray

When Marian Sang: The True Recital of Marian Anderson by Pam Munoz Ryan

Chapter 2

Assessment and the Framework for Four Types of Interventions

The purpose of an assessment is far more than a grade. Assessments let you know what students do and do not understand. When you assess throughout a unit, you have countless opportunities to celebrate students' successes and also intervene to help students who have difficulty applying the strategies you've modeled.

Once students practice a strategy, you can create an assessment to make sure each student understands the task. Some assessments result from the strategies you've modeled and students have practiced. Others can come from questions and prompts that apply to any text students have discussed.

For the fifth-grade unit *Obstacles*, students completed several types of assessments. Quizzes were developed from the notebook work, and students were asked to do the following:

➤ Identify three personality traits of their person and support each with text evidence.

➤ State two themes in their picture book biography and use text evidence to support each one.

➤ Use context clues to figure out three to four tough words from a short text that all students could read.

➤ Make three inferences using the person, other persons, decisions, problems, and solutions, and provide text evidence for each one.

Assessment in the form of writing included the following tasks:

➤ Plan and write a paragraph that explained what their person did that helped him or her become famous.

➤ Create an annotated timeline of four key events in the person's life.

➤ Plan and write a paragraph that explains how a person and an event influenced the achievements of the person featured in the biography.

Assessments will reflect success and improvement for all students as long as you have students practice before testing as well as provide targeted interventions for those who need support throughout the unit. In addition to unit assessments, it is important to use the strategy of "making the rounds" to determine where students need support and what interventions might be needed.

Teacher TIP

Store sticky notes that aren't reminders you give to students in a three-ring binder with dividers and notebook paper. The number of dividers depends on the number of classes or sections you teach. Start the year by writing the name of each student in a class on three sheets of notebook paper. During a planning period or at the end of the day, place sticky notes on appropriate pages.

Review sticky notes for developing readers, English language learners, and special education students every two weeks and use the notes as one formative assessment that can help you monitor their progress. Reread sticky notes for other students twice during a quarter.

Making the Rounds

One of the most effective methods teachers can use to stay abreast of students' progress is "making the rounds" (Allison 2009; Anderson 2000; Atwell 2014; Robb 2010). The teacher circulates among students providing immediate support for reading and writing through a shared conversation or jotting on a sticky note which students require one or a series of five-minute conferences. Tuning into how each student internalizes a lesson every day in your classroom keeps you abreast of the type of intervention each student needs to improve.

The Framework for Four Types of Interventions

As you continue to read, you'll explore the four intervention frameworks that are part of this book:

- ➤ 2- to 3-Minute Interventions
- ➤ 5-Minute Interventions
- ➤ 10- to 15-Minute Interventions
- ➤ 30- to 40-Minute Interventions

To help you decide how to support a student, start with a 2- to 3-minute intervention that includes observations and informal conversations. Keep in mind that the overarching goal of each type of intervention is to meet the learning needs of each student in your class.

2- to 3-Minute Interventions

The purpose of this brief intervention is to help you decide which students you can support during a two- to three-minute, informal conversation and who requires a five-minute exploratory conference. The word *exploratory* indicates that this first conference will help you determine how much scaffolding time a student needs to move to independence.

You can help repair students' small confusions by listening carefully while you make the rounds, asking questions, observing whether they are reading or off task, and skimming students' writing about reading. These daily interactions enable you to check on the progress of students you previously helped and continue supporting all students as they practice new tasks.

To determine the amount of intervention each student needs, circulate and pause at each desk, observe behavior and attitude, and watch how a student approaches a task. View these student behaviors as signals for you to investigate further: a student isn't writing, reading, or sharing during a pair-share; a student is doodling in his notebook, slumping in her seat, or resting his head on the desk. Have an on-the-spot informal conversation with each student and decide whether you need more than a short conversation to scaffold the learning.

While a student waits to confer with you, have the student work on a task he or she can complete independently, such as reading independently or rereading a section of a text at his or her instructional level. If you have time, schedule a five-minute conference that day or the next day, so you can decide the type of support the student needs.

The mini-lesson you presented and the expectations you and students have negotiated for silent reading, applying a strategy, or writing about reading provide the information you'll need to determine on-the-spot scaffolds. After you think aloud or model, have the student practice in front of you to ensure that he or she can work independently.

5-Minute Interventions

The purpose of this one-on-one conference is to help you decide how much support a student needs to move to independence with a task. You might be able to clear up the confusion in one to two conferences. However, there will be times when your observations of the student practicing finding text evidence or comparing and contrasting two characters indicate the need for a series of three or more short conferences so the student can achieve independence with the task.

These focused conferences between you and a student offer you time to model, have the student practice and think aloud in front of you, and then gradually release the responsibility for completing the task to the student. (See Chapter 3 for more information about gradually releasing responsibility.) These conferences are successful when you support the task that the student finds challenging. So if you're planning to scaffold text structure, narrow the focus to informational text or literature and pinpoint what the student needs to understand better.

Hold five-minute conferences in a quiet place in the classroom while other students are completing work independently. Set up a small table or a student desk away from other students so you have privacy while conferring. A student will be reluctant to share his or her feelings and concerns if everyone in the class can hear.

Your first five-minute conference can let you know what a student needs. Start with your observations during your informal conversation with the student and ask him or her, for example, how you can help with finding the author's purpose or identifying mood and tone. Teacher-to-student conferences are safe places for students to share what they find confusing or difficult. Watch the student's body language: continual yawning, asking you to repeat directions several times, or looking at the clock or a watch can indicate frustration over a lack of understanding of the lesson or anxiety about completing the task incorrectly. Consider these choices when you meet again: (1) repeat modeling the lesson and ask the student to stop you when he or she feels confused; (2) find an easier, more accessible text and reteach with it so the main challenge for the student is applying the skill or strategy and not struggling with a text.

Most five-minute conferences are between the teacher and one student. However, if there are two to four students practicing the same skill or strategy with you, you might bring them together once they are close to achieving independence. Often, at this point in the scaffolding, asking students to practice together and share and discuss their process can quickly move them to independence.

Five-minute conferences require planning on a conference form and keeping a written record of what transpired during each scheduled meeting. (Figure 2.4 shows the *Intervention Conference Form*. A full-size version of the form can be found in Appendix D and on the Digital Resource CD.) Pre-planning asks you to note the focus of

Figure 2.4 Intervention Conference Form

Intervention Conference Form

Student Name: _____ Date: _____

Focus of the Conference: _____

Materials:

Student's Comments:

_____
_____
_____

Teacher's Notes:

_____
_____
_____

Goal:

_____
_____

Check One:

☐ Works with a peer
☐ Works with the teacher
☐ Can work independently

Follow-up Conference Date: _____

Appendix D

Chapter 2

the conference and the materials you will use. Narrow the topic by breaking it into smaller parts. For example, ask yourself which part of inferring does the student need to practice? Subtopics for inferring might include: knowing an inference is unstated or implied; reviewing the prior knowledge the student has; deciding what details in an informational text will help with inferring; or using a literary element to infer. By pre-planning you can use all of the five minutes to support the student.

After the conference, note what the student said and accomplished, jot down your observations, negotiate a goal with the student for the next conference, and note the date the conference will occur.

The completed conference form in Figure 2.5 illustrates the breakthrough moment with Bernardo, a seventh-grade English language learner who had difficulty inferring with informational text. I used *Jane Goodall* by William B. Rice for Bernardo's reteaching lesson. We had been practicing making logical inferences using photographs from books, and after three conferences Bernardo was able to do this. Transfer occurred when I asked him to create a picture of what he read in his mind and use the mental picture to infer. For example, the cover of *Jane Goodall* shows Jane kissing a gorilla. Bernardo inferred that Jane loved gorillas and she wasn't afraid of them.

Figure 2.5 Sample Intervention Conference Form

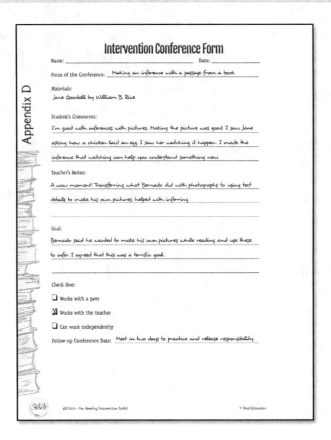

10- to 15-Minute Interventions

If you observe little to no progress during a series of five-minute conferences with a student, it's time to switch gears and consider scheduling a longer conference. You can also notice the need for a longer conference as you circulate among students and observe them reading or writing.

The purpose of a longer intervention is to provide more modeling to build background knowledge, or more time for a student to practice applying a strategy while the teacher monitors the student's progress.

Extra time allows the student to reflect on the task and figure out parts of the task he or she understands and areas that require more practice, as well as additional teacher modeling.

Usually, the teacher works with one student. However, if you plan to have the student transition to learning with a peer expert, it's beneficial to show the partners the type of practice you envision and have them work as you observe.

With this type of intervention, you can support a student who is not making progress after completing three or four five-minute conferences by extending the amount of time you work with him or her. The student might need extra time to process information, ask questions, and practice, or the student might need to learn and practice with an easier text. Switching to an easier text enables the student to focus on applying the strategy.

Classroom Snapshot: 10- to 15-Minute Intervention

I'm moving among eighth-graders who are identifying antagonistic forces about halfway through science fiction short stories. I notice Adam has set up his notebook page, but he's doodling. After a short conversation, I discover that Adam doesn't understand what *antagonistic forces* are. In fact, he is unfamiliar with other terminology such as *protagonist*, *rising action*, *conflict*, and *climax*. Based on Adam's candid feedback, I decide to arrange two consecutive 15-minute conferences to build his background knowledge of these terms and link them to a literary text. Adam's progress will help me decide whether to continue the longer intervention timeframe or move to a series of five-minute conferences.

Longer interventions work well with individual students and pairs or small groups of three to four students who struggle with the same reading challenge. Often, the interactions between pairs or among students in a small group can spark solid progress because students hear how their peers approach applying a reading strategy.

Longer interventions require more pre-planning in order to maximize the use of intervention time. Figure 2.6 shows my plan for a 15-minute conference with a fourth-grade student who retells the text when asked to identify a character's personality trait and use text evidence to support their thinking.

Figure 2.6 Plans for 15-Minute Intervention

Text: *Shiloh* by Phyllis Reynolds Naylor, Chapter 3

Procedure:

1. Review the meaning of personality traits.

2. Say, "To find characters' traits, it's important to focus on what characters say and do."

   ➤ Use Chapter 1. Model how I use what Ma says on the first page, and the conversation between Ma, Dad, and Marty on pages 17–18 to identify personality traits about Ma. Invite student to help identify a trait shown on pages 17–18.

   ➤ Use dialogue on page 29 with student. Reread it—student is Marty, I'm Dad.

   ➤ Tell student to try to step into Marty's skin and feel what traits Marty uses. Discuss.

3. Negotiate a goal with student.

4. Evaluate the lesson and goal and set up a second conference.

Chapter 2

This intervention is for a group of Tier 3 students who read more than two years below grade level. These students usually score below the 25th percentile on standardized tests. Often, they have an IEP and have already been designated as Tier 3 learners. If you have any doubts about a student's placement, then you or your school's reading specialist can administer an Informal Reading Inventory. See pages 41–42 for more about informal reading inventories.

The purpose of this intervention is to provide time for students to practice grade-level reading strategies using materials that are at their instructional reading levels. Instead of activity sheets, I recommend that students read high-interest books and short texts, and have discussions that interpret meaning with the support of a strategy, such as finding themes or making inferences. Writing about the reading in a notebook lets you know whether students can recall details, use details to analyze the text, and cite text evidence to support their thinking. Notebook writing also reveals the vocabulary students use, how they organize ideas, and their knowledge of spelling, usage, and punctuation.

If your school has a reading specialist or special education teacher who can work with students who need Tier 3 instruction, then this group can receive intervention lessons every day. Students who read far below grade level can use high-interest, easy-to-read books to practice and improve their application of reading strategies, analytical thinking about a text, and vocabulary, as well as enlarge their background knowledge. In addition to lots of practice with books at their instructional reading level, this group needs to read independently as much as possible to accelerate their reading achievement (Allington 2011; Krashen 2004; Miller 2010; Robb 2010 and 2013; Routman 2014).

Your plans for Tier 3 instruction should include a mixture of short texts and entire books at students' instructional reading levels. With some groups, you might be able to use the same book for all students. Other groups might have a wide range of instructional reading levels. For this situation, I recommend that you practice reading by using a short text every student can learn from. For the remaining class time, have students read books at their instructional reading levels. Confer frequently with students to monitor progress and adjust interventions.

Reflecting on the Four Types of Interventions

During the course of a school year, you might have to use each one of the four types of interventions several times to improve the reading and writing strategies of the students you teach. Keep in mind that one type of intervention is not better than another. It is impossible to categorize reading strategies under each type of intervention and claim that this or that intervention works best for inferring, determining importance, or using context clues to determine the meanings of unfamiliar words. You, the teacher, are the key to deciding the intervention that might work best for a student. By making the rounds every day, you can repair some confusion with short conversations, as well as identify students who need another type of intervention (Allington and Johnston 2000; Farstrup and Samuels 2011a; Howard 2009; Routman 2014).

Instructional reading, vocabulary building, and targeted interventions that meet individual students' needs combined with an independent reading curriculum can build students' reading strength and accelerate their achievement (Allington 2009; Allison 2009; Guthrie 2004; Hiebert 2013; Howard 2009; Miller 2010 and 2013; Krashen 2004). It's helpful to remember that a sixth-grader reading at a second-grade level most likely will not leap four years forward in one year. However, these developing readers can make significant progress when you scaffold their reading, provide expert reading instruction every day of the year, and have them self-select books for independent reading.

Continue the Conversation

Discuss these prompts and questions with your team or a peer partner. Reflecting on what you learn, what you know, and your students' performance can support your decision-making process regarding the kind of intervention plan you will develop.

1. Try making the rounds for at least 10 school days. What are the benefits of making the rounds and what have you learned?

2. Share how you differentiate reading, and discuss why differentiation is important.

3. What are the four types of interventions and how can each one support the students in your classroom?

4. Bring two completed conference forms to a second meeting with you and your colleague(s). Share what worked, and ask colleagues for feedback on aspects of the conference you felt didn't work. Suggest other interventions that could support the student.

Chapter 2

Chapter 2

Chapter 3

Intervention Tools for Teachers and Students

The intervention process can be easier to manage when you know the diverse intervention tools you have and which tools your students can access. Part of planning intervention requires that you understand the "how to do it" and the benefits for each of the tools you have available for modeling and overseeing guided practice.

You will also need a reliable tool to determine the instructional reading level of each student in your class. Knowing a student's instructional reading level helps you place him or her in an appropriate text for instruction and find the just-right text for guided practice during intervention.

Students' Instructional Reading Levels

It's helpful to consider multiple assessments when determining students' instructional reading levels such as standardized test scores, recommendations from the previous teacher, formative assessments you have, and the results of an Informal Reading Inventory (IRI). Using several measures can provide far greater insight into students' instructional reading levels than using one standardized test score.

An IRI can provide you with ways to address the instructional needs of students who need Tiers 2 and 3 instruction (Nilsson 2008). If your school has a reading specialist, try to enlist his or her help with administering IRIs to students who face the greatest reading challenges. Otherwise, you can administer an IRI, as it has clear and specific directions for administering and scoring.

Two Informal Reading Inventories to Investigate

1. The Flynt/Cooter Inventory (Cooter, Flynt, and Spencer 2014) uses narrative and expository passages in English and Spanish. Questions are literal, inferential, and evaluative. This IRI also includes questions about literary elements for narratives and text structures for expository selections. Retelling rubrics focus on literary elements for narratives and expository structures for informational texts. This IRI can be used with students reading at the pre-primer level through high school.

2. The Analytical Reading Inventory by Woods and Moe (2014) includes narrative passages and informational passages for social studies and science. Questions include inferential thinking, connecting ideas, evaluating, and supporting with text evidence. This IRI can be used with students reading at the pre-primer level through high school.

Quick Ways to Assess Instructional Reading Levels

Classroom-based assessments are most helpful if they are quick and efficient. As much as possible, it is helpful if finding instructional reading levels avoids interrupting teaching and students' learning (Serafini 2010). Here are four suggestions for easy ways to find students' approximate instructional reading level:

➤ If your school uses Fountas and Pinnell's Benchmark Assessment, then follow the directions for finding students' instructional reading levels.

➤ Teachers in some states receive students' Lexile scores along with reading scores. If you school doesn't have a summer reading requirement, you should allow for that "summer slide" backwards when starting the year (Allington and McGill-Franzen 2013; Miller 2010 and 2013).

➤ Nancy Padak and Tim Rasinski, both outstanding researchers, have published two books (2005) for quick reading assessments: *3-Minute Reading Assessments*, grades 1–4, and *3-Minute Reading Assessments*, grades 5–6.

➤ For grade-level and above-level readers, ask students to write the title and author of the last book they read for school in the previous year and rate it as easy, hard, or just right. If you're unfamiliar with the title, you can run it through Lexile.com to get a Lexile level or check Book Wizard (www.scholastic.com/bookwizard/), which has thousands of leveled books.

As you observe students reading at their instructional level, you'll decide which tools to access in order to support the interventions you plan.

Intervention Tools for Teachers

The tools for teachers that follow grow out of the needs that students demonstrate during lessons, when they work independently, or when they collaborate with partners or small groups. Having a menu of tools at your fingertips means that if one tool doesn't work, there's another one waiting in the wings that might help the student move forward.

The Think-Aloud

With this strategy, the teacher makes the reading process visible by thinking out loud so students can hear how he or she applies a strategy, as well as uses context clues to figure out the meaning of an unfamiliar word or the main idea using text details (Baumann, Jones, and Siefert-Kessell 1993; Robb 2010 and 2013; Wilhelm 2013). During a mini-lesson, the think-aloud allows the entire class to see how reading strategies work.

During guided practice, students can think aloud and show teachers their thought processes for comprehension skills such as inferring information or for showing how and why a character changes throughout the text. Moreover, the think-aloud is an effective strategy for partners practicing deep comprehension strategies because it helps them monitor their understanding and their ability to think at high levels (Baumann, Jones, and Siefert-Kessell 1993). As partners think aloud, they support each other and have multiple opportunities to hear how others solve the same reading problem.

Learning Reminders

As you circulate among students to observe while they read, write, and discuss texts with partners or small groups, you will observe learning issues that can be repaired with a short conversation. Provide on-the-spot interventions for students you can help within a few minutes by writing suggestions or reminders on a sticky note.

Each morning, prepare a clipboard with several sheets of notebook paper. On each sheet place dated sticky notes. When you chat with a student you can quickly help, jot the key points on a sticky note, give it to the student as a reminder, and require that the student keep the reminder on the work so you can measure improvement.

Sticky note reminders also refresh students' memories when they return to a task on another day. If a student requires more than a few minutes of support, set up a longer intervention. (See Chapter 2 for the framework for the four types of interventions.) As you make the rounds, look for the following cues and provide written reminders for students:

- ➤ **Interactive read-alouds:** Students' questions and/or comments show confusion or the student seems detached from the lesson.

- ➤ **Interactive mini-lessons:** Students don't participate during pair-shares.

- ➤ **Stamina during silent reading:** Students can't concentrate on reading, which could indicate that the text is too difficult or doesn't interest them and might call for offering a different text.

- ➤ **Difficulty settling down and concentrating on writing:** Written directions might seem unclear to the student or the student has little to no recall of the reading material.

- ➤ **Vocabulary:** Students have difficulty using context clues or linking figurative language to text meanings.

- ➤ **Prior knowledge:** Students need more prior knowledge to comprehend or need to preview a text to build prior knowledge.

- ➤ **Skimming a text to locate evidence:** Students need more support to see how skimming helps collect specific details.

- ➤ **Writing about reading:** Students need to talk more about a response before writing.

The goal of continually circulating among students and offering reminders is to prevent small confusions from becoming major obstacles to students' progress.

Gradual Release of Responsibility Model

Based on observations while making the rounds and from students' written work, the teacher can plan scaffolds that provide support through modeling, guided practice, and a gradual release of the responsibility for completing a task to the student (Buehl 2005; Duke and Pearson 2002; Fisher 2008). There are four stages of gradual release: *show me, help me, pair me,* and *let me.*

- ➤ **Show me** is used in a model lesson where you think aloud and show the student how you apply a strategy such as making logical inferences to a text. Clearly explain the process you use and how you find text evidence to support your thinking.

➤ **Help me** reflects guided practice that asks the student to apply a strategy to an easy text while you observe. During guided practice prompt the student, think aloud, ask the student to think aloud, and guide the student toward applying the strategy and finding text support. You might need to have more than one guided practice lesson to help the student become independent with the task.

➤ **Pair me with a peer** so we can practice together and observe and learn from each other's process. Once students are successful with guided practice, pairing them with a peer provides more opportunities to practice and discuss the strategy.

➤ **Let me work independently,** which is the goal of all instruction and interventions. Observe the student working on his or her own to determine whether additional guided practice or practice with a peer is needed.

Gradual release is not a linear model that asks students to move from one stage to another. You'll find that you will invite students to return to a stage to gain more practice so that they are secure enough with a task to work on their own. When you scaffold, keep in mind that students may not move to independence after the first round of interventions. That is a normal part of the process because some students, such as English language learners and developing readers, might be learning and practicing these skills for the first time. Revisit the scaffolds during the year, and keep in mind that it might take more than one school year for these students to achieve lasting independence with a task.

Reteaching Lessons

If the text students use during two scaffolding lessons is not helping the student improve, then it's time to reteach using a different instructional approach and a more accessible text (Fisher and Frey 2013; Howard 2009).

Develop a reteaching lesson when you observe any of the following:

➤ Guided practice is not helping the student understand how a strategy works.

➤ A series of 10–15 conferences has not worked.

➤ The text the student is using is too difficult. The text derails the student's focus away from the strategy because he or she cannot pronounce or understand the meaning of words, or cannot recall basic details.

➤ The student expresses frustration with the task or the student resists working on the task during guided practice.

Reteaching may include simply changing texts and using a student's independent reading book to model how a strategy works. Or you might break down a strategy into sub-steps and show the student how to apply the strategy as you identify each sub-step through a think-aloud. For example, sub-steps for finding theme are (1) state a theme in general terms, and don't use the names of persons or characters from your book; (2) know that a theme that applies to your book can also apply to other texts; (3) use what characters or persons do, say, and decide; their interactions with others; and their solutions to problems to figure out possible themes; (4) find text evidence to support the theme.

Word Study

Students who have difficulty pronouncing, spelling, and understanding words can grow as readers and thinkers with word study (Bear et al. 2011). Word study develops students' knowledge of the alphabetic principle, word patterns, and word meanings. Students learn to look at a word and consider its parts rather than guessing what the word is or means based on the first letter or syllable. In fourth grade and beyond, teaching phonics focuses on letter-sound relationships and pronunciation, while word study supports the alphabetic principle and pronunciation and also builds vocabulary and spelling power (Allington 2011; Bear et al. 2011).

In *Words Their Way*, a research-based approach to spelling and vocabulary, the authors describe a hands-on approach to word learning called word sorting (Bear et al. 2011).

First, you will need to assess students for placement in the appropriate spelling developmental stage. Figure 3.1 provides information about developmental stages of spelling.

You can gain confidence with using word study with students by studying *Words Their Way* with a colleague, trying the sorts, and discussing why this method is effective, especially for middle-grade and middle-school students who face reading challenges.

Figure 3.1 Developmental Stages of Spelling

Knowing these stages can help you identify the spelling needs of struggling readers and the kind of support they require to improve their vocabulary and knowledge of word patterns.

➢ **Emergent:** Students who lack phonemic awareness and can't hear and write beginning and ending consonant sounds.

➢ **Letter-Name Alphabetic:** This group, categorized as beginning readers, understands the left-to-right match-up of sounds to letters. They can hear and write beginning and ending consonant sounds in single-syllable words. Later in this stage, students place vowel sounds they hear in the middle of a word.

➢ **Within Word Pattern:** These students are transitional readers who have insight into the spelling of long and short vowel patterns.

➢ **Syllables and Affixes:** Intermediate readers fall into this group. Students look at patterns in two-syllable words and consider how words change when they add endings to a base word such as -ing to shop = shopping; -ment to judge = judgment.

➢ **Derivational Relations:** Students in this group are advanced readers. Word study for this group looks at word origins and includes studies of Greek and Latin roots and prefixes and suffixes with the goal of building a large and varied vocabulary.

One-on-One Conferences

Conferences between the teacher and a student can focus on scaffolding and reteaching. They can also be investigative conferences where the teacher tries to learn more about the student's instructional needs, attitudes, and reading life (Anderson 2000; Allington 2011; Allison 2009; Bomer 2011; Howard 2009; Robb 2008 and 2010). Prepare for and document conferences on a pre-planning form so you have a record of what you and the student practiced and negotiated. Figure 3.2 can be used to record information from these conferences.

There are many ways to start the conversation with students and encourage them to talk about their challenges. The following are suggestions for conferring with students.

Figure 3.2 Intervention Conference Form

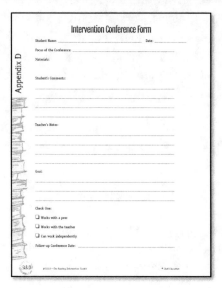

➤ **Choose a single topic.** Zoom in on one strategy such as making inferences, linking literary elements to themes, or determining important details and ideas.

➤ **Be positive.** Start by pointing out what the student has done well. It could be something you recently observed or the effort the student puts into analyzing texts.

➤ **Count to 100.** When you ask a question to start the conversation, count to 100 and give the student time to think. The tendency is for teachers to fill the silence with talk and solutions. This doesn't support students. Though your wait time might feel like an eternity, resist the urge to talk.

➤ **Listen carefully.** Avoid interrupting a student. Listen carefully and jot down questions you have; ask these once the student has finished talking. Throughout the conference, use your knowledge of this student to make comments and ask questions that boost the student's confidence and encourage him or her to talk.

➤ **Pose questions that prompt students to recall prior lessons.** Review a mini-lesson or a think-aloud that relates to the conference's topic. When you point students to a specific lesson, you shift the focus away from their own thinking, which sometimes frees them up to find the solution from the lesson.

➤ **Make your process visible.** Sometimes you'll need to think aloud to show the student how you apply a strategy to reading in order to refresh his or her memory and build enough confidence so the student risks completing guided practice.

➤ **Close a conference with positive comments.** Say something positive to the student at the end of the conference. Try the prompts that follow and adapt them to the content of your conferences.

> ➤ "I noticed that you have a solid understanding of literary elements (or informational text structure). I know you can use that knowledge to infer (or find themes, make connections, compare/contrast) when we meet tomorrow."

> ➤ "I like that you skimmed the text to find evidence to support your inferences."

> ➤ "I'm pleased that you reread several passages, for this strategy really helped you to determine important ideas."

➢ "You understand this strategy so well that I'm going to pair you with (name of student) so you can practice together."

➢ "Your hard work and revisiting parts of the text helped you compose a detailed plan for your paragraph."

➢ "I noticed that you listened to my think-aloud carefully and asked excellent follow-up questions."

➢ "Your writing now shows that you can use text evidence to support your inferences (personality traits, themes, mood or tone)."

Before-, During-, and After-Reading Checklists

Before-, during-, and after-reading checklists invite you to reflect, near the end of each quarter, on the progress students are making. Completing checklists after several weeks provides you with a broader view of a student's progress before, during, and after reading, and can move you beyond the focus of daily or weekly interventions (Robb 2010). Store checklists for each student in a file folder along with other conference forms and, after each quarter, compare your observations with students' written work, conference forms, and the checklists of previous quarters.

Observing the progress a student has made can build your confidence regarding the interventions you've planned and implemented, but it can also help you help the student understand his improvement. Showing a student's progress and success can motivate that student to complete more self-selected, independent reading books and, at the same time, enlarge vocabulary and background knowledge as well as continue to apply the strategies you've modeled to instructional-level texts (Allington 2009 and 2011; Guthrie 2004; Guthrie and Wigfield 2000).

Checklists enable you to reflect on what students do well and highlight needs. You don't have to complete a checklist for grade level and above readers. However, it's helpful to complete a checklist for all students reading two or more years below grade level. Figures 3.3, 3.4, and 3.5 show before-, during-, and after-reading checklists.

Figure 3.3 Before-Reading Checklist

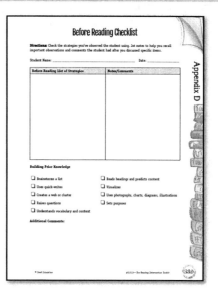

Figure 3.4 During-Reading Checklist

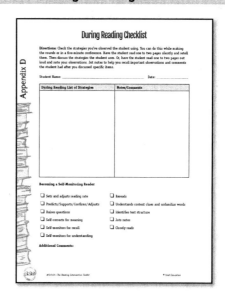

Classroom Snapshot: Before, During, and After Reading

The before, during, and after reading checklists for a fourth-grade student reading three years below grade level revealed some progress after seven weeks of instruction and intervention. The *Before-Reading Checklist* indicated that the student was using informational text features to build prior knowledge and better understand text details. Though several mini-lessons focused on asking questions and self-monitoring to check recall, the only strategy that I had observed was rereading to deepen recall. As I reflected about the *After-Reading Checklist*, I noted that the student was discussing questions about parts of the text in his guided reading group. In addition, I had moved the student from retelling informational texts to summarizing parts of a text. There was some progress, but like all teachers, I wanted more. When I completed the checklists from the second quarter and compared them to the checklists from the first quarter, the student was back on track. Here's why:

Figure 3.5 After-Reading Checklist

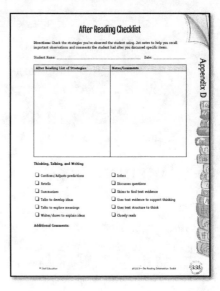

➢ **Before Reading:** The student could brainstorm a list of prior knowledge, raise questions, and set purposes for reading.

➢ **During Reading:** The student used context clues to figure out unfamiliar words, and he was able to monitor comprehension and reread to recall more information. He also knew when he didn't comprehend a sentence or passage and would ask for support if close reading didn't help.

➢ **After Reading:** The student returned to the text to find evidence for questions.

By comparing first and second-quarter checklists, I was able to see the gains this student had made. I showed him the checklists so he could celebrate his effort and improvement in reading. Moreover, I don't believe I would have had such a clear picture of this student's progress without taking the time to complete the checklists and compare them.

Interpreting Assessments

There are times when I review before, during, and after reading checklists and conference forms that document interventions, and I don't see enough progress. This does not frequently happen, but when it does occur, it's helpful to have a strategy that can deepen my understanding of the student's process, attitudes, and needs. I often complete the Interpreting Assessments Form, which I developed and have used for many years. Because completing the form takes a lot of time, I fill it out only when I've tried different interventions and I'm not seeing progress. Figure 3.6 shows a sample Interpreting Assessments Form.

Figure 3.6 Sample Interpreting Assessments Form

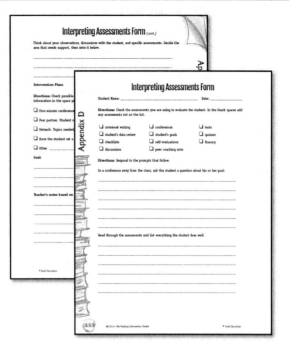

Classroom Snapshot: Interpreting Assessments

The notes in this snapshot come from my interaction with a seventh-grade student who reads four years below grade level. During independent reading, he turns the pages of books and magazines, but he isn't reading. My primary goal is to find books the student wants to read. I have used notebook writing, conferences, and checklists as well as worked with the student on personal goals prior to the interaction described here. All of these evaluations have shown that the student is not interested in reading.

First, I ask the student questions about my goal.

Robb: Why don't you read during independent reading?

Student: Not interested.

Robb: What are you interested in?

Student: Baseball.

That's the first time he shares his interest; I've asked that question many times. Usually, he says, "Dunno." To me, this is a breakthrough moment. I decide to try something "out of the box" and tell him that the fifth-grade teacher needs an older student to help a fifth-grade boy who loves sports do more independent reading. I suggest that the seventh-grade student choose a picture book biography about a baseball hero to read with the fifth-grade boy. The next day, I bring several to the class, and the seventh-grade student chooses a biography of Jackie Robinson. He and I work together to help him set a goal based on the discussion. We decide that we would read the biography out loud together so that he could then read it successfully to the fifth-grade student. We also decide where to stop, so the fifth grader can predict what will happen next.

The student's honesty about his interests was one key; the second key was that a fifth-grade boy needed help with independent reading. The relationship flourished, and the seventh grader improved his reading by teaching the fifth-grade boy some basic strategies that he and I rehearsed. However, by sharing books on baseball and other sports, both read books together and watched and discussed video clips about sports. You never know when a breakthrough moment for a student will occur, but when it does, capitalize on it.

Intervention Tools For Students

To assist the intervention process, there are things that students can do to support teachers' efforts. Consider the following section as a menu of tools from which you can pick and choose.

Have Students Track Their Progress

The research of Marzano clearly demonstrates that when students track their own progress using formative assessments there is a greater gain than when teachers do the tracking (Marzano 2009b).

A combination of student and teacher tracking in grades four and up is favorable because conclusions about progress can differ between adult and student, but together they can set reasonable and achievable goals. Negotiating and reaching these goals can enhance students' levels of self-efficacy, that feeling of "I can do it" (Duckworth and Eskreis-Winkler 2013).

In 14 different studies conducted by Marzano, teachers in one class had students track their progress on a simple chart. In a second class, teachers taught the same content for the same amount of time to students, but the teachers did not have students track their own progress. Results of the study showed that, on average, when students tracked their own progress, there was a 32-percentile point gain in their achievement. Figure 3.7 shows a sixth-grade student's progress over three months of tracking the number of books completed for independent reading. The student started with no books read and during the third month had completed four books. In a conference, the student said, "Seeing the line move up was great, and I wanted it to go up more. Besides, I enjoyed the books I chose."

Figure 3.7 Student's Progress: Independent Reading

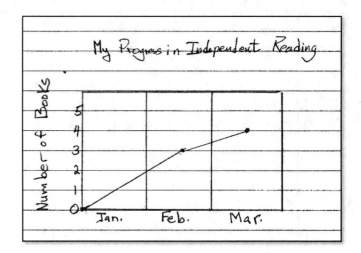

Marzano (2009b) identifies three things that can produce strong results when you ask students to track their progress:

1. **Have all assessments address one goal so that results are clear and reliable.** From the previous example of the sixth-grade student, the teacher had three goals for independent reading: (1) the student would read three to four books a month; (2) the student would complete one book talk a month; (3) the student would write the title and author of completed or abandoned books correctly on a book log and, in his notebook, explain why he abandoned the book.

2. **Use a rubric instead of points, but give students the rubric before they complete assessments and track their progress.** Marzano states that in all 14 studies when teachers used a rubric the best results occurred. Marzano recommends the rubric go from 0 to 4 and then decide what each number means. For example, with independent reading, the teacher's goal was for students to read four self-selected books a month. A 0 to 4 rubric tracked the number of books a student read each of three months. If you use the 0 to 4 rubric to help students track their progress with making logical inferences, it might look like this: A score of 4 means that the student can infer and support the inference with two pieces of text evidence. A score of 3 means the student inferred but used one piece of text evidence; a score of 2 means the student inferred but included no text evidence; a score of 1 means that the student made an inference but retold the text for support.

3. **Use different kinds of assessments.** Instead of the traditional tests and quizzes, try assessing written paragraphs, essays, personal narratives, a speech, an annotated timeline, or a reader's theater script.

Data Review

A data review is a self-monitoring strategy that asks students to track their progress using three or more performance assessments. Every six to eight weeks, students select three or more performance artifacts, list them on the Student Data Review Form (Figure 3.8), and reflect on their progress (Bomer 2011; Robb 2010; Valencia 2011). For the review to provide helpful information about a student's progress, performance artifacts should all relate to the same learning experience. For example, students have practiced finding two persons or characters and two events that change the protagonist during a narrative. They were required to clearly explain each change using text evidence. In Figure 3.9, a student has listed three notebook entries to review. The student notes the assignment's guidelines, decides whether he met the guidelines, and explains why or why not. Finally, if guidelines were not met, the student notes what needs to be done based on your instructions. This could be revising one notebook entry or completing a new entry that includes all of the guidelines.

Figure 3.8 Student Data Review Form

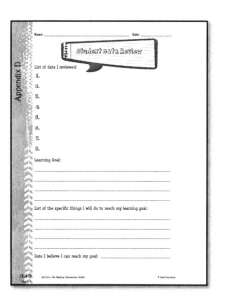

You can adapt the data review to reflect the diversity of students in your classroom. For example you can reduce the number of text examples for Tier 3 students to one person or character and one event, ensuring that these students experience success (Guthrie 2004; Guthrie and Wigfield 2000). Moreover, your students will probably be practicing different strategies to improve their reading, resulting in data reviews that address individual student's needs.

Just as you provide additional support to your Tier 3 students with setting goals, they will require help with selecting pieces, recalling the guidelines for the task, and noting their progress.

Figure 3.9 Sample Student Data Review Form

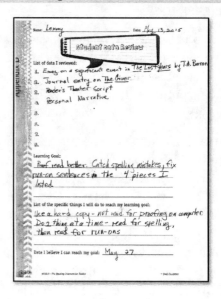

INSERW Self-Monitoring Strategy

INSERW stands for Interactive Notation System for Effective Reading and Writing. This strategy encourages students to interact with a text and offers them a way to determine, on their own, what they do and do not comprehend. Once students pinpoint a passage or word that's confusing, they can use close-reading strategies, reread and connect to other text details, or seek help. Becoming self-aware is the first step to making progress and boosting comprehension.

INSERW Notations

I understand = +

I'm confused = ?

This is important = *

Students can write notations lightly in their texts with a pencil and erase these, allowing others to interact with the same material, or use mini-sized sticky notes.

Bookmarks

Students can self-monitor their comprehension by making explicit the thinking they do while reading. Completed bookmarks enable the teacher to reflect on student thinking during and after reading.

To create a bookmark, fold a piece of notebook paper in half lengthwise. Have the student write his or her name, date, the title of the book, and the page number where he or she stopped to write his or her thinking. Avoid overusing the bookmark strategy as it can add an element of tedium to reading. Think of the strategy as a way to check a student's application of a strategy after you've intervened and provided support. Here are some idea for things that students can monitor using bookmarks:

➢ Make a prediction and support with text evidence.

➢ List the important details and the main idea.

➤ Visualize and draw what you see or use words to describe what you see.

➤ Explain unfamiliar words using context clues.

➤ Draw conclusions about a character or an event.

➤ Make inferences as you read about a person or character, decision, conflict, interaction, or information.

➤ Generate questions before, during, and after reading, and jot answers.

➤ Record a problem encountered while reading and how you repaired it.

Classroom Snapshot: Bookmarks

While reading *Shiloh*, by Phyllis Reynolds Naylor, fourth-grade students completed bookmarks so their teacher, Paul Green, and I could monitor how they identified and supported, with text evidence, three character traits and three emotions. The bookmarks revealed the reading capacity of each of the students. The work sample in Figure 3.10 shows that the student could provide some text evidence for emotions, but not for personality traits. Moreover, there was no text evidence to support the character traits and the traits listed—heart, sweet, mean— could be more thoughtful.

Figure 3.10 Text Evidence for Emotions

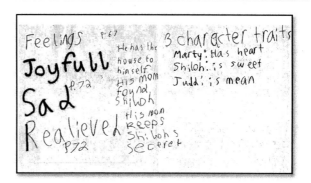

I believe that this student would benefit from a series of 5-minute interventions. We would work on organizing the bookmark and citing specific evidence to support each emotion and trait. A goal would be to help this student transfer her learning from the bookmark strategy to similar tasks recorded in her notebook. Figure 3.11 provides a list of personality traits that students could use.

Figure 3.11 Adjectives That Describe Personality Traits

adventurous	dutiful	joyful	sarcastic
aggressive	empathetic	kind	secretive
aloof	evil	knowledgeable	sensitive
ambitious	exacting	lazy	silly
anxious	excitable	lively	sincere
assertive	fearful	loving	snobby
bitter	fearless	loyal	sociable
bland	fierce	meek	spiteful
bloodthirsty	foolish	modest	stubborn
boisterous	friendly	moody	suspicious
bossy	fussy	morbid	timid

brave	gentle	mysterious	tolerant
brutal	grouchy	naughty	treacherous
calm	gullible	nosy	tyrannical
capable	harsh	obnoxious	unfaithful
careful	hasty	optimistic	ungrateful
careless	haughty	overbearing	unhappy
cheerful	helpful	patient	unique
clever	heroic	pessimistic	unpopular
conceited	hopeful	popular	unruly
confident	humane	practical	unsociable
confused	humble	proud	unwise
controlling	imaginative	pushy	vain
courageous	impatient	quick-tempered	villainous
cowardly	impish	rash	violent
cruel	impulsive	rational	vivacious
daring	innocent	realistic	weak
determined	insensitive	reasonable	willful
dignified	insincere	rebellious	wise
distrustful	intolerant	reckless	wishy washy
domineering	inventive	rowdy	witty

Setting Goals

Whenever students set performance goals, it's important to help them figure out the work they'll need to complete to reach the goal. For a performance goal to be effective, it should be within the student's learning zone and with enough of a challenge to be reachable (Vygotsky 1978; Zimmerman 2000). According to Schunk (2009), these kinds of goals can motivate students to work hard in order to reach the goal. Figure 3.12 shows a form that can be used for setting goals.

Figure 3.12 Setting a Goal Form

Classroom Snapshot: Goal Setting

A fourth-grade student having difficulty with summarizing a short literary text set this goal: Practice summarizing by first taking notes on the Summarizing Fiction, Memoir, and Biography Form and then using the notes to write a summary. Figure 3.13 shows the form the student wants to use to summarize.

Figure 3.13 Summarizing Fiction, Memoir, and Biography Form

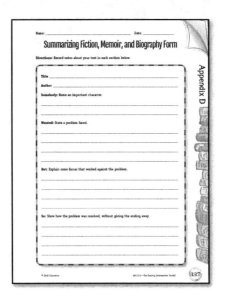

Initially, the student resisted using the form and was writing long retellings instead of selecting details for a summary. At the end of a five-minute conference on summarizing, the student agreed to take notes on the form. In addition, I asked the student to think about what she had to do to achieve her goal. Together, we created this list that she wrote on the goal form.

➤ Reread the story.

➤ Complete the form.

➤ Show the form to Mrs. Robb for feedback.

➤ Write a sentence that introduces the summary, and include the title and author of the story in the sentence.

➤ Write the summary by turning notes into sentences.

She also estimated that she could complete the form during one class period and write the summary during independent work time in the next two classes.

Keep short-term goals within a reasonable timeframe to motivate students so they can visualize themselves reaching the outcome. Providing progress feedback during the goal can lead to completing the task successfully (Zimmermann and Kitsantas 1999).

When students experience success with goal setting and meeting the goal, they learn that with hard work, and teacher feedback and guidance, goals can be reached (Guthrie 2004; Guthrie and Wigfield 2000). Once a student attains a goal, take a few moments to recap what he or she did and verbally praise the student's efforts or write positive comments on a sticky note. Here's what I said to the student in the previous classroom snapshot: "You added details to your notes that resulted in a summary that helped me know the key parts of the story. You experienced how a planning form can support this task. Your hard work helped you reach your goal!"

Chapter 3

Goal Setting for Students Receiving Tier 3 Instruction

Until Tier 3 students internalize the goal-setting process, you will need to provide solid support. You can support these students in the following ways:

➤ Keep timeframes very short so these students don't feel overwhelmed and lose motivation to accomplish the goal.

➤ Help students by breaking a goal into sub-goals. For example, you want some Tier 3 students to find text evidence to answer a question about evaluating an important decision a character or person made. You might set the sub-goals and have the student check in with you for progress feedback after completing each item.

➤ Make sure students understand that *evaluate* means judging the decision and explaining why it was or was not a good decision.

  ➤ Limit the pages or paragraphs that students need to skim or reread to pinpoint the decision. Have them locate the passage in the text and show it to you.

  ➤ Ask the students to write the decision in their own words.

  ➤ Have students note whether they believe the decision was a good or poor one and give two reasons to defend their position.

➤ Use the gradual release model to slowly release more of the responsibility for completing a goal to the student.

Peer Support Through Peer Partnerships

A peer partner is a mentor, a wise and trustworthy student-guide who can coach and support a classmate's learning. Because middle-grade and middle-school students value peers' perspectives, peer partnerships can have positive results. Moreover, partnerships make learning social and interactive.

Peer partnerships support both students and teachers. While several partners help each other develop text-dependent questions or plan and write an explanatory paragraph, the teacher is free to support students who need his or her expertise (Bomer 2011; Burke 2010; Robb 2012). Peer partnerships work when you consider these guidelines:

➤ Establish partnerships about four to six weeks into the school year, after students have worked with you and have gained insight into the conferring process.

➤ Give each pair of students clear directions that explain what they need to do.

➤ Negotiate a timeframe for partners to complete a task. Limiting the time to complete a task helps keep students focused.

➤ Check in with partners at work after you have helped some students. Provide progress feedback and suggestions.

➤ Let students know how they did and offer positive feedback by recognizing their progress and hard work.

Organize students into reading partners and change partnerships every time a new unit starts so students experience working with a variety of classmates. Often, an explanation from a peer can provide the support that enables a student to continue to move forward. Peer partners can be assigned by the teacher or selected by the student (Robb 2012; Ryan and Ladd 2012). Combined with you overseeing partners' work and providing progress feedback, peer partnerships can give developing readers the extra practice needed to help them improve strategies and push their reading achievement forward.

Struggling Readers Need to Practice Reading Strategies

In reading classes, comprehension strategies are often taught to students in the three tiers of instruction throughout the school year (Allison 2009; Bomer 2010; Fisher and Frey 2013; Howard 2009; Robb 2010 and 2013). Readers who struggle benefit from repeated practice with reading strategies, such as making logical inferences, understanding text and genre structures, identifying themes and big ideas, summarizing, and using context clues to determine the meaning of unfamiliar words.

Set priorities and have students practice a challenging strategy for a specific task. For example, a seventh-grade student can infer with literature, but her teacher discovers that she has great difficulty inferring with informational text. Since the next unit for this class is informational text, the teacher decides to focus on three strategies to support this student and others: making logical inferences with informational text; building background knowledge of the genre, including text structure; and building background knowledge of text topics. This teacher's decision supports the observations of Pinnell and Fountas who explain that teaching reading strategies is not linear with a prescribed sequence (2003).

Students in each tier of instruction benefit from applying strategies to texts to improve their recall and analytical thinking. However, there are four strategies that readers who struggle need to develop in order to improve their reading: prior knowledge, vocabulary, fluency, and prosody.

Build Students' Prior Knowledge

Students' prior knowledge differs widely because the background information, amount of independent reading, and vocabulary they bring to texts differs. Responsive teachers understand that students' motivation to build background knowledge before reading increases when they create situations that are social and interactive (Boss and Krauss 2007; Duke 2014; Guthrie 2004).

You can organize students into pairs or groups of four and send each pair or group to a website to watch specific video clips or to study a set of photographs that enhance prior knowledge of a topic. Students then share what they have learned with the entire class. Another strategy invites students to read the first chapter of their book, reflect on photographs or illustrations, and mentally recap what they've learned. Designing student-centered lessons engages them and builds a commitment to invest in the reading (Bomer 2011; Duke 2014; Fountas and Pinnell 2013; Gay 2000).

Expand Students' Vocabulary

If we want students to succeed at reading grade-level literary and informational texts, we need to embrace vocabulary instruction in all subjects. One of the main reasons that students are below grade level in their reading and struggle to catch up is their vocabulary deficits (Hart and Risley 2003; National Assessment of Educational Progress 2012; Rowe 2008 and 2012).

Excellent vocabulary instruction has the power of closing the huge gap between students who do well in reading and those who don't. Knowing a much bigger bank of words, especially general academic vocabulary, will give a huge boost to our English language learners, students living in poverty, and students reading three or more years below grade level (Beck, McKeown, and Kucan 2013; Verhoeven and Perfetti 2011; Robb 2014).

Chapter 3

In all subjects, when teachers consistently teach vocabulary and have meaningful conversations with students about words throughout a unit, they can enlarge students' word knowledge. In my book, *Vocabulary Is Comprehension* (2014), I recommend daily 10- to 15-minute lessons that relate to the reading and research students do. For example, during a unit of poetry, the teacher moves beyond asking students to memorize definitions of simile, metaphor, and personification, to requiring that students understand how each figure of speech works, what it means, and how it enhances their understanding of author's purpose, theme, or mood.

In *The Great Fire* by Jim Murphy, the author describes Chicago in 1871 as being "bound by a highly combustible knot." First, students discuss the word *knot* and agree that a knot ties or holds things together. The class also agrees that the word *combustible* relates to the wood buildings, wood sidewalks, and wood roads, that if ignited, can trap people in their homes and prevent firefighters from dousing flames. Moving beyond definition to analytical thinking can prepare students to read complex grade-level texts.

Develop Students' Fluency and Prosody

Prosody, reading with expression, also demonstrates readers' fluency and comprehension of a text (Rasinski and Griffith 2011; Rasinski 2004). Instead of struggling to find the time to have students complete repeated readings of short passages to build their fluency, Rasinski recommends teachers use practice and performance (2004).

Use poetry for fluency practice and performance, and have partners read a poem to each other for the first four days of the week. On the fifth day, students read their poems with expression and fluency to the class. In order to improve fluency, it is important for students to practice and present poems during most of the school year. Rasinski's research shows that not only does students' fluency improve, but their understanding of their reading also progresses (2004).

To help students read with expression and fluency, read aloud a poem posted on your board, and then point out to students how the punctuation supported how you read with expression. As pairs practice each week, circulate, listen, and offer suggestions that increase prosody. You will need about 20–30 minutes for performance (Rasinski and Griffith 2011; Rasinski 2004).

Write About Reading

In 2010, the Carnegie Institute published a landmark study by Steve Graham and Michael Hebert called *Writing to Read: Evidence for How Writing Can Improve Reading*. The conclusions of this study point to a simple but truthful concept: Students recall better and improve reading comprehension when they write. This study reviews the methodology Graham and Hebert used to develop their recommendations for the kinds of writing that boosts reading comprehension.

> **Teacher TIP**
>
> To collect a rich and varied selection of short poems for your students to perform, work as a grade-level team or department. You can type *poetry by grade level* into an online search engine and find dozens of poems that students can easily read. Or you can photocopy poems from anthologies in your school's library.
>
> Organize poems by readability levels and place sets in file folders and continually add poems to each folder. Each week, groups can select from a new poem to practice and perform from a specific folder.

According to Graham and Hebert, writing can enhance reading in three ways:

➤ Improve the comprehension of texts.

➤ Strengthen students' reading skills.

➤ Boost students' analytical thinking.

You can download a free copy of this report by Googling *Writing to Read* by Graham and Hebert. In the report, the authors discuss each recommendation and the theory behind it.

What follows is a summary of the recommendations Graham and Hebert make for using writing to improve reading (2010, 11). One of the most important aspects is to have students write about texts they read in science, social studies, mathematics, and language arts. Students can write about texts in the following ways:

➤ Respond to a text in writing (personal reactions and analyzing and interpreting the text).

➤ Write summaries of a text.

➤ Write notes about a text.

➤ Answer questions about a text in writing or create and answer questions about a text in writing.

Teachers should integrate the following into their instruction:

➤ Teach the process of writing including text structures of writing, paragraph, and sentence construction (improves reading comprehension).

➤ Teach sentence construction skills (improves reading fluency).

➤ Teach spelling skills (improves word reading skills).

➤ Increase the amount of time that students write at school (improves reading comprehension).

The actual writing that goes on in middle and high-school classes today still focuses on fill-in-the-blanks, worksheets, copying teachers' notes, and formulaic essay structures (Applebee and Langer 2011; Gillespie and Graham 2015; Graham and Hebert 2010). The research on the importance of writing and its correlation to reading comprehension shows a need for more writing time at school. However, the kinds and amounts of authentic writing about reading that students do at school needs to be re-evaluated and revised.

Assessment Observations and Conversations

I find that it's best to assess students' reading comprehension every day that students are in class. I understand that daily assessment can be daunting, but "making the rounds" makes it doable and even enjoyable once you get the hang of it. (See Chapter 2 about making the rounds.) Each day you will find me moving around the room, clipboard in hand, answering students' queries and jotting down my observations. During this time questions fly though my head: *Does the student need scaffolding? Should I set up a conference? Would working with a partner on this skill benefit the student more? Is the book too challenging?* This is what responsive teaching looks like in action.

Classroom Snapshot: Assessment Observations and Conversations

I am working with fifth-grade teacher Sandi Kim and her students on a research project. Students have selected topics they are passionate about and have been reading and rereading materials for almost two weeks. Ten minutes before class ends, students turn and talk to a partner, telling one another everything they learned and recalled from their reading. My goal is to have students read, reread, and discuss until they are itching to take notes based on what they recall.

After a mini-lesson where I model jotting notes from memory, I ask students to write what they recall in their notebooks. Then I circulate, stopping at each student's desk to check on the note-taking progress. I notice Camila drawing cartoons in her notebook. I walk over, bend down, and ask, "Can I help you get started?"

Camila looks at me, eyes brimming with tears, "I can't do this. I don't remember anything I read about Paul McCartney. I need the books in front of me. That's the only way I can take notes."

I pull over a chair and sit next to Camila. "Talk to me. Tell me anything you remember about Paul McCartney."

And Camila talks and talks. And I write her words in her notebook. "You do know so much about him," I say. "Reread what I wrote."

"I guess I do remember," says Camila.

"Try saying what you know in your head or whisper it. Then, stop and write what you just said. After you collect notes, you can reread parts of books and add more details." Camila asks if she can find a quiet place to talk and then write.

"Go for it," I say and move on to check out other students.

Had I not interacted with Camila that moment and instead waited one or two days, her anxiety about remembering information could have escalated, Camila would have no notes to use to create a project plan, and she might not have discovered the "talk-to-note-taking" strategy that worked for her. Since students selected their topics and Ms. Kim and I helped them find materials they could learn from, differentiation played a key role in completing successful projects to share with classmates.

Continue the Conversation

Discuss these prompts and questions with your team or a peer partner. Reflecting on what you learn, what you know, and your students' performance can support your decision-making process regarding the kind of intervention plan you will develop.

1. Discuss the value you see in making the rounds.

2. Discuss the Gradual Release Model. How do you move students to independence with applying reading strategies?

3. How do you decide that a student requires reteaching? Discuss the changes you make in a lesson in order to support the student.

4. Discuss how you improve students' vocabulary, and share one or two lessons that students learned from and enjoyed.

Chapter 4 | Interventions for Reading Informational Texts

During my travels to train teachers in districts around the United States, I always ask this question: *How many informational text units are you completing in a school year?* Most teachers respond that they do one unit; some only complete novel studies with students. Units on biographies seem to be most popular for studying informational text. However, biography is more like fiction as it contains dialogue, true plot lines, and the protagonists are famous or infamous people. "I avoid informational texts," a sixth-grade teacher told me, "because they're unfamiliar. I do fiction because I know the genre, am familiar with the structure, and my students like it." I believe this teacher's candid comment accounts for a subtle resistance to incorporating informational units of study in a yearlong reading curriculum—a resistance born from teaching a genre that teachers are uncomfortable using.

Students receive a large diet of narrative texts in the primary grades, but due to changing state and national standards, new assessments, and the recommendations from quality research (Duke 2003), this trend is changing.

It's crucial to add informational reading units to the reading curriculum for students to experience success on today's tests, as well as in high school when they will read a myriad of informational texts in science, social studies, and English classes. Only when students read and analyze informational texts can you identify who requires interventions with this type of reading.

Help Students Dive Deeply Into Informational Texts

In the English language arts classroom, informational texts that teachers offer students should have excellent literary quality and include outstanding authors of this genre such as Jim Murphy, Albert Marrin, Russell Freedman, Kathleen Krull, and Steve Sheinkin. (See Appendix C for a list of recommended nonfiction books/informational texts.)

To develop students' enthusiasm for reading informational texts and to motivate all students to read widely in this genre, design units that offer students choice of topics and books. To engage students who focus reading on fantasy and realistic fiction and have not experienced an in-depth unit on informational texts, include print and ebooks, magazine and online articles, and newspaper articles.

One way to get students engaged in reading informational texts is to have them list three topics they would like to become experts on or topics that interest and/or fascinate them. Then, have students list the topics in order of preference from one to three. Use the topics students listed on these papers to determine available resources, and meet with your school librarian to identify the topics the library can support. In addition, discuss the readability of materials to ensure that students can read and learn from diverse texts on their own. Once you have researched what is available at the library, explain to students that the topic you circle on their papers reflects the materials available. Note that sometimes, your school library has funds waiting to be spent. One year, my librarian, Traci, ordered materials so that every fifth-grade student could investigate his or her first choice topic. However, I find that students are pleased with any of the choices they provided.

Because it is important for students to feel a sense of ownership for this informational text project, consider negotiating the following items with them instead of creating the parameters on your own: amount of reading, use of class time, getting help, and possible projects.

Amount of Reading—Students work on this informational unit for four weeks and complete all the reading and note taking at school. In four weeks, students agree to read parts or all of two books and a magazine or online article. Students usually read far more than this minimum. As Lucas pointed out: "If you love your topic, you want to read about it."

Use of Class Time—Students agree that settling down and reading or taking notes would not be an issue because they are learning more about topics that are important to them. They also agree that if they work hard during each 45-minute class, and they need more time to complete their project, teachers would hear and act on their request.

Getting Help—Students suggest that they first seek help from a classmate in their group. If they still need support, they would ask the teacher. If a teacher continually makes the rounds, he or she should always be available for a quick repair or a five-minute intervention conference.

Possible Projects—Students brainstorm the list of projects by spending five minutes on this during two class periods. Note that when you invite students to build a list of projects that interest them, you learn the types of projects that interest them and that they believe they can complete with enthusiasm. Here are suggestions for possible projects:

Possible Projects

➤ Create a web page with information about your topic.

➤ Design a visual and discuss your project using it.

➤ Make a video and show it.

➤ Write a series of poems.

➤ Design a PowerPoint Presentation.

➤ Create an infomercial.

➤ Plan and write a graphic text.

➤ Design a poster and discuss it.

➤ Write a photographic essay.

➤ Set up an interactive blog and write two to three blog posts.

Assessing Students' Needs for Interventions with Informational Texts

My primary goal of having students select a topic and read informational materials related to the topic is to introduce them to informational texts and develop an enthusiasm for this kind of reading. For this short project, as I make the rounds, I am focusing on the following four skills:

➤ Comprehension

➤ Paired conversations

➤ Note taking

➤ Organization

Comprehension

Here, the main question I ask is: Are students using a text they can read and learn from? Listening to students' paired conversations about the book can help you decide whether they can read and learn from it. If they have difficulty, find alternate texts that students can learn from independently. If listening doesn't give you a clear idea about a student's recall, try having the student retell to you directly.

To do this, meet with the student in a quiet place, and invite him or her to reread and retell two to three pages of the text. Document this conference on a Retelling Checklist for Informational Texts, which will enable you to decide whether the text is appropriate for the student. Figure 4.1 shows the Retelling Checklist for Informational Texts.

Equally important, you can discuss your notes with the student to help him or her understand why choosing a more accessible text can make the reading enjoyable. For example, a sixth grader retells pages 22–24 in *Unforgettable Natural Disasters* by Tamara Leigh Hollingsworth (2013). To document the student's retelling, I use the Retelling Checklist for Informational Texts shown in Figure 4.1. The retelling, even after a second silent reading, shows little recall, no connections to other texts, and lots of comments of "I don't remember." Figure 4.2 shows that the book for retelling was too difficult for the student, and I will have the

Figure 4.1 Retelling Checklist for Informational Texts

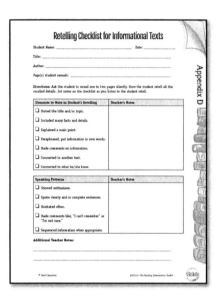

Figure 4.2 Sample Retelling Checklist for Informational Texts: Unforgettable Natural Disasters

student retell again with an easier book. Based on the retelling assessment, the first intervention for this student is to find a book about natural disasters that he or she can learn from and gain the prior knowledge needed for more challenging texts.

Paired Conversations

Here, the main question I ask is: Can students recall and discuss what they read? The level of details that students offer will enable you to determine what the student learned and recalled from the material. First have students reread two pages and then retell to you. If the retelling is detailed, remind the student that rereading is a great strategy to use.

Note Taking

Here, the main question I ask is: Do notes reveal a rich set of details? Before taking notes, students find a comfortable place to read for up to 30 minutes. Then, they discuss everything they recall with a partner. This talk creates an "oral text," which supports recall and helps clarify information. Once they complete reading and talking about a text, students jot a list of recalled information in their readers' notebooks. This method grows out of how authors like Russell Freedman and Jean Craighead George say that they read and talk to an editor or have an in-the-head conversation and write when they feel they are sweating the information—when the details have been absorbed by every cell (Robb 2004).

Sometimes the talk is rich and detailed, but the notes are minimal. This can be due to a student having difficulty with the physical act of writing. If this is the case, have the student record notes on a computer or tablet. In addition, you can do part of the writing and have the student complete the rest so that the task is not overwhelming.

Organization

Here, the main question I ask is: Can students create categories for their audience and organize notes under these? Students' projects and the audience they're writing for (novice or experienced with a topic) determine the categories or headings they develop to organize their notes.

For example, Lorna's project was on the assassination of Abraham Lincoln. She organized her notes under nine headings: Civil War, John Wilkes Booth, Why Killed Him, Assassination, Where He Died, Peterson House, Abraham Lincoln, Photo of Shooting, and Ford's Theater Now (see Figure 4.3). This organization tool enabled Lorna to plan a PowerPoint that her classmates learned from and enjoyed.

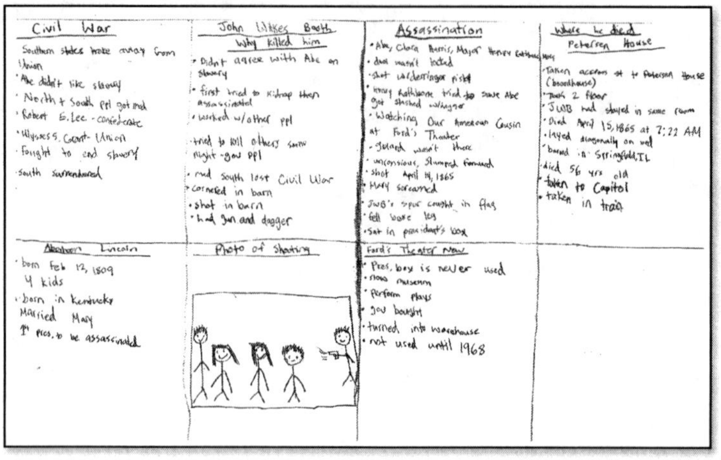

Make sure the student has a clear picture of his or her audience's needs, and what a category is and does. Think aloud and show the student how

Figure 4.3 Lorna's Project

you use the lists of notes and the audience's needs to determine categories or big ideas in headings. After showing how you find two categories, turn the task over to the student. If he or she struggles, return to thinking out loud and then try to release only part of the responsibility for developing categories to the student.

Supporting Students' Reading of Informational Texts

A key goal of reading is to enable students to achieve independence as they read more challenging instructional materials as well as easier independent reading texts. To help students move to greater independence, help them use these 10 suggestions. Also present these suggestions to students who require additional practice within the context of mini-lessons. A student version of these tips is found on pages 228–229 in Appendix D.

Ten Tips to Help You Comprehend Informational Texts

1. **Do a quick text preview before reading.** Before you start reading, do a quick preview that can build your background knowledge of a topic. Read the title, the first and last paragraphs of a short text, or the first chapter and last page of a book. Study text features such as bold vocabulary, photographs, and captions. Have an in-the-head conversation that reviews what information you learned from the preview. Now you have background information that can support recall and understanding.

2. **Study text features.** Read and think about text features such as boldface headings and vocabulary, photographs and captions, maps, diagrams, charts, snippets of letters or diary entries, and boxed sets of facts related to the topic. Doing this introduces you to information in the text and builds prior knowledge about the topic.

3. **Set a reading purpose.** Make your purpose to read to discover why the author used this title. You can also use what you learned from the preview to set a reading purpose.

4. **Raise questions.** Before reading, use text features to raise a few questions that, along with your purpose, drive the reading and enable you to focus on important details.

5. **Use context.** Try to determine the meaning of a word that is unfamiliar by looking for clues in the sentence that contains the word, by reading a few sentences that come before the word and sentences that come after the word. Sometimes the author defines the word immediately after using it by separating the word and definition with a comma or with "or."

6. **Consider informational text structure.** Informational text writers use these text structures: description/sequence, question/answer, problem/solution, compare/contrast, and cause/effect. Usually, writers mix structures so that a paragraph might be descriptive but also include comparisons and contrasts. Your knowledge of text structure can assist comprehension because you know what to expect as you read and think about why the author chose sequence or why he or she compared and contrasted, etc. Reflecting on structure can focus you on the way the writer organizes information as well as help you consider how the organization improves understanding of the author's purpose, the themes of the piece, and how details connect.

7. **Stop, check, recall, assess, reread, or read on.** To ensure that you can paraphrase information you've read, it's helpful to pause at the end of a section or page to see how much information can be recalled. If you recall little information, then reread and test yourself again. As you reread,

pause to evaluate recall, to better comprehend information in a sentence or section, and to deepen your knowledge of a text. Rereading is an excellent repair strategy.

8. **Skim to find important details.** It's helpful to understand that skimming to locate key details under text headings is an excellent review strategy that highlights important details. Skimming can also help you pinpoint information that answers text-dependent questions.

9. **Discuss text-dependent questions.** It's important to return to specific parts of the text to answer questions. You might use several passages to answer a question. To demonstrate understanding, paraphrase text details—put the ideas into your own words to show comprehension of facts and also use the facts to draw inferences. When you read a text with layers of meaning, there will be diverse interpretations among classmates.

10. **Close read.** Close reading is a useful tool to figure out the meanings of unfamiliar words and to unpack meaning from sentences and passages that are confusing. It is a repair strategy that helps you unpack meaning from challenging parts of texts. Review your handout on close reading (See Figure 4.4).

Figure 4.4 Close Reading Guidelines for Informational Text

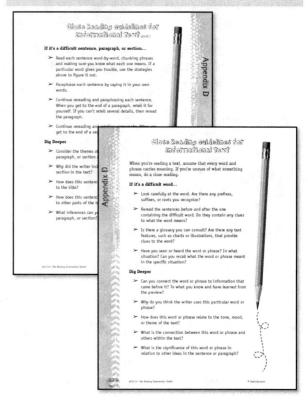

Classroom Snapshot: Discussing Text-Dependent Questions

When you show students how text-dependent questions have key words that can help them quickly locate information in a text, you enable them to skim and identify specific details. This excerpt from a conference with a sixth-grade student is an example of this strategy that you can use in a whole-class mini-lesson or as an intervention with a small group or individual.

Text: *Lightning* by Seymour Simon (first two pages of text)

Focus: Student avoids skimming and makes many errors when answering text-dependent questions.

Scaffolding Plan: To model how I refresh my memory of the information in the text, I read the first sentence of each paragraph and discuss what I've learned with the student. I also point out that I now know where different details are located. Then, I show how choosing key words from a question enables me to skim the text looking for these words. After modeling, I will turn the process over to the student. We will discuss the benefits he sees in skimming to locate the details that answer questions.

Goal: To boost skimming skills for locating text details where the text doesn't have headings.

Text-Dependent Questions:

➢ How fast does lightening travel?

➢ How much power does a flash of lightning contain?

➢ Why can't we harness the electricity in lightning bolts?

➢ How does lightning begin?

➢ What are step leaders?

➢ How do step leaders cause the birth of a lightning bolt?

Robb: Even though there are no headings and bold words in this text, you can use key words in the questions to skim for answers in the text. To help you recall the information on a page, read the first sentence of each paragraph. For the first question, I'm looking at how fast lightning travels; my key words will be *fast* and *travel*. I see *travel* and *speed* in the first sentence. I skim and can answer: "Lightning bolts travel as much as 60,000 miles a second." If I read the next sentence I learn that this is 6,000 times faster than the fastest spaceship we have. Now you locate the details for the second question. The key words to skim for are *power* and *flash of lightning*.

Student: I found it! There's lots of information here. (Rereads text.) It says a flash is brighter than 10 million 100-watt light bulbs. That flash has more power than there is in all the electrical power plants in the U.S.

Robb: How long does that energy last?

Student: Ummm. Okay. I got it. A split second. That is a millionth of a second for each flash.

Robb: I noticed how well you located the information each time. Now that we've practiced using key words in questions to locate details, can you name the key words in the last question?

Student: (rereads question) *Step leaders, birth, lightning bolt.*

Next Steps:

1. Have the student practice skimming to discuss and then write answers to text-dependent questions with a peer. The student's written work will let me know whether he can move to independence or if he should practice with me again or a peer. Before having him work on this skill independently, I will ask him to show me how to identify key words in a question, locate information in the text, and then skim to find details.

2. Document each intervention using the Scaffolding Conference Form in Figure 4.5. Having a written record of what transpired during a series of conferences will help me plan additional interventions and decide when he is ready to work independently. At the next short conference, I'll turn the entire process over to the student.

Figure 4.5 Scaffolding Conference Form

Scaffolding Conference Form

Appendix D

Student Name: _____ Date: _____

Focused Topic: _____

Teacher's Preparation Notes and Observations:
_____
_____
_____

Materials used with student:
_____
_____

Student's comments:
_____
_____
_____

Teacher records outcomes:
_____
_____
_____

Negotiated goal:
_____
_____

Check one:

❏ schedule another conference

❏ have student work with a peer

❏ student can work independently

233 | #51513—The Reading Intervention Toolkit | © Shell Education

Focus Your Intervention Lessons

It is important to focus your intervention lessons on the standards and skills that students need most to improve their reading. Here is a process to follow to help you do this:

1. Review the student's written work, your observational notes, and any conferences.

2. Focus on one aspect of the informational text focus standards that will most benefit the student. See focus standards and suggested scaffolds on the pages that follow.

3. Monitor the student's progress through scaffolding conferences and written work.

4. Record each focused scaffolding lesson on the *Scaffolding Conference Form* on page 232.

5. As soon as possible, gradually release responsibility to the student until he or she can complete the task independently.

Reading Standards and Interventions for Informational Texts

The interventions in this chapter follow key focus standards for reading informational text. They were selected based on analysis of a variety of current standards. Additionally, I've selected writing elements that enable students to focus on content. Content becomes primary because what students write can assist you in deciding whether they need help with developing a claim or topic sentence, finding text evidence for a paragraph, or short response or planning and thinking through ideas before writing.

For each strategy, one of these interventions will be provided: a quick, 2- to 3-minute intervention, a 5-minute intervention, a 10- to 15-minute intervention, or a 30- to 40-minute intervention. To help break the process down into steps that can ultimately support students' progress, a menu of scaffolding tips is included so that you can decide which ideas might help a student move to independence with the task.

Teacher TIP

When you make the rounds, you will be able to decide which students can benefit from a 2- to 3-minute intervention. You can determine which level of intervention other students require, by scheduling a five-minute investigative conference to observe how students manage and complete a task.

You can assess students' performance and determine the kind of intervention you'll try first by observing them while they plan and write as you make the rounds or in a conference that you document. Look for the following "red flags":

➢ The student doesn't talk during pair-shares.

➢ The student completes no writing or very little writing.

➢ The writing support doesn't relate to the claim or topic sentence.

➢ The student says, "I can't do this."

➢ The student shows anger towards writing about reading.

➢ The student refuses to plan or plans have little detail.

➢ The student doodles or draws cartoons.

➢ The student's head is on the desk.

Focus Standard 1

{ Determine what the text says explicitly and make logical inferences from the text using close reading; when writing or speaking, support conclusions drawn from the text by citing specific textual evidence. }

The skills and strategies that follow are crucial for students to master in order to achieve proficiency with this standard.

Strategy	Intervention Timeframe	Resource Page(s)
Identifying Details (page 72)	5 minutes	*Bug Builders* (bug.pdf)
Retelling Text (pages 73–74)	30–40 minutes	*Rome* (rome.pdf)
Skimming to Locate Key Details (pages 75–76)	5 minutes	*Amazon Rainforest* (amazon.pdf) *Scaffolding Conference Form* (page 232)
Making Logical Inferences (pages 77–78)	15 minutes	*Unforgettable News Reports* (news.pdf)
Using Text Details to Support Discussion and Writing (pages 79–80)	5 minutes	*Roberto Clemente* (roberto.pdf)
Building Prior Knowledge (pages 81–82)	30–40 minutes	*Rome* (rome.pdf)

Identifying Details

Chapter 4

Overview

In this intervention, students learn how text features can be used to identify details.

Materials

➨ *Bug Builders* (bug.pdf)

Procedure

1. Model how titles, headings, captions, and boldface words help determine important details.

2. Make the rounds and observe students practice with a page from their informational books.

3. If you observe that a student thinks that every detail is important, once again model how to use the text features to find important details.

Scaffolding Suggestions

➢ Model how you reread a paragraph and pinpoint key details.

➢ Show how you use the title and headings to find and cite details.

➢ Have students use photographs, captions, charts, and diagrams to think of details these features highlight. Have them find more details in the text that relate to the features.

➢ Explain that the title, headings, and boldface words can be used to find specific details. Then, model the process for students.

➢ Have students reread paragraph by paragraph and cite details also showing how details link to the title and headings.

➢ Ask students to read two to three paragraphs and tell the details, after you observe success when you offer support.

➢ Show students details from the text and discuss what details are.

➢ Have students read headings and predict the kind of details they will find in a section.

➢ Ask students to read a paragraph and identify details in the text. Keep adding more text until they show they are comfortable identifying details.

Classroom Snapshot

"I think everything is an important detail," Mena says as I pause at her desk. She's reading *Bug Builders* by Timothy J. Bradley.

"Let me model again," I say. I read the heading *Underwater Living* and the caption: *This aquanaut lives and works in an underwater habitat*. Then I explain that I'll pull out details that relate to both.

"I get it," says Mena. "Aquanauts live underwater in a habitat that has oxygen. Scuba divers might not need oxygen in the future; we might be able to get it from the water like fish."

"You used the heading and caption to help you select key details. Now jot your ideas in your notebook," I say, and I move on.

Retelling Text

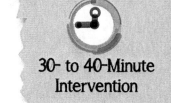

Overview

In this intervention, students look at specific parts of a text to support them in retelling the key facts from their reading.

Materials

➦ *Rome* (rome.pdf)

➦ *Retelling Checklist (optional)*

Procedure

1. Review that a retelling means you say, in your own words, the key facts.

2. Build background knowledge by studying the photograph of an aqueduct in the text.

3. Model with the last paragraph of the text. Have students ask questions and say what they noticed.

4. Organize students into pairs. Have students read the information in the sidebar under *Aqueducts*.

5. Have students start with retelling one sidebar from the text at a time. Students read the section twice and retell to their partner. The partner has the text and checks the level of detail.

6. Circulate and listen to pairs. Give feedback that explains what they did well and how they can improve.

7. After modeling the process for students, have them look at the photograph of an aqueduct and discuss it. Then, listen carefully to pairs' retellings.

Scaffolding Suggestions

➢ Review the term *sequence* with the student.

➢ Monitor with the *Retelling Checklist*, one per student.

➢ Ask the student to jot down retelling details in sequential order and use these to retell.

➢ Model how you reread short sections and retell each one in sequence.

➢ Have the student reread and retell paragraph by paragraph.

➢ Have the student reread a section or page and retell when they are able to retell one paragraph at a time.

➢ Have the student set a purpose for reading and use the purpose to select and retell important details.

➢ Show the student how the captions and information in the sidebars can help with retelling. First, practice with text, and then add retelling information in sidebars.

➢ Show the student how you reread the passage you retold to check whether you have included enough details.

Retelling Text *(cont.)*

Classroom Snapshot: Retelling

The following is Tony's retelling for information under *Aqueducts*:

Tony: Umm. Romans built aqueducts. They're pipes and carry water.

Robb: Why did Romans build these?

Tony: Not sure.
(I tell Tony that he's made a good start and ask him to reread and add details). They bring water to places—cities. People in cities had water because of these (aqueducts).

Robb: When you retell information under *Building Materials,* reread and check that you have all the details. Your partner can remind you to reread to recall more. Rereading is an excellent strategy for remembering more details and one all good readers use.

Skimming to Locate Key Details

Chapter 4

Overview

In this intervention, students learn how to skim the text to help them remember key details rather than using memory alone.

Materials

➤➤ *Scaffolding Conference Form* (page 232)

➤➤ *Amazon Rainforest* (amazon.pdf)

Procedure

1. Make the rounds to determine whether students are able to locate key details.

2. If you notice that a student is relying on memory rather than finding text evidence, meet with the student.

3. Determine whether the student is having difficulty with the strategy or the student is avoiding the extra steps.

4. Pre-plan on the *Scaffolding Conference Form* what you and the student will do for any necessary follow-up conferences.

Scaffolding Suggestions

➤ Show how these features enable you to locate details: headings, bold words, photographs and captions, diagrams, and charts.

➤ Model how text structure enables you to skim to find passages that compare/contrast, use problem/solution, question/answer, or have the main idea and details.

➤ Ask the student to locate a specific text structure and discuss how the structure increases comprehension.

➤ Practice until the student can use structure to skim for information.

➤ Practice until the student can show how a text structure improves his or her understanding of the material.

➤ Have the student use text-dependent questions to support skimming. Show him or her how to pinpoint key words in a question and search the text for the same key words.

➤ Help the student understand that skimming enables him to locate information, and that the next step is to reread the information.

Chapter 4

Classroom Snapshot: 5-Minute Intervention

Two fifth-grade students are relying on their memories to cite text evidence. As I make the rounds, I notice that they do not locate and skim parts of the text to make sure their text evidence is complete, accurate, and detailed. I'm unsure whether their resistance arises from some difficulty with this strategy or if they want to avoid extra steps. To determine what kind of intervention I'll select, I hold a five-minute investigative conference with each student because, even though they exhibit the same behaviors, their challenges might differ. Whenever you are unsure about what to do, the five-minute conference can help determine what to do because you can observe the student working and ask probing questions. I use the *Scaffolding Conference Form* to work with the student. Here are the questions I choose to ask:

1. Why is the Amazon known all over the world?

2. Why do people say the Amazon is huge?

3. Why is water from the Amazon River so important?

I notice that for question 3, the student writes: "It's fresh water." I ask the student to skim the text and boxes on pages 12 and 13 of the text. He tells me that there's more fresh water in the Amazon than in the next seven largest rivers in the world. There's more than nine feet of rain in the Amazon forest. The river supplies lots of fresh drinking water.

When I ask him which strategy, skimming or using memory, helps him provide more detail when citing text evidence, he replies, "Skimming—I get more information. I remember more. My answer is more complete."

The student recognized the benefits of skimming, but I feel more practice is needed. I schedule two more five-minute conferences with me. If the student continues to use the strategy, I'll pair him with a partner for extra practice. At our two short conferences, the student also needs to show me how he locates the pages that have appropriate text evidence.

Making Logical Inferences

Overview

In this intervention, students look at text features to support them in making inferences.

Materials

➤ *Unforgettable News Reports* (news.pdf)

Procedures

1. Model how to use "Civil War Letters" from *Unforgettable News Reports* to collect details and make an inference. Share questions that you use to make an inference, such as the following: What do I learn about the writer? What do I learn about Erastus, the wounded boy? What do I learn about the effects of war?

2. Use the following think-aloud to model how to select details: "Here are the details I select: Whitman, a friend, writes to the parents of Erastus to tell them of their son's final days. Whitman spends time with Erastus every day until the soldier dies. From these details I can infer that Whitman is empathetic and caring about Erastus's condition. I can also infer that Whitman is considerate and kind because he writes to Erastus's parents to soothe their pain by giving them as many details as possible about their son."

3. Have the student use the photographs from the text to infer.

4. Have the student read the paragraph under *The Televised War* and select details.

5. Help the student generate questions about the details that can lead to making an inference.

6. Ask the student to read the heading and the text in the box on page 22. Have the student think about what he or she has learned about war from television news and movies. Have the student generate questions about the details and then use answers to infer.

7. Repeat the process using the box on page 45 of the text.

8. Ask the student to explain what he or she learned about inferring with informational texts.

9. Have the student practice with another section of text.

Scaffolding Suggestions

➤ Explain that an inference is not stated in the text. It is an unstated or implied meaning.

➤ Make sure the student has enough background knowledge to be able to select text details and make a logical inference.

➤ Think aloud and show how you use a section of a text to infer.

➤ Have the student reread a different section and you select key details. Ask the student to use these details to infer.

➤ Continue practicing until the student can select details and use them to infer.

➤ Show the student details from the text and discuss what details are.

➤ Have the student read headings and predict the kind of details they'll find in a section.

➤ Have the student use photographs, captions, charts, and diagrams to think of the details these features highlight.

➤ Ask the student to find more details that relate to the text's features.

Making Logical Inferences *(cont.)*

Chapter 4

➢ Help the student select key details from a passage if the student has difficulty doing this.

➢ Have the student reread the details, discuss how they relate to one another, and develop an inference that grows out of them.

Classroom Snapshot: A Strategy for Interventions

As I make the rounds, I notice that an eigth-grade student is having difficulty making inferences with informational texts. During our conversation, I observe that the student can pinpoint text details, but is unable to develop an inference from these. I decide to schedule two consecutive 15-minute conferences before school starts as this student is on an early bus. This option offers me time to prompt the student so he can use a set of details to develop an inference. If I observe progress, I will move to a series of five-minute conferences during class.

Using Text Details to Support Discussion and Writing

Overview

This is a series of three 5-minute interventions where students examine text details to paraphrase their understanding.

Materials

�» *Roberto Clemente* (roberto.pdf)

Procedures

Day 1

1. Have the student read the text and record any questions he or she might have in his or her notebook.

2. Under each question in his or her notebook, help the student find the page that provides details to support his or her answer.

Day 2

1. Discuss paraphrasing and model how to paraphrase information.

2. Have the student practice paraphrasing parts of text he or she needs to cite and orally explain his or her answer to each question.

Day 3

1. Release responsibility to the student. Ask the student to skim the sections that have details he or she needs to answer each question. Have the student explain orally what he or she intends to write in his or her notebook.

2. If the student still needs support with paraphrasing, pair the student with another who is proficient with using text evidence, and monitor their progress.

Scaffolding Suggestions

➤ Show students details from the text and discuss what details are.

➤ Have students read headings and predict the kind of details they'll find in a section.

➤ Have students use photographs, captions, charts, and diagrams. to think of the details these features highlight.

➤ Practice paraphrasing details.

➤ Help students find parts of the text where details are located and reread.

➤ Have students locate the details that support a specific question or idea.

➤ Find similar support in another text, a teacher's read-aloud, or a common class text.

➤ Help students understand that they need to paraphrase text details and put the information into their own words. Paraphrasing shows comprehension.

➤ Scaffold the process by telling students how many text details you want them to locate.

Chapter 4

Using Text Details to Support Discussion and Writing *(cont.)*

Chapter 4

Classroom Snapshot: Identifying and Planning an Intervention

Seventh-grade English language learners have generated and discussed questions for their guided reading book: *Roberto Clemente*. I have asked students to select two questions, write each one in their notebooks, then, in their own words, answer each question using text details. As I make the rounds I notice that Ben has written the questions in his notebook, but is not skimming his book to find text details. My brief conversation shows me that Ben understands what details are, but he's having difficulty putting them in his own words. "Why can't I just copy?" he asks me.

To support Ben, I set up three consecutive five-minute conferences using the plans above and the *Roberto Clemente* text. I'll work with Ben during the 15 minutes of silent reading the group does each day.

Building Prior Knowledge

Overview

This is a series of three 30- to 40-minute interventions to support building prior knowledge. Students watch a video clip, review images and captions, and bolded terms to support their understanding.

Materials

➤ *Rome* (rome.pdf)

➤ chart paper (*optional*)

➤ video clips and images of Ancient Rome

Procedures

Day 1

1. Have groups of four watch video clips about ancient Rome and look at photographs.

2. Have students share in their groups what they learned and record a list of information and vocabulary in their notebooks.

3. Allow students to share out as a class, and support them by jotting their ideas onto the board or chart paper.

Day 2

1. Have students review what they learned. Organize the group into pairs, and have pairs study and discuss the photographs and read the captions in the text.

2. Have partners share what they've learned.

Day 3

1. Review the key points that students learned on the second day. Focus on boldface words, and have pairs discuss their meanings.

2. On the board or chart paper, have partners help create a list of what they learned from the book.

Scaffolding Suggestions

➤ Model how you preview the text to build your prior knowledge: read the title and any features such as charts, diagrams, photographs, maps, etc.

➤ Read the first paragraph after previewing features, and think aloud to show what you've learned.

➤ Give the student a different short passage and ask him or her to complete a preview and tell you the prior knowledge he or she gained.

➤ Point out that if the topic is unfamiliar, even with a preview, the student should read slowly and check recall often.

➤ Have the student reread and/or close read to improve comprehension.

➤ Have the student read the features carefully.

➤ Ask the student to explain what he or she learned from each feature.

➤ Have the student write a list of the prior knowledge gained from the preview.

➤ Ask the student to read the first few paragraphs of a short text that doesn't have features or the first chapter of a book.

➤ Tell the student to explain what he or she learned from this preview reading.

➤ Ask the student to make a list of prior knowledge notes based on the preview reading and use these notes to set a purpose for reading.

Building Prior Knowledge *(cont.)*

Classroom Snapshot: 30- to 40-Minute Intervention

A group of fifth-grade students receiving Tier 3 instruction will be studying ancient Rome, a required curriculum topic. None of the students have background knowledge about ancient Rome and the goal of this intervention is to build students' vocabulary and background knowledge so they can learn from this book. The goal is to have students actively involved in building their background knowledge, so the plans are for three consecutive lessons. The first lesson taps into visual learning that students relate to and enjoy.

Focus Standard 2

Determine central themes or ideas of a text and analyze their development across the text; summarize the key supporting ideas and details.

The skills and strategies that follow are crucial for students to master in order to achieve proficiency with this standard.

Strategy	Intervention Timeframe	Resource Page(s)
Using Details to Identify Main Idea (pages 84–85)	15 minutes	N/A
Using Details to Identify Central Idea (pages 86–87)	5 minutes	N/A
Summarizing the Text (pages 88–89)	30–40 minutes	*Nelson Mandela: Leading the Way* (mandela.pdf) *5 Ws Organizer for Summarizing* (pages 234–235)

Using Details to Identify Main Idea

Overview

This is a series of two 15-minute interventions to support students as they use details to help identify the main idea.

Materials

➡ Any informational instructional-level text

Procedures

Day 1

1. Model how the main idea can grow out of two or more paragraphs.

2. Discuss that the main idea is a key point or concept in the text.

3. Show how details and text features such as headings, photographs, and boxes can help you figure out the main idea. For example, break the thinking process into a few steps. Show how the image supports the text and the main idea or how the subheadings break the details into pieces to support the main idea.

4. Have the student explain what you did and how text features support your thinking.

Day 2

1. Ask the student to use photographs, text features, and text to figure out the main ideas in several other parts of the book.

2. By the end of the intervention session, the student can hopefully figure out main ideas without any prompting from you. If that is the case, schedule two five-minute conferences to have the student practice with different texts to ensure independence.

3. If he or she cannot work independently, return to modeling and find a different text to use, making sure that the student had enough background knowledge to learn from the new text and to identify main ideas.

Scaffolding Suggestions

➤ Review the meaning of the main idea: the central purpose or key concept that one or more paragraphs express.

➤ Show the student how you use details in a paragraph to determine the main idea. Explain that, often, the main idea of a paragraph is in the first or last sentence.

➤ Have the student practice finding the main idea paragraph by paragraph, always pointing to details that helped.

➤ Show the student details from the text and discuss what details are.

➤ Have the student read headings and predict the kind of details he or she will find in a section.

➤ Have the student use photographs and captions, charts, diagrams, etc. to think of the details these features highlight. Have him or her find more details in the text that relate to the features.

Using Details to Identify Main Idea (cont.)

Classroom Snapshot: 15-Minute Intervention

While making the rounds, I discovered that a fifth-grade student found finding the main idea challenging. First, I conducted a five-minute investigative conference to determine the type of intervention I felt would benefit the student. I discovered that the student, Emma, expected the main idea to be the first sentence of each paragraph. My plan was to schedule two consecutive 15-minute conferences, assess where the student was with the process, and decide how to proceed.

In the first intervention, I showed how details and text features such as headings, photographs, and boxes can help you figure out the main idea. Then I had Emma repeat/explain what I did. She responded by saying, "The main idea is an important idea. You found it by looking at photos, captions, boxes, and headings. It looked easy for you. I'm not sure I can do this."

To boost her self-confidence, I praised her for listening carefully and recalling what I did. Then, I broke the thinking process into a few steps. First, I asked her to study the photographs and illustration on pages 8–9 and think of a main idea: "She [Jane] loved all kinds of animals." I tell her that if she can find a main idea with pictures, she can do it by reading page 8 and the box on page 9. "I got one about the mom—she respected Jane's love of animals and encouraged Jane's love of animals."

I ask, "How did you figure that out?"

"Well, when her mom found that Jane had earthworms in bed with her, she (her mom) didn't get angry. I think it's because her mom loved animals." I tell the student that I notice how well she used details to figure out a main idea.

By the end of the intervention session, Emma could figure out main ideas without any prompting from me.

Using Details to Identify Central Idea

Chapter 4

Overview

In this intervention, students practice identifying the central idea in the text using instructional-level text.

Materials

➡ a model text used for read-aloud

➡ any familiar instructional-level text

Procedures

1. Make sure the student understands that a central idea is supported by most of the text and that texts can have more than one central idea.

2. Think aloud using one of your completed read-aloud texts and show the student how you determine the central idea. Point out how most of the information in the text supports the central idea.

3. Have the student use a guided reading book or any instructional material he or she has discussed and have the student find the central idea.

4. Ask the student questions to point him or her to a central idea. For example, What is an idea that most of this book supports? Can you explain what _____? Why are _____ important? Why is _____?

5. Continue modeling, helping the student with questions and gradually move the student to independence.

Scaffolding Suggestions

➢ Review the meaning of central idea: similar to the main idea, but the central idea threads through most of the text.

➢ Start with a short text so students can deal with using an entire text to pinpoint the central idea.

➢ Model how you use details through most of the text to pinpoint the central idea.

➢ Using a new text or different part of the same text, select details from several paragraphs and have the student use these to state a central idea.

➢ Continue practicing using different texts until the student can select details and state a central idea.

➢ Show the student how you identify similar and related details in a text, and use these to state a central idea.

➢ Have the student use a short text and find related details throughout the text.

➢ Ask the student to state the central idea for all the details.

Using Details to Identify Central Idea (cont.)

Classroom Snapshot: 5-Minute Intervention

A sixth-grade student should be able to find the central idea using a short text and explain how he or she tests a central idea by examining the entire text to see if most of the details support the thinking. Ralph's guided reading group has completed *Amazon Rainforest* by William B. Rice. I move the student to reviewing the book and finding a central idea because he has participated in discussions, developed and answered text-dependent questions, and discussed main ideas.

During our short conference, I ask the student to skim written text and text features, think about the discussions the group had, and ask himself: What is an idea that most of this book supports? Here's the central idea that he suggested: We need to protect the Amazon Rainforest and stop cutting down trees because it has lots of fresh water for our Earth and plants and animals that only live there. The student nailed the central idea, and I complimented his ability to use what he learned from this book to develop a central idea. Next, I will pair this student with a peer in his guided reading group and ask them to find central ideas in a book they read.

Summarizing the Text

Chapter 4

Overview

This is a series of three 30- to 40-minute interventions where students use a graphic organizer to support them in summarizing the text.

Materials

➡ *Nelson Mandela: Leading the Way* (mandela.pdf)

➡ *5 Ws Organizer for Summarizing* (pages 234–235)

Procedures

Day 1

1. Have students read the text. Think aloud and show how the *5 Ws Organizer for Summarizing* helps you select details to write on the form in my own words.

2. Encourage students to ask questions and make observations about the process.

Day 2

1. Have the group reread the text and study the photographs.

2. Organize students in pairs and have pairs suggest notes for each *W*. Write students' responses on a whiteboard or chart paper. Ask students to reread the responses for one *W* at a time and suggest adjustments and revisions.

3. Show students how to take the ideas for each *W* and turn them into one or two complete sentences. Then, demonstrate how to add a topic sentence.

Day 3

1. Distribute a copy of the *5 Ws Organizer for Summarizing* to each student.

2. Have students take notes on the organizer, and write a topic sentence and summary. Observe and scaffold students as they work.

Teacher TIP

Your observations of students taking notes and composing a summary will help you decide how the intervention should proceed. Students who can take detailed notes and use these to write a summary can practice with a partner. However, students whose notes are sketchy and summaries lack details will need additional practice with their teacher. For example, if a student writes one word next to each of the *W*s, it is helpful to support the student before he or she writes a summary, explaining that the more detailed the notes on the *5 Ws Organizer*, the better the summary.

Summarizing the Text *(cont.)*

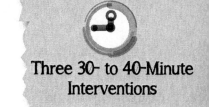

Chapter 4

Scaffolding Suggestions

➤ Explain that a summary contains facts and is short. To summarize, it's important to select key details.

➤ Show the student how to use the *5 Ws Organizer* to collect facts from the text.

➤ Model how to turn the notes from each *W* into a sentence for a summary.

➤ Have the student turn some of your notes into sentences.

➤ Use a new selection or part of one already read and have the student take notes and write the summary. The topic or opening sentence should contain the title and author of the piece.

➤ Continue practicing until the student can complete a *5 Ws Organizer* independently as well as use the notes to write a summary.

➤ Help the student understand that detailed notes for each *W* can be turned into one to two sentences.

➤ Have the student write sentences for one *W*, then add two, three, and so on, until the student can turn all the notes into sentences.

Focus Standard 3

> Interpret words and phrases as they are used in a text, including determining connotative, figurative, and technical meanings; analyze how specific word choices shape tone and meaning.

The skills and strategies that follow are crucial for students to master in order to achieve proficiency with this standard.

Strategy	Intervention Timeframe	Resource Page(s)
Using Context Clues (pages 91–92)	2–3 minutes	*Six Kinds of Context Clues* (page 233)
Identifying Connotative and Denotative Meanings (page 93)	2–3 minutes	*Unforgettable Natural Disasters* (disasters.pdf)
Using Figurative Language in a Text to Comprehend (pages 94–95)	5 minutes	N/A
Show How Word Choice Affects Meaning and Mood (pages 96–97)	15 minutes	*Jane Goodall: The Early Years* (goodall.pdf)
Using Roots to Infer Meaning (pages 98–99)	2–3 minutes	N/A

Using Context Clues

Overview

This intervention describes how to use a series of brief mini-lessons on context clues over a period of several days to support students' understanding by making the rounds. The types of mini-lessons are based on the *Six Kinds of Context Clues* resource page.

Materials

➼ *Six Kinds of Context Clues* (page 233)

➼ any read-aloud text

Procedures

1. Select a difficult word from a read-aloud text. Think aloud to show students how you use clues in the sentence that contains the word to determine its meaning.

2. Explain that if the sentence doesn't contain clues, you will have to read a few sentences that came before the word or after the word. Show students how this works using a word from the read-aloud text or their guided reading book.

3. Present additional mini-lessons that illustrate each of the context clue types on the handout *Six Kinds of Context Clues,* and make sure to categorize the kinds of clues the authors provide.

4. After completing all of the mini-lessons, distribute copies of the *Six Kinds of Context Clues* to students to use as a resource. Have them place the handout in their notebooks.

5. In the days that follow, make the rounds as students read their own texts and ask questions to see how they are using context clues to determine word meaning. Remind students to use their handout for support.

Scaffolding Suggestions

➢ Explain that context clues are words and punctuation in a sentence or sentences that can help you determine a tough word's meaning.

➢ Model how to use clues in a sentence to determine a word's meaning.

➢ Have the student practice by assigning a sentence from a text.

➢ Explain that sometimes the clues are in a sentence that came earlier and model how you reverse and find clues in a previous sentence(s).

➢ Provide the student with a passage that asks him or her to read sentences that come before the one with the tough word.

➢ Review how reading on for clues helps figure out a word's meaning and model with a short passage projected onto a white board.

➢ Invite the student to practice using a different passage from the text.

➢ Continue having the student practice until he or she can use context clues independently.

➢ Have the student decide where the clues for figuring out the word's meaning are—in the sentence, sentences that come before or after the sentence with the word, etc.

➢ Show the student how commas and words like *or* and *is* signal the definition of a challenging word.

Using Context Clues *(cont.)*

Classroom Snapshot: Making the Rounds

As students practice using context clues with their instructional books, I make the rounds and support them. One student has difficulty linking the word *pandemic* to airplane travel; after rereading the text, the student says, "People can bring germs into a country from anywhere in the world. It's easy and fast to get to any place." I praise the connection he made and continue to circulate. A student is having difficulty finding a clue to figure out the meaning of *domesticated*. "It's not in the sentence," she says. When I ask her to read on, she get's it: "They don't live in the wild," she says. I ask her to explain what that means. And she says it means they're like cows and live on a farm with people. "Good example," I say, and move on. I schedule a 5-minute intervention for students who need more than two or three minutes of my time.

Identifying Connotative and Denotative Meanings

Overview

In this intervention, the teacher asks a series of brief questions to check student's understanding of connotative and denotative meaning.

Materials

➡ *Unforgettable Natural Disasters* (disasters.pdf)

Procedures

1. Make sure students understand denotative and connotative meanings of words. Have students practice using words from your read-aloud text.

2. Invite students to work with a partner and determine the denotative, or literal, meaning of the word *volcano* and then discuss connotations, or associations, with the word.

3. Distribute copies of *Unforgettable Natural Disasters*. Have students read the text and study the photographs and captions.

4. Instruct pairs to connect connotations to information in the text. As you make the rounds, support students by asking questions that help them connect a connotation to an idea in the text: Can you link *power* to information in the text? Can you link *explosive fire* to something you read? How does *destruction* connect to details on these pages?

5. Questions can help students see the relevance of connotative meanings to information about Mt. St. Helens. If questions don't help a student, schedule a 5-minute investigative intervention.

Scaffolding Suggestions

➤ Review the meanings of *denotative* and *connotative*. Explain that authors want readers to think of connotations for key words because these support and expand readers' understanding.

➤ Choose a word from the title of a text or a word that's in a text and show students how you find words and phrases associated with the word.

➤ Prompt students with questions to help them gather connotative meanings: Can you find associations from your reading? From a movie or video you've watched? From conversations with friends? From texting?

Using Figurative Language in a Text to Comprehend

Chapter 4

Overview

In this intervention, students examine figurative language to help them understand the big idea of the text.

Materials

➤ Any read-aloud text that includes figurative language

Procedures

1. Read aloud a portion of the selected text that demonstrates figurative language.

2. Think aloud and explain the type of figurative language in the text and show how to link the figure of speech to information or ideas in a text. For example, here is a passage from *Bug Builders* by Timothy J. Bradley:

   Leafcutter Ants

   Leafcutter ants are farmers. They have very sharp mandibles. They use them to chew plant leaves into small pieces. Then they carry the leaves to the nest. The leaves become food for a fungus that the ants use to feed their young.

   Say, "The author uses a metaphor which is a comparison without like or as: Leafcutter ants are farmers. The author wants us to think about how these ants are like farmers. They cut leaves just as farmers cut corn and harvest other crops. The ants feed their young this way and farmers feed their families and people all over this country."

3. Explain that a writer uses figurative language to help readers better understand big and important ideas in a text.

Scaffolding Suggestions

➤ Help the student move from knowing the definitions of figurative language to understanding how each one improves visualization and comprehension.

➤ Model how a simile and/or metaphor from a text helps you visualize an event, machine, or description.

➤ Show the student how alliteration and repetition can emphasize a point or main idea.

➤ Have the student use a different passage with figurative language and ask him or her to show connections to key ideas as well as describe visualizations.

➤ Review the main and central ideas of the selection.

➤ Ask the student to connect a figure of speech to a main and/or central idea.

➤ Ask the student to show how figurative language enhances an understanding of specific details.

Using Figurative Language in a Text to Comprehend *(cont.)*

Chapter 4

Classroom Snapshot: 5-Minute Intervention

To support a student who had difficulty connecting figurative language to ideas in the text, I used the following passage from a book titled *Rome: Performances in theaters were also a popular pastime. Roman plays were based on plays from ancient Greece. Successful actors were popular like movie stars are today*. The student quickly identified and explained the simile by showing me what makes movie stars today popular.

When I asked her to link the simile to information later in the book, she shrugged her shoulders. "It's not written here," she says. So, I asked a question to help the student explain what popularity might have meant for actors in ancient Rome: What kinds of popularity that actors experience today could apply to ancient Rome? "I get it," she says. Maybe if a popular actor was in a play, it sold out and everyone in Rome knew about the actor. Maybe people wanted the actor's autograph and dressed like him." I tell the student that she connected what she knows about the popularity of actors today to ancient Rome. "You inferred and chose ideas that could relate to actors in ancient Rome."

Based on the student's responses, I decide to do one more 5-minute intervention on figurative language. If progress continues, I would have the student work with a partner to gain confidence with the strategy.

Show How Word Choice Affects Meaning and Mood

Overview

In this intervention, students practice identifying key words that portray the mood of the text and connect that to the main idea.

Materials

➡ *Jane Goodall: The Early Years* (goodall.pdf)

Procedures

1. Display the following paragraph from the text:

   When Jane was four years old, she visited a farm. While there, she became curious about where eggs come from. How could an egg come from a chicken? She asked the grown-ups about it, but no one gave her a good answer. So, she hid in a henhouse for several hours to find out for herself. When she finally saw a chicken lay an egg, she excitedly ran to her mother to tell her what she had seen. Even, when Jane was a little girl, she knew that with patience she could find the answers she wanted.

2. Have students read and discuss the paragraph and find the main idea. Students should find the main idea in the last sentence and say that patience can help you find answers to questions.

3. Ask students to reread and identify words that could help them determine the mood and then connect mood to the main idea. (Possible student responses: *curious, find out herself, excitedly*.)

Scaffolding Suggestions

➤ Explain that mood is the emotions the reader feels from a passage, paragraph, or page.

➤ Make sure the student can explain emotions such as happy, unhappy, jealousy, tension, anger, fear, etc.

➤ Select one or a few paragraphs, and think aloud to show the student how you use the author's word choice to figure out the mood.

➤ Select a passage the student has read, choose the words, and ask the student to share the emotion the words conjure. Then, let the student select the words from a passage and pinpoint the emotion.

➤ Ask the student to read a group of words and explain what they have in common.

➤ Have the student turn the common meaning of a word into an emotion that reveals mood.

Show How Word Choice Affects Meaning and Mood (cont.)

Classroom Snapshot: 15-Minute Intervention

Three students could select groups of words from a passage, but they were unable to explain the feeling or mood the words imply. I tried two 5-minute interventions and realized that the students needed more time to practice, so I scheduled one 15-minute intervention.

When I worked with the students on this intervention lesson, they agreed the mood was curiosity and excitement. One student said that curiosity helped Jane Goodall find a way to learn about how chickens lay their eggs and excitement happened when her patience paid off. Clearly, the longer lesson worked. However, I decided to follow the lesson up with two 5-minute interventions to make sure students could work independently. That day, these students taught me a lesson. They agreed that once they had the main idea, finding words that related to it and figuring out the mood was easier. That process works well for all tiers of learners.

Chapter 4

Using Roots to Infer Meaning

Chapter 4

Overview

In this intervention, students use their understanding of roots, prefixes, and suffixes to infer word meaning.

Materials

→ dictionaries (print or online)

Procedure

Prior to this intervention, students should have had a mini-lesson about roots, prefixes, and suffixes, and understand that they are tools for figuring out the definition of unfamiliar words.

1. Organize students into pairs and have pairs use word parts to define a set of words that come from the same root. For example, you can use words that come from the Latin root *spec* (to see or look at): *inspect, inspector, inspection, disrespect, spectacles, spectator, respect, retrospective, introspection, circumspect.*

2. Give each pair one word to define using what they know about the meaning of the word's parts. Have students use an online or print dictionary to check the meaning of prefixes and the part of speech a suffix indicates.

3. Have the entire class share what they learned.

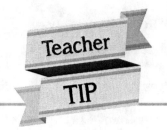

Teacher TIP

Enlarge students' vocabulary by studying roots, prefixes, and suffixes for eight to 10 consecutive weeks. Choose eight to 10 roots that relate to your curriculum. Have students use the root to generate words the first two days. On the third day, use the root, prefixes, and suffixes to define the word. Think of situations each word could work in on the fourth day—for example, *inspect* could work when you discuss a detective, an inspector of homes and restaurants, or parents checking to see if your room is clean. On the fifth day, have pairs compose sentences for two to three words and share with the class. To learn more about this method, see my book *Vocabulary Is Comprehension* (2014).

Using Roots to Infer Meaning (cont.)

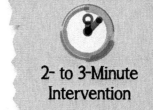

Scaffolding Suggestions

➤ Explain that prefixes can change the meaning of root or base words. Offer the student examples and show how the prefix and root or base word help a reader figure out meaning.

➤ Have a student define words based on a particular root. For example, the Latin root *port*, to carry: *deport, import, report, portfolio, importer, portable, transport, transportation, porter, portal*.

➤ Ask the student to separate the prefix and suffix from the root or base word.

➤ Have the student use the meaning of the prefix and root or base word to define the word.

➤ Ask the student to use the suffix to determine the part of speech.

Classroom Snapshot: Moving to Longer Interventions

When students struggle with using word parts, I work with a group of three to four in two 15-minute interventions so there's enough time for them to practice, build understanding of word parts, and share their knowledge. Providing extra time for students to generate words from a root, then defining each word using word parts and the root can clarify the process. You'll have to help these groups identify situations each word works in, so students can write a sentence that shows they understand the word.

Focus Standard 4

> Analyze the structure of a text, including how specific sentences, paragraphs, and larger portions of the text (e.g., a section or chapter) relate to each other and the whole.

The skills and strategies that follow are crucial for students to master in order to achieve proficiency with this standard.

Strategy	Intervention Timeframe	Resource Page(s)
Recognizing and Interpreting Text Features (page 101)	15 minutes	*Unforgettable Natural Disasters* (disasters.pdf) *Informational Text Features* (pages 236–237)
Understanding the Structure of Informational Text (pages 102–103)	30–40 minutes	*Roberto Clemente* (roberto.pdf) *Informational Text Structures and Text Meanings* (page 238)

Recognizing and Interpreting Text Features

Overview

This is a series of two 15-minute interventions where students examine text features in order to understand their function and purpose in informational text.

Materials

➨ *Unforgettable Natural Disasters* (disasters.pdf)

➨ *Informational Text Features* (pages 236–237)

Procedure

Day 1

1. Organize students into pairs and distribute copies of *Informational Text Features* and *Unforgettable Natural Disasters*.

2. Have partners study the text features and use their handout to better understand each feature and how it helps readers comprehend the information.

3. Ask students to share one thing they learned about text features.

Day 2

1. Have students explore pages 14–18, discuss the features on these pages, and refer to the handout to learn more about the feature.

2. Have students share what they've learned about text features by pointing out specific features in the book. If some students require additional support to identify text features, pair them with a peer for support or schedule one to two 5-minute interventions.

Scaffolding Suggestions

➤ Explain to the student that text features enhance and relate to the main and central ideas.

➤ Think aloud about one feature at a time, explain the information each provides, and connect it to a main idea.

➤ Select specific features in a text that the student has read, show the information, and ask the student to link the information to a main idea.

➤ Repeat this intervention periodically to help the student reach independence.

➤ Give the student a book with text features and ask him or her to identify each one. Model how you make these connections and then ask the student to try making connections using one feature at a time.

➤ Help the student interpret text features by asking prompts: How does the information in the feature connect to a heading? A boldface word? A diagram? A photo and caption? A big idea?

Understanding the Structure of Informational Text

Chapter 4

Overview

This is a series of two interventions where students examine a piece of informational text to determine its structure and how that affects the content of the text.

Materials

➡ *Roberto Clemente* (roberto.pdf)

➡ *Informational Text Structures and Text Meanings* (page 238)

Procedures

Day 1

1. Explain that, often, authors include more than one informational text structure in a passage and that it's what the author wants to say that determines which structures an author uses.

2. Distribute copies of *Roberto Clemente* and *Informational Text Structures and Text Meanings*.

3. Read aloud the box on page 4 titled *Commonwealth of Puerto Rico*, and explain that this is an example of description. Next, read aloud the section "Business in Puerto Rico," and point out that description and cause/effect can work together. The cause statement is that industry replaced farming. An effect is that tourism became very important.

4. Organize students into pairs and have them practice identifying the three informational text structures using pages 10–13 in *Roberto Clemente* or any text you select.

   ➢ On page 10, have students identify cause/effect and explain the mental pictures the words created for them.

   ➢ On page 11, compare and contrast the information under "Milk Bottles" with how families obtain milk today.

   ➢ On page 13, identify cause/effect in the first paragraph, and use the description in the second paragraph to create a mental picture.

5. Wrap up by asking students to explain how these text structures helped them understand Clemente's childhood.

Day 2

1. Review the three text structures and the information on the *Informational Text Structures and Text Meanings* handout.

2. Have students use these pages to discuss specific structures and how they improve an understanding of Clemente.

   ➢ Page 16–17: Description

   ➢ Page 16: "What an Arm!"—cause/effect

   ➢ Page 19: "Pride of the Pirates"—compare/contrast

   ➢ Pages 20–21: Organize students into pairs and have partners figure out the text structure and how it helps them better understand Clemente. Encourage students to use their handout to support their thinking.

3. If students can connect text structures to deepen their understanding of Roberto Clemente, then introduce the three other informational text structures during another 30- to 40-minute intervention. However, if some students require additional practice, schedule a series of 5-minute interventions for them.

Understanding the Structure of Informational Text *(cont.)*

Scaffolding Suggestions

➤ Help students understand that informational texts can have features and that all use some or all of the structures.

➤ Help students recall the four purposes of informational texts: argue for a position or opinion; present information on a topic; provide procedures or directions; explain the why behind an event. These purposes are genre characteristics.

➤ Think aloud and show students the genre characteristics of a recently completed informational text.

➤ Have students read a section of an old favorite or new text and discuss its genre characteristics.

➤ Review the characteristics of Informational Texts: Informational texts are based on research and true occurrences. Many have text features such as photographs and captions, sidebars with extra information, maps, charts, diagrams, and snippets from diaries and newspapers. The text includes these structures: description, cause/effect, compare/contrast, problem/solution, question/answer, and sequence.

➤ Help students understand that knowing text structure is like having a map that enables them to better navigate the text because they know what to expect.

➤ Ask students to use the handout on informational text structures to help them make connections to main ideas and concepts.

➤ Have students reread one paragraph at a time and discuss the text structures.

➤ Model how knowing a structure improves comprehension. For example, compare and contrast shows likenesses and differences; sequence presents the time order of an event or experiment and can reveal the connections between items; or, if the author presents a problem, the reader looks for the solution.

Teacher TIP

To prevent frustrating students with too much information, work with three informational text structures at a time. The first three, description, compare/contrast, and cause/effect, are often easier for students to identify. Once students can identify these structures in passages, they can work on sequence, problem/solution, and question/answer. Students have practiced main idea/details as well as studied examples of cause/effect and compare contrast with fiction. The challenge for students is often to transfer what they learned using fiction to informational texts.

Focus Standard 5

{
Assess how purpose or point of view shapes the style and content of a text.
}

The skills and strategies that follow are crucial for students to master in order to achieve proficiency with this standard.

Strategy	Intervention Timeframe	Resource Page(s)
Identifying the Author's Point of View (page 105)	5 minutes	Excerpt from *Bug Builders* (bugexcerpt.pdf)
Determining the Author's Purposes for Informational Text (page 106)	2–3 minutes	N/A

Identifying the Author's Point of View

Overview

In this intervention, students examine boldface words, adjectives, and comparisons to help determine the author's point of view.

Materials

➼ Excerpt from *Bug Builders* (bugexcerpt.pdf)

Procedures

1. Have students read the text silently. Then, have them reread the text to determine the author's point of view about bugs.

   ➤ Ask students to focus on the boldface words—engineers and skyscrapers.

   ➤ Ask students to figure out why the author compares what bugs can do to what engineers can do. (He calls bugs animal engineers, so the point of view is that bugs are great thinkers and builders.)

2. Wrap up the intervention by explaining that boldface words, comparisons, and adjectives the author uses can show the author's point of view.

Scaffolding Suggestions

➤ Help students understand that studying point of view is effective with history/social studies and science topics. Explain that text represents the point of view or attitude toward the topic of the author and not necessarily the truth.

➤ Make sure students understand adjectives and can select them from a passage or paragraph or section of a text to figure out point of view.

➤ Explain to students the importance of reading texts on the same topic by different authors. Share with students that the information an author chooses to present on a topic or information omitted can also give readers a handle on point of view.

➤ Model for students that to discover an author's point of view, study the adjectives used. Select adjectives from a text and ask the student to explain what the adjectives reveal about the author's attitude or point of view toward the topic.

➤ Invite students to read a selection and work with a partner to determine the author's point of view.

Teacher TIP

As a follow-up to this intervention, have students practice with texts that require a closer reading to study adjectives the author includes and to find phrases that reveal opinions about facts.

Determining the Author's Purposes for Informational Text

Overview

In this intervention, students use their own text to identify author's purpose and support their reasoning with text evidence.

Materials

➡ any read-aloud informational text

➡ any informational text at students' instructional reading level

Procedure

Prior to this intervention, read aloud the selected informational text, and make sure that students understand the purposes for informational texts: to explain, entertain, inform, argue for a position, persuade, convince, or change your opinion.

1. Point out to students that headings, text features, and text details can help students determine the purpose. Think aloud and show how you use headings, boldface words, and other text features to decide on the author's purpose.

2. Have students practice identifying author's purpose using their instructional-level texts and providing text evidence to support their reasoning.

Scaffolding Suggestions

➤ Show how you can look at text structure by thinking about whether a section argues, explains, informs, describes, shows compare/contrast, shows cause/effect, or contains a problem/solution.

➤ Divide a text into sections, skim a section, and show how you determine the purpose of the section by using evidence and word choices from the text. Give a section to the student, have him or her reread and decide the purpose of the section offering evidence from the text.

➤ Provide students with the transitional words that signal an argument: *on the other hand, according to, in fact, furthermore, most convincingly*.

➤ Provide students with the words that signal explaining or informing: *such as, for example, characteristics, for this reason, before, after, similar to*.

➤ Provide students with words that signal comparing and contrasting in the text: *alike, different from, on the contrary, unlike, same as, as opposed to*.

➤ Show students how using section headings and the author's word choice can let readers know the author's purpose.

➤ Show students details from the text, discuss what details are, and model how the purpose can be found in details.

➤ Have students read headings, predict the kind of details they'll find in a section, and explain what the details reveal about purpose.

➤ Have students use photographs, captions, charts, and diagrams to think of the details these features highlight and what they illustrate about purpose.

➤ Start by giving students a text that has one purpose, and ask students to identify the author's purpose and explain how they determined that. When students are comfortable with one purpose, offer a text with two to three purposes and ask them to identify each purpose.

Reteaching Lessons for Informational Texts

If the text and/or instructional approach used during your interventions is not helping students improve, then it's time to reteach using a different instructional approach and a more accessible text (Fisher and Frey 2013; Howard 2009). You can present these reteaching lessons to one student, a pair, or small group. It's possible that there will be times when the entire class or most of the class would benefit from a reteaching lesson. These lessons will support them, too. **Note:** Document each reteaching lesson with the *Reteaching Lesson Form* on page 239. Documenting each lesson will enable you to make decisions about future interventions.

When to Move On

➢ There will be students who don't absorb the process. Sometimes, it's helpful to move on to other skills and strategies and return to inferring after a few weeks have passed.

➢ Remember, some students might not become independent with a specific strategy during the year you have them. Keep practicing and planting seeds of understanding, because eventually the students will be able to move to independence.

Writing in Notebooks

Before students complete their notebook writing, have them plan by recording two to four points they want to include. Check these points *before* students write to make sure they are detailed. If their notes are too general, ask students to add specific details and let you see their plans again. Then, they can write using their plans as guides.

The following reteaching lessons are provided in this chapter.

Lesson Title	Resource Page(s)
Making Logical Inferences (pages 108–109)	*Nelson Mandela: Political Prisoner* (political.pdf)
Summarizing (pages 110–111)	*Amazon Rainforest* (amazon.pdf) *5 Ws Organizer for Summarizing* (pages 234–235)
Denotative and Connotative Meanings (pages 112–113)	*On the Scene: A CSI's Life* (scene.pdf)
Analyzing Structure (pages 114–115)	*Bug Builders* (bug.pdf) *Informational Text Features* (pages 236–237) *Informational Text Structures and Text Meanings* (page 238)
Author's Point of View (pages 116–117)	*Roberto Clemente* (roberto.pdf) *Rome* (rome.pdf)

Reteaching Lesson 1

Making Logical Inferences

Chapter 4

Materials

➤ *Nelson Mandela: Political Prisoner* (political.pdf)

Goal

To help students understand that inferences are unstated or implied meanings and to model how to infer using details from an informational text.

Teaching the Lesson

1. Open the lesson by providing background information about Nelson Mandela and recap key information about inferring. If desired, read aloud the background information provided on page 109.

2. Distribute copies of *Nelson Mandela: Political Prisoner*.

3. Read the following think-aloud to students: "Today, we're going to practice making inferences using an excerpt from a book about Nelson Mandela. Because an inference is not stated in the text, I have to use details to help me infer and find unstated meanings that grow out of the details. Listen as I read the first four sentences out loud.

4. Read the first four sentences of the text. Then continue the think-aloud: "The details that the government arrested Mandela, found him guilty, and put him in prison for five years help me infer that the government feared Mandela's power among his people and those living outside of South Africa. The next set of details—that Mandela and his friends sabotaged or destroyed prison property and were sentenced to life in prison—resulted in me inferring that the government knew Mandela's popularity and strength and wanted him isolated from others. I can also infer that these were fake charges because what was there to destroy in a prison cell."

5. Have students discuss the think-aloud. Try to determine whether they understand how you used specific details to infer. If necessary, repeat your thinking and show them that your inferences were not in the text. Accept any inference that the details support.

6. Ask students to read the rest of the second paragraph. You select details and ask students to pair-share to use the details to infer.

   ➤ Details: At first, Mandela refused to eat to protest the sentence. Eventually, he ate to live so he could end apartheid. Possible inferences: (1) Mandela was a clear thinker. When not eating didn't work, he ate to stay healthy so he could eventually end apartheid. (2) Mandela had a dream of equality, and he ate to stay alive hoping he could help bring about his dream.

   ➤ Details: Mandela became more passionate about his cause. He believed if he kept trying to change legal segregation, his people would live in a better place. Possible inferences: (1) Mandela was selfless because he put the welfare of his people above himself. (2) Mandela had perseverance and determination, and being in prison could not change that.

7. If students have difficulty using the details to infer, continue modeling for them.

8. Have students read the last two paragraphs on prison life. Ask them to pair-share to figure out key details and share these, and then use the details to infer.

9. Write the key details students offer on chart paper or display them on a whiteboard.

10. Invite partners to use the details to infer. Possible inferences: (1) Mandela's jailors were cruel; they withheld books and letters and made him work under "tough conditions." (2) Mandela must have been lonely because he only saw a family member once every six months and did not always receive their letters. (3) Mandela felt isolated from the world; he lived in a tiny cell, did not always receive letters and couldn't be sure his letters were delivered. (4) Mandela lived without comforts; his cell was 7 x 7 feet, and he had a uniform, a mat for sleeping and 2 blankets—there was no mention of a toilet or a sink with water.

Journal Response

Explain why Nelson Mandela was able to survive his harsh prison conditions and continue to think of helping his people. **Tip:** Use some of the inferences you made about Mandela to support your explanation.

Assessment Tips

➤ Determine who can infer and who requires scaffolding or another reteaching lesson.

➤ Use a text the student is reading to scaffold the process and move to a gradual release to the student.

➤ Use this selection to model using details to infer and focus on the parts that created difficulties for students.

➤ Prepare another reteaching lesson using a different text.

Nelson Mandela Background Information

Nelson Mandela, son of a tribal chief, worked hard to end apartheid in South Africa. Apartheid, legalized segregation, resulted in Africans living in certain parts of cities. Apartheid controlled the kind of jobs Africans could obtain, where they went to school, and even who they could marry. In South Africa, during apartheid, whites had freedom to choose where they lived, went to school, and their ability to earn money was greater.

After becoming a lawyer, Nelson Mandela worked with others to end apartheid and bring equality to all people in South Africa. With others, Mandela planned strikes, boycotts, and peaceful protests. The South African government threatened Mandela, but he continued to protest with others. In 1962, Nelson Mandela made a decision that was illegal for him; he traveled outside of South Africa to speak about freedom and against apartheid. After Mandela returned to South Africa, the government arrested him and sentenced Mandela to five years in prison.

Reteaching Lesson 2

Summarizing

Materials

➤ *Amazon Rainforest* (amazon.pdf)

➤ *5 Ws Organizer for Summarizing* (pages 234–235)

Goal

To show students how to take notes using the *5 Ws Organizer for Summarizing* and turn the notes into a summary; to help students understand that at times they will only use three or four of the *W*s because information fits under a few of them.

Teaching the Lesson

Day 1

1. Begin the lesson by reading the following think-aloud to students: "Summarizing means that you choose the important details and put these into a summary paragraph. It's different from a retelling, which asks you to recall as many details as possible. Summarizing is selective!"

2. Distribute copies of *Amazon Rainforest* and the *5 Ws Organizer for Summarizing*. Have students read and discuss the short selection.

3. Continue the think-aloud: "Together, we'll complete a *5 Ws Organizer for Summarizing* note-taking form. We will fill in parts that work for this selection. This helps us choose key details and make sure the details are specific." Complete the graphic organizer as a team. Possible student suggestions:

➤ What: The Amazon Rainforest—known all over the world

➤ Where: It covers the northern half of South America. It crosses several countries, but the largest part of the Amazon Rainforest is in Brazil.

➤ When: the present

➤ Why: Lots of plants and animals are there that other parts of the world don't have. More kinds of plants and animals live there than anywhere else in the world.

Day 2

1. Read the following think-aloud to students: "Today, we will write a summary by turning the notes from your *5 Ws Organizer for Summarizing* into one or more sentences. The first sentence needs to contain the title and author."

2. Have students review their notes from the previous lesson. As a group, work on transforming their notes into sentences one *W* at a time.

3. Invite students to refine each sentence before you write it on chart paper or project it onto an interactive whiteboard. This reminds students that writing is a process and that sentences can be improved.

✿ Have students read the summary out loud and listen for possible edits and revisions, such as adding transition words, missing words, or rewriting the sentence to make it clearer. Here is a sample response from a group of students: *In* Amazon Rainforest *by William Rice, he says that this is one of the world's greatest rainforests. It's in the northern part of South America. The rainforest goes over lots of countries. Most of it is in Brazil. The Amazon Rainforest has more kinds of plants and animals than other places in the world. Some of these plants and animals are only in the Amazon.*

Journal Response

Have students reread the text selection about the Amazon and ask them to explain why the Amazon Rainforest is important to all people.

Assessment Tips

➢ Determine which students demonstrated difficulty with taking notes and/or transforming notes into sentences, continue with short texts until they can work on their own.

➢ Decide whether students can make progress with this task by working with a peer expert. Have students work through the note-taking and writing process with a partner, as additional practice can move them to independence.

Teacher TIP

When students have difficulty taking notes on an entire chapter or long article, start the reteaching with a short, manageable text. Gradually increase the amount of text that students summarize always pointing out how the 5 *W*s help them select key details. It's helpful to complete the lesson over two days to separate note-taking from writing.

Denotative and Connotative Meanings

Materials

➤ *On the Scene: A CSI's Life* (scene.pdf)

➤ chart paper (*optional*)

Goal

To understand the difference between denotative and connotative meanings and use connotations to improve comprehension.

Teaching the Lesson

1. Review the difference between the denotative and connotative meanings of words. Explain that denotative meanings are the literal meaning—ones you find in a dictionary. Connotative meanings include everything you associate with a word. Associations can come from a movie or video, a book, conversations, song lyrics, experiences, and so on. To gather connotative meanings, students need to think freely without censoring their ideas.

2. Share the following think-aloud with students: "Sometimes the reading of a text is richer if the teacher has you focus on the connotative meanings of key words. I will model the process for you. Connotations can improve and deepen your understanding of what you read because the diverse associations with a word can emphasize a main idea, help you infer, and connect important ideas. Here are some connotations for the word *evidence*: details to answer a question, details for an inference, items that show changes in seasons, aging, hair color, clothing, weather, food, footprints, tire tracks, a diary or note, fibers, hair, a weapon, or blood."

3. Explain to students that not all of these connotations apply to a text on CSI investigations. But by selecting those that apply to the text, students can discuss how each connotation links to what they are reading. The connotations not only supply thinking and talking points, but they can lead to pinpointing main ideas and important details.

4. Divide students into pairs.

5. Invite pairs to find connotative meanings for *crime scene investigators* and *tracks*. (Possible student suggestions for crime scene investigators: police, detectives, photographers, doctor, evidence collectors; Possible student suggestions for tracks: tracks from tires from a truck, car, motorcycle, or bicycle, person, or animal)

6. Have pairs share what they have explored and record these ideas on chart paper or project them onto a whiteboard.

7. Distribute copies of *On the Scene: A CSI's Life* to students and have them read the text in pairs.

8. After students have read the text, return to the connotations to discuss how they enhance comprehension of key details, main ideas, inferences, and connections.

Journal Response

Help students find key words in their instructional and/or independent reading text and write the denotative and connotative meanings for each word.

Assessment Tips

➤ Check to make sure students have generated enough connotative meanings. This is more difficult with an individual or small group because the more students are involved in the lesson, the greater the number of responses. Ask questions to encourage students to provide more connotations, such as: What television shows that you watch can help you? Have you seen information on the Internet that can help? Focus questions on possible experiences. If this doesn't help, then you can offer two to three suggestions.

➤ Can students skim a text to find details that connect to specific connotations? If this poses a challenge, then think aloud and show students how you do this. Then, invite pairs to skim, locate a speciftic passage, and make connections to text details using a different connotation.

Analyzing Structure

Materials

➤ Excerpt from *Bug Builders* (bugexcerpt.pdf)

➤ *Informational Text Features* (pages 236–237)

➤ *Informational Text Structures and Text Meanings* (page 238)

➤ blank paper

Goal

To help students identify some structures in informational texts and be able to explain how the structure improves comprehension.

Teaching the Lesson

Day 1

1. Distribute copies of *Informational Text Features* and *Informational Text Structures and Text Meanings* to students.

2. Review the information on each resource sheet and explain that most, but not all, paragraphs have more than one structure.

3. Distribute copies of the excerpt from *Bug Builders* to students. Explain that as you discuss the text structures in the text, students should use the handouts that explain how each one supports comprehension.

4. Have students read the text in pairs and discuss what they learned.

5. Read aloud the paragraph under *Making It Work*. Have students consult the resource sheets to see whether they can determine the structures used.

6. Explain to students that the structure in the paragraph reflects main idea/details. The first sentence states the main idea of the paragraph. The author provides details that apply to engineers and ends with a surprise by telling readers that the engineers in this text are bugs!

7. Have students read the text under *Trapdoor Spider*. Ask them to determine a structure and offer evidence from the text. (Text Structure: sequence and description.)

8. After students share their thoughts, point out that the sequence helps readers visualize the steps the trapdoor spider takes to catch its prey. It also shows what a remarkable engineer the spider is: it camouflages that hole and places silk strands around the trap to feel the vibrations of a caught bug.

Day 2

1. Ask students to read the *Great Diving Beetle* section, and have them discuss the text structures they observe.

   ➤ Text structure—sequence, main idea/details, some description

   ➤ Sequence helps readers picture the adaptations of a land bug living in water, how it finds food and how it breathes.

   ➤ Main idea is stated in the first sentence, and readers explore the support as they continue reading. The final sentence is a surprise because these beetles can also fly. Descriptive parts tell the food the beetles eat and how it collects more air.

2. Introduce the word *aquanauts* prior to asking students to read the selection. Point out that the Latin root *aqua* means water, and in Greek the root *nauts* refers to sailors. Have students skim the word aquanauts, and find and read the sentence in the passage "Underwater Living." Have students discuss what they know about people living underwater.

3. Ask students to read the last selection and discuss text structure. (Text structure: question/answer.) Explain that the author poses two questions and the information in the paragraph answers these. This structure provides information to readers—information that relates to the posed questions.

4. Distribute a blank sheet of paper to each students. To summarize their understanding, have students make a T-chart. On the left side, have students list these structures: question/answer, sequence, description, compare/contrast. On the right side, instruct them to explain the purpose of each structure.

Journal Response

Invite students to select two of the four sections in *Bug Builders*. In their notebooks, students write the section title and the text structures the author used.

Assessment Tips

➤ Continue to think aloud to show students how to determine text structure.

➤ Continue practicing with students who are unable to identify informational text structure and explain how the structure helps comprehension.

➤ Consider pairing a student who almost gets it with a peer expert and have them practice analyzing text structure together.

Reteaching Lesson 5

Author's Point of View

Materials

➤ *Roberto Clemente* (roberto.pdf)

➤ *The Great City of Rome* (greatrome.pdf)

Goal

To show students that the adjectives and verbs an author uses as well as the way the author presents the content can reveal point of view.

Teaching the Lesson

Day 1

1. Explain to students that the author's word choice, such as adjectives and verbs, can help determine point of view. Readers can also look at the information the author chooses to include to help understand author's point of view.

2. Distribute copies of *Roberto Clemente* to students. Read the first two paragraphs aloud, and then show students how you use word choice and content to determine point of view.

3. Say, "The text has two points of view—the author's and Roberto Clemente's. The author uses phrases such as: *nothing but love, good person, respect and dignity*, and *importance of hard work*. These words illustrate how the author feels about Clemente's home life: *The family was loving and taught their values of being good, working hard, and being respectful*. Roberto Clemente's words: *I never heard any hate in my house. Not for anybody*, reinforces the loving and positive point of view that the author expresses in the section headed *Nothing But Love*."

4. Have students read the last two paragraphs and identify adjectives and verbs and well as factual information and point of view in the text. (Adjectives and verbs: *generous, blessed, share, make a difference for himself and others;* information and point of view: mom fed poor children who visited, Clemente helped children raise money to put a protective fence around their school, saved a person from a burning car.)

5. Ask students to explain the author's point of view in the text and use text evidence to explain how they determined it.

Day 2

1. Distribute copies of *The Great City of Rome* to students.

2. Have students read the first two paragraphs and select words that provide the author's point of view. Students should be able to identify two points of view about Rome.

   ➤ Author's word choice, paragraph 1: grand, beautiful, impressive

   ➤ Author's word choice, paragraph 2: noisy, dirty, dangerous, close quarters, run-down, collapsed

3. In pairs, have students discuss the point of view that the adjectives and verbs express. Make the rounds to listen to student conversations and support as necessary.

Journal Response

On Day 2, after students discuss the words in paragraphs one and two, have them write about the author's point of view for each paragraph using the words in the text to guide their thinking.

Assessment Tips

➤ Help students who have difficulty pinpointing adjectives and verbs by pointing these out to them. English language learners and developing readers will definitely need this type of support to think through point of view.

➤ Have students who need additional practice use a different text to work on point of view.

Continue the Conversation

Discuss these prompts and questions with your team or a peer partner. Reflecting on what you learn, what you know, and your students' performance can support your decision-making process regarding the kind of intervention plan you will develop.

1. Share an example of scaffolding you used with a student. Which intervention did you use? How did you move the student to independence?

2. Share a reteaching lesson that worked and discuss why.

3. Share an informational text unit that worked well for you and students. Explain why it worked well and what you would do again.

4. Discuss the *Ten Tips to Help You Comprehend Informational Texts* (page 65). How did these inform your teaching practices?

Chapter 5

Interventions for Reading Literary Texts

Stories define us: they recount who we are: our beliefs, hopes, and dreams. They have the power to transform us as we live the events through the lives of others. Stories frame our thinking and talking; we are a story-telling people (Wells 1985). Our literate lives start with the amount of meaningful talk and oral stories we hear and tell from birth on and from the number of storybooks read to us before entering school (Hart and Risley 2003; Wells 1985).

Katherine Paterson (2012), an award-winning author who served as our nation's ambassador for children's literature, said this about literature: "It's not enough to simply teach children to read; we have to give them something worth reading. Something that will stretch their imaginations—something that will help them make sense of their lives and encourage them to reach out toward people whose lives are quite different from their own."

Robert Coles pointed out in *The Call of Stories* (1990), that readers are truly engaged with a story when they are "in cahoots" with a character (64). Paterson describes this reading as having the ability to transform lives. When readers "become" the character, they step into the character's shoes and live life as if they had entered the character's world and thoughts.

When I work with students in grades four to eight, I always survey the genres they love and read. Fantasy and realistic fiction are usually at the top of the list, followed by mystery, suspense, and adventure. Science and historical fiction are not what this age group usually chooses, unless the book is by a beloved author on a historical period they are burning to know more about, or a peer strongly recommended the book. Some of the units that you plan should introduce students to literature that they're not reading by choice.

Supporting Students as They Read Fiction

Reading instructional-level materials should stretch students so that they enlarge their expertise by applying skills and strategies needed to comprehend. Following are ten tips that can help students unpack meaning from instructional-level and independent-level materials. You can use the tips with whole-class and small-group mini-lessons. A student version of these tips can be found in Appendix D.

Ten Tips for Reading Fiction That Work!

1. **Do a Preview Before Reading.** This includes reflecting on the cover illustration, the title of the book, and first chapter. Read the first chapter and think about what you have learned. In your reader's notebook, record what you recall about the setting, the protagonist, problems and conflicts, and other characters. Skim and reread sections to collect specific details. You can turn and talk to a partner and try to connect the book and chapter's title to what you have learned from the preview. Titles provide clues that focus you on themes and what's important.

2. **Set Reading Purposes.** Having a purpose for reading can make the process motivating and engaging. With fictional texts, a first purpose for reading can come from a text preview, or you can use the title and read to discover why the author used that title. Purposes can change while you continue reading and can include predictions about plot, characters' decisions and interactions, and how setting changes will affect the plot and characters. It's helpful to adjust your reading purpose before starting a new chunk of text.

3. **Check Out Chapter Titles and Themes.** Since chapter titles usually point out a key theme in the chapter, the title can help you identify that theme and locate the details that support it. Here's how to state a theme: The statement is general and does not mention a character or specific event. The theme applies to the book you are reading but also can apply to other books. Themes are also statements about life, relationships with others and self, decisions, events, problems, and reactions to settings.

To figure out themes of books that don't have chapter titles or to find multiple themes in a chapter, you can use these questions:

- How do characters' actions and words lead to themes?
- What decisions have characters made that can support themes?
- What relationships in the book can lead to discovering themes?
- Do characters have rich inner lives that can lead to themes?
- How does setting contribute to theme?

Next, use the chart that follows to pinpoint general topics. These common topics can be transformed into themes.

Common Topics That Can Become Themes

abuse	freedom	love	self-reliance
childhood	friendship	loyalty	stereotyping
courage	growing up	nature	success
death	hate	patience	trust
devastation	hope	patriotism	truth
dreams	identify	prejudice	unhappiness
faith	independence	race relations	violence
family	justice	self-improvement	war

4. **Use Context.** There are six different types of context clues: definitions and synonyms, concrete examples, restated meanings, comparison, words or phrases that modify, and conjunctions that show relationships and link ideas. Use these to find examples from your instructional and independent reading. You can avoid letting an unfamiliar word stump you by ask a peer partner for help. The more often you "meet" a word in your reading, the better you'll understand how it works in different situations or context.

5. **Consider Literary Elements or Narrative Structure.** Knowing literary elements means that you have the tools for understanding literature or narrative texts. An important goal is to know the definition of each element and demonstrate your understanding by identifying from a specific text the protagonist, antagonist(s), conflict, and problems, and offering evidence from the text that supports your understanding of a specific element.

6. **Stop to Check Recall and Make Predictions.** Stopping to think and reflect on one or two chapters in a fictional text enables you to check recall of events and to keep track of characters. Stopping to think at the end of one long chapter or two short chapters also enables you to decide if you have recalled enough details or whether you need to reread. This self-monitoring strategy supports independence while reading and enables you to savor the story, word choice, and literary elements.

7. **Make Inferences.** With fictional texts you can infer using a wide range of elements: dialogue, interactions between characters and with various settings, reactions to problems, antagonists, what other characters say, decisions characters make, their motivation for actions, resolving or not resolving conflicts or problems, and their inner thoughts.

8. **Discuss Text-Dependent Questions.** Discussing text-dependent questions can deepen your knowledge of the narrative as well as literary elements or text structure. Use the skimming technique for locating details that answer questions by identifying key words in a question and skimming a text to find those words. In addition, you can use chapter titles to locate information and skim a character's name or a specific setting to locate details that answer a question.

You can create your own text-dependent questions by using verbs that create interpretive, open-ended questions: why, how, evaluate, explain, compare/contrast, defend, etc. For you to be able to create your own open-ended questions, you need a solid knowledge of the plot and characters. You can determine whether your questions are interpretive by testing each one to see if it has two or more different responses.

9. **Think about Relationships.** A work of fiction contains characters, and as the plot unfolds relationships between and among characters develop. Reflecting on relationships and how these affect decisions the protagonist makes can enrich your reading of literature. In addition, relationships can lead to determining themes, as well as help you understand how relationships affect conflicts and the protagonist's ability to solve problems. It's also beneficial for you to pinpoint antagonistic or adversarial relationships and consider how these affect the plot, problems, decisions, and conflicts.

10. **Closely Read.** A close read can help you make sense of confusing passages and deepen your understanding of figurative language and connotations. Close reading asks you to reread and analyze a passage phrase-by-phrase and sentence-by-sentence in order to link ideas and improve your comprehension. Keep your copy of the handout *Close Reading Guidelines for Fiction* close by and use it as a resource and reminder to help you comprehend tough passages.

Focus Your Intervention Lessons

It is important to focus your intervention lessons on the standards and skills that students need most to improve their reading. Here is a process to follow to help you do this.

1. Review the student's written work, your observational notes, and any conferences.

2. Focus on one aspect of the literary (fiction) text focus standards that will most benefit the student. See focus standards and suggested scaffolds on the pages that follow.

3. Monitor the student's progress through scaffolding conferences and written work.

4. Record each focused intervention lesson on the *Scaffolding Conference Form* on page 232.

5. As soon as possible, gradually release responsibility to the student until he or she can complete the task independently.

Reading Standards and Interventions for Literary/ Fiction Text

The interventions in this chapter follow key focus standards for reading literary text. They were selected based on analysis of a variety of current standards. In Chapter 4, I discussed in depth the following standards that apply to both informational texts and literature: building prior knowledge, using context clues to find meanings of tough words, connotative and denotative meanings, figurative language, how word choice affects meaning and mood, and using prefixes, roots, and suffixes. Include these in your lessons on literature, as well.

Teacher TIP

When you make the rounds, you will be able to decide which students can benefit from a 2- to 3-minute intervention. You can determine which level of intervention other students require, by scheduling a five-minute investigative conference to observe how students manage and complete a task.

For each strategy, one of these interventions will be provided: a quick, 2 to 3-minute intervention; a 5-minute intervention; a 10- to 15-minute intervention; or a 30- to 40-minute intervention. To help break the process down into steps that can ultimately support students' progress, a menu of scaffolding tips is included. You can decide which ideas might help a student move to independence with the task. If one suggestion doesn't support the student, try another.

You can assess students' performance and determine the kind of intervention you'll try first by observing them while they plan and write as you make the rounds or in a conference that you document. Look for the following "red flags":

- ➤ The student doesn't talk during pair-shares.
- ➤ The student completes no writing or very little writing.
- ➤ The writing support doesn't relate to the claim or topic sentence.
- ➤ The student says, "I can't do this."

- ➤ The student shows anger toward writing about reading.
- ➤ The student refuses to plan or plans have little detail.
- ➤ The student doodles or draws cartoons.
- ➤ The student's head is on the desk.

Focus Standard 1

{ Determine what the text says explicitly and make logical inferences from the text using close reading; when writing or speaking, support conclusions drawn from the text by citing specific textual evidence. }

The skills and strategies that follow are crucial for students to master in order to achieve proficiency with this standard.

Strategy	Intervention Timeframe	Resource Page(s)
Identifying Key Details (pages 124–125)	30–40 minutes	*The Raven And His Young* (raven.pdf)
Retell The Text (pages 126–127)	10–15 minutes	*The Bremen Town Musicians* (bremen.pdf) *Retelling Checklist for Narrative Texts* (page 246–247)
Skim to Locate Information (page 128)	5 minutes	N/A
Make Logical Inferences (pages 130–131)	30–40 minutes	*The Raven and His Young* (raven.pdf)
Make Logical Predictions (page 132)	10–15 minutes	*The Bremen Town Musicians* (bremen.pdf)

Identifying Key Details

Overview

This is a series of three 30- to 40-minute interventions where students examine the protagonist to identify and understand key details in the text.

Materials

➡ *The Raven and His Young* (raven.pdf)

➡ chart paper (*optional*)

Procedures

Day 1

1. Pre-teach the following vocabulary: *island, mainland, toil, raven.*

2. To build background knowledge, ask students to discuss the following question: What are problems older animals face? (possible responses: get tired, can't do as much work, are alone)

3. Review the meaning of the following literary terms: *protagonist, antagonist,* and *problem.*

4. Distribute copies of *The Raven and His Young* to students and read the text aloud to model fluency.

5. Have students reread the text silently to think of the meanings of the pre-taught literary terms and identify the protagonist.

6. Allow students time to discuss what they learned about the protagonist in pairs. (possible responses: The raven is old, he gets tired, he's weak and worries that when he gets older his kids will notcarry him over the sea) Explain to students that these are key details about the raven.

7. Conclude the lesson by pointing out the excellent discussions students had and how

they used the term *protagonist* to identify key details about the raven.

Day 2

1. Provide students time to reread *The Raven and His Young* in pairs.

2. Review how identifying the protagonist of the story on Day 1 enabled students to find key details about the raven. Have students discuss antagonists and share what they learned. Here are possible explanations:

   ➤ The raven's sons: The first two said they'd carry the raven, but they lied so he dropped them into the ocean. The third son said he couldn't help because he would be caring for his own babies.

   ➤ The ocean: It was far to get to the mainland. The raven got tired and had no place to rest.

   ➤ The raven was worrying about getting old: He said that when he was old and weak he couldn't fly over the ocean alone. He woukd need help.

3. Ask students to record each antagonist in their notebooks and next to each one write the key details they recalled from their discussion.

4. If your students have difficulty identifying the antagonists, ask them questions, such as *What happened to the first two sons? Why did this happen? Why did the older raven let the third son live? What do you learn about crossing the ocean?* Questions can point students to specific details. You might also point them to the parts of the text that answer each question and have them skim or reread each part.

5. Conclude the lesson by pointing out how well students found key details about each protagonist.

Identifying Key Details *(cont.)*

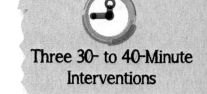

Day 3

1. Plan to release responsibility to the students. First, ask them to reflect on what they did on Days 1 and 2. On the board or chart paper, write questions that will support their recall. For example, What details did you learn about the protagonist? What details did you learn about the antagonists? Consult your notebooks to refresh your memory. How can literary elements help you find key details?

2. Organize students into pairs. Instruct pairs to identify the problems each character in the story has, the outcome of each problem, and key details.

3. Make the rounds to see how students are progressing with this task. If students have difficulty working on their own, return to supporting them with questions. Point out that they can raise questions to help them explore literary elements and key details.

Scaffolding Suggestions

➢ Model how you use plot events to identify key details about characters, setting, conflicts, and problems.

➢ Show students how chapter titles can help them pinpoint important details.

➢ Show students how a knowledge of literary terms can help them find details.

➢ Have students practice with you or with a peer partner working on literary elements, details, and chapter titles to find key details.

➢ Work with one literary element at a time and show students the details that can be gathered.

➢ Have students use settings to find details related to time and place.

➢ Have students use information about the protagonist and other characters to find important details and develop understandings about characters.

➢ Ask students to pinpoint conflicts and/ or problems and the details learned for each element.

➢ Introduce other literary elements in a lesson. This should take less time if students understand the process they've practiced. Have the entire class continue practicing with your daily read-aloud and with instructional reading materials.

Retell The Text

Chapter 5

Overview

This is a series of two 15-minute interventions where students examine literary elements (characters, setting, problem, outcome) to help them retell the text.

Materials

➡ *The Bremen Town Musicians* (bremen.pdf)

➡ *Retelling Checklist for Narrative Texts* (pages 246–247)

➡ chart paper (*optional*)

Procedures

Day 1

1. Distribute copies of *The Bremen Town Musicians* to students. Explain that when retelling, it's important to reread a text and think about identifying the following literary elements: characters, setting, problem, and outcomes.

2. Read aloud Chapter 1. Tell students that once you identify the key elements in the text, retelling is easy. Also explain that it is helpful to record notes after you have read or reread a selection and use them to retell the text. As a class, discuss the four literary elements below and record students' ideas on chart paper or the board. Possible responses for each literary element include:

   ➤ characters: the farmer and the donkey

   ➤ setting: farm

   ➤ problem: the donkey grew old and weak, the farmer decided to send the donkey far away

   ➤ outcome: the donkey decides to run to Bremen and become a musician

3. Sharing out loud, use the notes to retell the events of Chapter 1. Ask students to compare the notes with the actual retelling. (Students will likely notice that the retelling is longer than the notes and that you added details when you retold the chapter.)

4. Conclude the lesson by pointing out what you did: (1) reread Chapter 1; (2) used literary elements to think about the story; (3) jotted key elements on paper; (4) used notes to retell; (5) added details to the retelling.

Day 2

1. Have students read Chapter 2, "Escape!"

2. Ask students to find the pattern in the story. Discuss these literary elements and then have students record notes next to each one: title, characters, setting, problem, outcome. If students struggle with writing, have them dictate the notes for you to write. Talking before writing supports recall.

3. Remind students to reread their notes before retelling out loud. Sometimes having the student reread the notes and the chapter/text selection before retelling can help them recall more details.

4. Provide time for students to retell the chapter. Use the *Retelling Checklist for Narrative Texts* to assess student progress.

Retell The Text (cont.)

Scaffolding Suggestions

➤ Demonstrate how to retell a short narrative text. You can use a story, a short book, or an excerpt/chapter.

➤ Have the student look at the *Retelling Checklist for Narrative Texts* to know what you're expecting.

➤ Invite the student to reread the selection before retelling.

➤ Ask the student to jot some notes that can support the retelling.

➤ Increase the amount of information to be retold as the student gains confidence and experiences success.

➤ Explain why it's helpful to know to include elements such as title, name of protagonist and other characters, and sequential events in a retelling.

➤ Help the student understand that recall is the key to retelling and to let you know if he or she struggles with recall. If that's the case, find a text that is more accessible and/or one where the student has a great deal of background knowledge about the genre or topic.

Classroom Snapshot: An Adaptation for English Language Learners

A fourth-grade student has difficulty including details and literary elements in her retelling. After a 5-minute investigative intervention, I decide to plan these two consecutive retelling lessons because more time meant that I could listen to the student's retelling, prompt her if necessary, and gather enough data to decide what to do next. Because she is still limited with her writing proficiency level, I allowed her to dictate her notes before retelling. Here is what I wrote for the student:

Title: *The Bremen Town Musicians*, Chapter 2, "Escape!"

Characters: donkey, dog

Setting: field, road to Bremen

Problem: dog can't round up sheep—master will send dog away

Outcome: dog joins donkey—go to Bremen to become musicians

This student makes solid progress over the two days, but she still depends on me for jotting notes, which suggests the need for a second rereading. To move the student to independence, I schedule two 10-minute interventions and have her read, take notes, and retell chapters 3 and 4. However, since the story of *The Bremen Town Musicians* follows a pattern, a goal for this student is to have her retell from a text that isn't patterned and has longer chapters.

5-Minute Intervention

Skim to Locate Information

Overview

This intervention should be used after a mini-lesson on locating details in a text. It focuses on using the table of contents and key words in questions to help the student locate information in the text.

Materials

➡ any student instructional text

Procedures

1. Present a mini-lesson on locating details in a text as a strategy to find evidence for responding to text-dependent questions.

2. Provide students with a set of text-dependent questions relating to their guided reading book.

3. Model what you do to locate information in the text for the first question. Think aloud and demonstrate how to choose which chapters you will skim and what key words in the first question can help you locate information to answer that question.

4. Have students practice skimming the text to locate answers to the remaining questions.

5. Make the rounds to check on each student's progress.

6. Schedule longer interventions for students who require more assistance and modeling.

Scaffolding Suggestions

➤ Show students how skimming using the names of characters can help them locate details.

➤ Show students how chapter titles can help them locate details.

➤ Have the students practice skimming for details using characters' names, proper nouns, and/or chapter titles.

➤ Provide text-dependent questions and have students skim the text for names and key words.

➤ Explain that knowing what happened in a chapter can enable students to find the event or situation that has the specific details.

Skim to Locate Information (cont.)

Classroom Snapshot: Making the Rounds

A group of students is reading *Stone Fox* by John Reynolds Gardiner, and I ask them to locate information using these text-dependent questions:

➢ Why does Willy want Doc Smith to check out Grandfather?

➢ How does Willy make Doc Smith understand that something's wrong with Grandfather?

➢ What do you learn about Willy from his attitude toward Grandfather?

As I make the rounds, I notice that two students have difficulty locating the parts of the text that answer these questions, so I set up a 5-minute intervention, work with each student separately, and follow the headings on the *Scaffolding Conference Form*. I decide to work with each student separately because together one could dominate the discussions, and I wouldn't be able to discover the support each one needed.

Here is a completed *Scaffolding Conference Form* for one of the students with whom I worked:

Scaffolding Conference Form

Appendix D

Student Name: _____ Date: _____

Focused Topic: Using the table of contents and key words in questions to help the student locate information in the text.

Teacher's Preparation Notes and Observations:

Ask the student: Which chapters will you skim? What key words in the first question can help you locate information? Model and show student what I do to locate information in the text for the first question. Ask the student to identify key words in the second question and locate the place in the text that answers the question.

Materials used with student:

Stone Fox

Student's comments:

I wasn't using words in the question or chapter titles. Then I used chapter 1 (titled Grandfather) and Doc Smith, Willy, and grandfather in the second question. I skimmed page 6 Going to bed early and no music got Doc Smith to come.

Teacher records outcomes:

Student located details for the second question. No time for third questions.

Negotiated goal:

Use key words in questions and chapter titles to locate information to answer questions.

Check one:

☒ schedule another conference

☐ have student work with a peer

☐ student can work independently

Chapter 5

Make Logical Inferences

Overview

In this intervention, the teacher uses questioning to prompt student thinking and help them make inferences from a text with supporting text evidence.

Materials

➤ any read-aloud text to model inference

➤ *The Raven and His Young* (raven.pdf)

➤ chart paper

Procedures

1. Explain that an inference is not stated in the text; it is implied. Use your read-aloud text to show students how you make an inference using a dialogue between characters and/or a literary element such as the story's problem.

2. Distribute copies of *The Raven and His Young* to students. Read the text together. On the board or chart paper, provide students with a series of prompts to help them infer:

   ➢ How did the raven's words and actions help you understand his personality and feelings?

   ➢ Use the raven's words, actions, and personality traits to make an inference.

   ➢ Support the inference with details from the text.

3. Organize students into partners. Have students reread the first six paragraphs and with their partner think of one inference along with details from the text that support the inference.

4. As students answer, organize their thinking on a T-chart. This will serve as a resource when you ask them to write inferences in their notebooks using their instructional reading books. Possible student responses include:

Inference	Text Evidence
1. The raven is afraid of getting old.	1. The raven thinks about if his son will help him when he's old—carry him to places when he's tired and weak.
2. The raven is heartless.	2. He drops the first two sons in the ocean.
3. First two sons fear their dad.	3. They lie and say they'll carry the dad to stay alive.

Make Logical Inferences *(cont.)*

Scaffolding Suggestions

➤ Help students understand that an inference is an unstated meaning.

➤ Explain that students can use literary elements to support making logical inferences. Model how you use a literary element to infer and then ask students to practice.

➤ Start with dialogue and help students understand how to infer characters' personality traits from what they say.

➤ Have students study decisions a character made or actions taken to solve a problem and consider what inferences can be made with these.

➤ Pair students who need additional practice with inferring, and have them use the same text.

➤ Have students learn to infer using one literary element at a time. Move to practicing inferring with a new literary element only when students can infer with the one they are practicing.

➤ Teach students how to organize their inference and text support in a T-chart.

Classroom Snapshot: Support from the Story

To help a group of eighth-grade students make logical inferences, I used *The Raven and His Young* by Leo Tolstoy. Students had used this text to identify key details, and they had the background knowledge necessary to make logical inferences. It's helpful to use a text students have read and discussed when practicing a challenging strategy because they can focus their energy on the strategy instead of decoding and recall.

Students had so much prior exposure to this text that I decided to have them work independently. I asked them to read paragraph 7 to the end, then make one inference and support it with details from the text. This was tough for students. All of them made the obvious inference—that the third son lived because he told the truth. However, I wanted students to dig deeper, so I returned to the strategy of asking questions: Why did the raven like the third son's answer? What do you think the third son's answer made the raven think about? What will eventually happen to the old raven and how does that connect to the third son's answer?

The last question created that click of comprehension that teachers desire. Here's what a student said: "The inference is that none of the ravens can live forever. Having babies makes sure ravens stick around." I told students that they not only made a terrific inference, but they also identified the theme of this short tale.

If none of the questions you pose support students' thinking, then return to the think-aloud model, and show them how you made the connections.

Make Logical Predictions

Overview

In this intervention, students use a text that has both predictable and unpredictable story patterns to practice making their own predictions about plot events.

Materials

➡ *The Bremen Town Musicians* (bremen.pdf)

Procedures

1. Read aloud the first four chapters of *The Bremen Town Musicians*. Model how to make logical predictions based on the information included in those four chapters.

2. Distribute copies of *The Bremen Town Musicians* to students. Then, have them read Chapter 5 independently or in pairs.

3. Have students discuss Chapter 5, and use the chapter to predict what will happen next. Be sure students use text details to support their predictions. Possible student predictions:

   ➢ The robbers will beat up the animals and the animals will run away.

   ➢ The singing is so scary and loud, the robbers will run away.

   ➢ The robbers ignore the singing and keep eating.

4. Have students read to the end of the third paragraph of Chapter 6 and adjust their predictions based on what happens in the story. Have students share their predictions.

5. Allow students time to finish reading the text. After students complete the story, discuss the difference between predicting with a predictable story pattern

(Chapters 1–4) and without one (Chapters 5–6). Students will likely say that without the pattern they had to think about what happened in that chapter and also think about why the animals were going to Bremen in order to predict what would happen next.

Scaffolding Suggestions

➢ Model how to stop at the end of a chapter to think about what you've learned and know in order to make a prediction. Help students understand that developing the habit of stopping at the end of a chapter and making a prediction can keep them interested in reading because they want to discover whether their prediction is on target or if they need to adjust it.

➢ Explain that predictions can be about what characters might do, a decision the character might make, how he or she might solve a problem, or what will happen next in the story.

➢ Explain the difference between a guess and a logical prediction. A logical prediction uses details and inferences from the text to predict what might happen next. A guess is made without specific evidence and can use the reader's past experience.

➢ Have students practice making predictions about one element at a time: a character, a solution to a problem, or a plot event. Predicting about characters is usually the easiest for students to learn first.

➢ Model how you can predict a plot event or what might happen next. Ask students to predict what will happen next.

➢ Provide enough practice until students feels comfortable making logical predictions. Partner students with peers reading the same text for extra practice.

Focus Standard 2

{
Determine central themes or
ideas of a text and analyze their
development across the text;
summarize the key supporting
ideas and details.
}

The skills and strategies that follow are crucial for students to master in order to achieve proficiency with this standard.

Strategy	Intervention Timeframe	Resource Page(s)
Identify Theme (pages 134–135)	15 minutes	*Composing a Theme* (page 248) *The King and the Shirt* (king.pdf)
Summarizing Fiction (pages 136–137)	15 minutes	*The King and the Shirt* (king.pdf) *Summarizing Fiction, Memoir, and Biography Form* (page 225–226)

Identify Theme

Chapter 5

Overview

In this intervention, students use a short text to identify theme.

Materials

➺ a recent read-aloud text

➺ *The King and the Shirt* (king.pdf)

➺ *Composing a Theme* (page 248)

➺ projector or document camera

Procedure

1. Display *Composing a Theme* and review the tips provided. Model for students how to use the tips to figure out the theme from the selected recent read-aloud text. Explain to students that themes are stated in general terms and can apply to many texts.

2. Distribute copies of *The King and the Shirt* and *Composing a Theme* to students. Pre-teach the word *emissaries* using context clues from the text.

3. Have students read the text in pairs or independently.

4. Organize students into pairs and have the pairs use the steps to find a theme. Sample student responses:

   ➤ The point is to find happiness for a sick king who's unhappy.

   ➤ The king believes that money can buy him happiness.

   ➤ Theme: Money can't buy happiness.

   ➤ Theme: Wearing the shirt of a happy person can't make you happy.

   ➤ Theme: You have to find happiness yourself.

5. If students have difficulty, ask questions such as, "Why was the king unhappy? How did the king propose to find happiness?" Show how these questions lead to a theme. You can also ask, "Why can't the happy poor man help the king? What did the king and his emissaries learn from the poor man?" Help students understand how these last two questions lead to a theme.

Teacher TIP

Make sure that students understand that themes can grow out of specific parts of a book or text, but the central theme connects to most of the book. For example, in *The King and the Shirt* a theme is that people are not happy all of the time, but the central theme is that each person has to find happiness.

Identify Theme *(cont.)*

Scaffolding Suggestions

➤ Help students see that when stating a theme you don't name a specific character but use the terms "characters" or "people."

➤ Think aloud and show students how you use a literary element to figure out theme. Then, ask students to use the same element but in a different part of the text to find theme.

➤ Help students use the main character's decisions and think about what the character does or says to find a central theme.

➤ Help students think about what the book is saying about all characters or people and the lives they live to find a theme.

➤ Ask students to identify a significant or pivotal event, and then consider the importance of this event to plot or characters and develop a theme statement.

➤ Help students understand that in a long text, such as a novel or a play, there can be more than one central theme.

➤ Use these prompts to help students figure out a central theme: What did the character learn about friendship? About family? About solving problems? About coping with conflict or fears?

Classroom Snapshot: Deciding Who Needs Intervention

From making the rounds, I identify a large group of sixth-grade Tier 2 students who need help with theme. Students keep naming characters and specific plot events in their book when stating the theme. I divide the eight students into two groups of four and work with each group for 15 minutes using the steps provided in this intervention. I chose to use this short text to offer students success with this strategy and build on their success, so they can apply the strategy to a longer text at their instructional level.

Summarizing Fiction

Chapter 5

Overview

This is a series of three 15-minute interventions where students use a graphic organizer to take notes about the text in order to support their summary.

Materials

➹ a recent read-aloud text

➹ *Summarizing Fiction, Memoir, and Biography Form* (page 225–226)

➹ *The King and the Shirt* (king.pdf)

➹ any short text to match instructional reading level

➹ projector or document camera

Procedures

Day 1

1. Display a copy of the *Summarizing Fiction, Memoir, and Biography Form*. Using your most recent read-aloud text, model how to take notes on the form. Explain what you will write for each of the four words: *Somebody, Wanted, But,* and *So*. Point out how you return to the text to collect specific details.

2. Distribute copies of *The King and the Shirt*. Have students read the text to get the basic plot of the story.

3. Display a new copy of the *Summarizing Fiction, Memoir, and Biography Form*. Instruct students to reread the short tale and help you take notes on the form. Remind students that it's important to use their own words when offering specific details and to skim parts of the text so they can be specific.

Day 2

1. Display the completed *Summarizing Fiction, Memoir, and Biography Form* and quickly review the note-taking process used in the previous lesson.

2. Show students how you compose a topic sentence that includes the title and author of the text (e.g., "In the tale, *The King and the Shirt* by Leo Tolstoy, the author tells a story about finding happiness.").

3. Demonstrate how to turn the notes next to *Somebody* into one or two complete sentences. Then, have students help you turn the rest of the notes into sentences.

4. If students show that they are not ready to try this strategy on their own, schedule one or two more collaborative lessons.

Day 3

1. Distribute the selected new text and copies of the *Summarizing Fiction, Memoir, and Biography Form* to students.

2. Have students read the text and complete the activity sheet.

3. Make the rounds and support students as they work.

Summarizing Fiction (cont.)

Scaffolding Suggestions

➤ Model how to summarize fiction using the *Summarizing Fiction, Memoir, and Biography Form*. Summarize in front of students with a short narrative poem, or a short, short story, myth, or legend.

➤ Explain the terms on the form in more detail and have students record information as you discuss: The *Somebody* section represents the protagonist or main character. The *Wanted* section is something important that the protagonist wanted. The *But* section is what got in the way of what was wanted. The *So* section represents what happens as a result of both the *Wanted* and *But* sections. However, it's important to NOT give away the ending of the story.

➤ Have students work in pairs with a common text. Ask students to plan and write a summary on their own once they can successfully work with you and/or a peer partner.

➤ Have students practice with a chapter from a novel, a short story, anarrative poem, a myth, or a legend. The novel can be from the student's independent or instructional-level reading.

➤ Have students observe you model the entire note-taking process with a short text both of you have read.

➤ Demonstrate how to turn notes for each section of the *Summarizing Fiction, Memoir, and Biography Form* into one to three sentences.

➤ Point out that summarizing is about being selective, and the four words in the *Summarizing Fiction, Memoir, and Biography Form* support the selection of key details.

Chapter 5

Focus Standard 3

{ Analyze the structure of a text, including how specific sentences, paragraphs, and larger portions of the text (e.g., a section or chapter) relate to each other and the whole. }

The skills and strategies that follow are crucial for students to master in order to achieve proficiency with this standard.

Strategy	Intervention Timeframe	Resource Page(s)
Literary Elements Support Comprehension (pages 139–140)	2–3 minutes	*Literary Elements and Text Meaning* (pages 249–250)
Text Structure: Cause and Effect (pages 141–143)	10–15 minutes	*The Bremen Town Musicians* (bremen.pdf)
Genre Characteristics of Literature (pages 144–145)	2–3 minutes	N/A

Literary Elements Support Comprehension

Overview

In this intervention, a series of mini-lessons is utilized. The teacher listens and questions students as they apply their learning using texts from their instructional level to determine if longer intervention is needed.

Materials

➡ any completed read-aloud text

➡ instructional texts from guided reading/book club groups

➡ *Literary Elements and Text Meaning* (pages 249–250) *(optional)*

Procedure

1. Using a recently completed read-aloud text, organize a series of mini-lessons such as the suggestions that follow:

   ➢ Identify the protagonist and explain what an important decision shows you about his or her personality or relationship with another character. Instead of a decision, you can substitute problems solved or interactions with other characters.

   ➢ Choose a situation that was tough or challenging for the character. Explain how the character handled the situation and what you learned about the character.

   ➢ Select an important antagonist. Discuss how the protagonist dealt with the antagonist and what you learned about the protagonist's personality or a theme.

2. After each mini-lesson, show students how you link a literary element (e.g., protagonist, antagonist, problem, decision, or setting) to build deeper understanding of the text. Work with one literary element at a time, as having students work with more than one can confuse them.

3. Have students work in their guided reading/book club groups with their instructional texts to mirror the process you modeled. Make the rounds to listen to students' discussions. Ask questions of students/groups who struggle to decide whether a longer 5-minute investigative intervention is needed.

Scaffolding Suggestions

➢ Provide students with copies of *Literary Elements and Text Meaning*. Review the literary elements to make sure students understand them.

➢ Show students how you link a literary element, such as the protagonist, to a specific text to illustrate your understanding.

➢ Focus on elements that confuse students and support them as they practice applying an element to a text.

➢ Discuss literary elements as you read aloud to students, and model how a specific element improves your comprehension.

➢ Pair students who require extra practice applying literary elements and showing how an element improves comprehension. Have students use a common text such as your read-aloud or instructional-level materials.

Literary Elements Support Comprehension *(cont.)*

Chapter 5

Classroom Snapshot: Making the Rounds for 2- to 3-Minute Interventions

Fifth-grade students have practiced linking these literary elements to read-aloud texts and short narratives: protagonist, antagonist, problem, decision, and setting. Today, students use the guided reading books they recently completed: *Esperanza Rising* by Pam Munoz Ryan, *Shiloh* by Phyllis Reynolds Naylor, and *Because of Winn Dixie* by Kate DiCamillo. Students work in guided reading groups; discuss each literary element, connecting it to the book; and discuss how these literary elements lead to an understanding of a character's personality, decisions, and coping strategies with adversity or tough situations.

For about 15 minutes, I go back and forth among groups and listen to their discussions. I observe that students do well with linking a literary element to their book, but have difficulty showing how the element deepens their comprehension of a character's personality, etc.

At this point, I stop the discussions, compliment students on linking each literary element to their books, and decide to have students work with partners on one connection at a time. They will link the protagonist's main problem to two important decisions he or she made. I continue making the rounds, pausing to support pairs by asking questions. Focusing on one literary element at a time and pairing students enabled them to experience success. Out of 24 students, I identify three who need additional support, so I schedule a 5-minute investigative intervention for each one of them. Being able to use your observations to immediately adjust plans is what responsive teachers do because the teaching is not about the plans; it's about helping students experience success while they learn.

Text Structure: Cause and Effect

Overview

In this intervention, students identify text structure and use it to determine information about the characters and the events in the story.

Materials

➤➤ familiar read-aloud text

➤➤ *The Bremen Town Musicians* (bremen.pdf)

➤➤ any simple text (lower than instructional reading level)

Procedures

1. Model how to identify cause/effect in a familiar read-aloud text and explain that writers use this technique to show why things happen.

2. Distribute copies of *The Bremen Town Musicians*. Ideally, the student has read this text at least once or twice prior to this intervention. If needed/desired, read the text aloud. Have the student practice identifying cause and effect from the events in the text.

3. Discuss how the text structure shows characters' personality traits as well as how it can show the relationship among themes and events.

4. Schedule a five-minute conference for the next meeting. Have the student identify cause/effect in Chapter 6 of the text and explain what the cause/effect showed about the characters and their decisions.

5. Have the student practice cause/effect with a different easy text. If he or she can work independently, ask the student to identify cause/effect using his or her instructional text.

6. Then, have the student explain what he or she learned about the character or the plot when reflecting on the causes and effects.

Scaffolding Suggestions

➤ Show students that text structures, such as cause/effect, compare/contrast, description, and sequence, that are found in informational texts are also part of literature (fiction).

➤ Work on these structural elements one at a time with students, always helping them to understand the following:

➤ **cause/effect:** authors want readers to consider the effects of characters' words, actions, interactions, decisions, approach to problem solving

➤ **compare/contrast:** authors show how settings and/or characters are alike and different

➤ **description:** descriptive details enable readers to visualize settings and characters

➤ **sequence:** authors choose to tell events in a specific sequence; this is often found in mystery, fantasy, historical fiction

Text Structure: Cause and Effect (cont.)

Chapter 5

Classroom Snapshot: Questioning to Go Deeper

A seventh-grade English language learner, reading at a mid-third-grade instructional level, has difficulty identifying cause/effect and relating effects to what readers learn about characters. What follows is the conversation I have with the student who has read Chapters 1–4 of the text. Instead of saying "good" or "correct" when he answers, I notice the thinking he did because I want him to focus on his process and use what he has learned again. When the student can't respond, I ask a question to direct his thinking.

Robb: Writers can use cause/effect to explain why things happen in a story. It's often helpful to think back on what you have read to see if there is a cause/effect relationship. The event that happens first is the cause. The event or events that happen as a result are the effects. Let me think aloud and show you cause/effect in Chapter 1 of *The Bremen Town Musicians*. Here's a cause, event, or statement from Chapter 1: "As years passed on the farm, the donkey grew old and weak and couldn't help the farmer anymore." Here are two effects: The farmer decided to send the donkey far away and the donkey grew sad and worried.

I ask the student to reread Chapters 1–5.

Robb: Can you think of a third effect?

Student: The donkey got an idea—he would go to Bremen and become a musician.

Robb: I noticed that you figured that out quickly! What do you learn about the donkey from the cause/effect relationship?

Student: He could solve his problem. He didn't just accept what the farmer would do. I think the farmer didn't care about all the work the donkey did.

Robb: I noticed that you understood the cause/effect pattern here. Reread Chapter 5 and see if you can find one more cause/effect relationship.

Student: Well, they're tired from all the walking—I think that's a cause. (I nod.) There are lots of effects. Donkey leans against a tree. Dog and cat lie down. Rooster sees a light glowing and says it could be a cottage and it's close. Donkey says, "Let's go to the cottage," and they all do.

Text Structure: Cause and Effect *(cont.)*

Robb: I noticed how thorough you were. Can you tell me what you learn about the animals? (No response.) Let me ask a question to help you think about what the cause and effects help you understand about the animals. What does the fact that all the animals go to the cottage let you know about them?

Student: They do things together.

Robb: Can you think of other ideas that relate to their decision?

Student: They'd rather be in a warm cottage than sleeping in the woods.

Robb: I noticed that you were able to go beyond identifying the cause and effects to better understand the animals and their decision.

The student recaps what he learned about cause/effect and says: "It's hard to think about the characters and cause/effect." I agree, but point out the solid thinking that he did. I tell him that with more practice, he'll find this part of cause/effect easier.

Genre Characteristics of Literature

Overview

In this intervention, specific questions are used to call students' attention to the characteristics of the studied genre.

Materials

➡ any fictional read-aloud texts to support genre study

Procedures

1. Use your selected read-aloud text to remind students about the characteristics of fiction and the terminology: setting, plot, protagonist, antagonist, problem, conflict, outcome, climax, and a return to normalcy.

2. Introduce students to the desired literary genres (e.g., mystery, historical fiction, realistic fiction, or folk/fairy tale) they will be reading in guided and independent reading by using your read-aloud texts and the books students read for instruction.

3. Have students discuss each genre structure and then ask groups to collaborate to make a list of the characteristics of each. Make the rounds during this time to listen in and question students who seem off track or unsure of the genre characteristics. Sample questions to ask/statements to use to guide students' thinking are as follows:

   ➢ What in the text makes you think that?

   ➢ Think about the books you've read. Do they all share that characteristic?

   ➢ What makes this book a _____?

   ➢ How is this different than _____?

4. Allow students time to share their ideas. Have students categorize picture books by genre for additional practice.

Scaffolding Suggestions

➢ Review the genre characteristics that students are presently working on to make sure that students understand the elements.

➢ Help students understand that literary elements are part of all fiction, whether it's science fiction, fantasy, mystery, realistic fiction, etc.

➢ Discuss genre characteristics as you read aloud to students. It's helpful for your read-aloud to be the same genre as students' instructional books.

➢ Have students reading the same genre for independent reading pair up and discuss the elements of the genre they've selected. You can also organize students into groups of four.

➢ Help students recognize that understanding genre can improve comprehension, but it can also support writing in a specific genre.

Genre Characteristics of Literature *(cont.)*

Classroom Snapshot: Making the Rounds and Asking Questions

To help fourth-grade students understand the genre characteristics of realistic fiction, I explained that the word *fiction* signals these genre characteristics: setting, plot, protagonist, antagonist, problems, conflicts, outcomes, climax, and a return to normalcy. This mini-lesson introduced realistic fiction, mystery, historical fiction, and folk/fairy tale. Students used their most recently completed independent fictional book to categorize their books and then discussed with partners what makes a book realistic, historical, mystery, or a folk/fairy tale. At the end of the lesson, students built an explanation of each of the four types of genres they were reading. I made the rounds and listened to partners. One student said that realistic fiction is real. I asked, "What makes it real?" Her partner helped by saying that it could happen today—the plot, the problems—and the characters are like us. "You made the connections," I said, and move on.

Two students were having difficulty with folk tales and they came up with the definition, "a make-believe kind of fiction."

"What makes it a folk or fairy tale?" I asked. "Think of the books you read."

One student said that the stories have magic and animals can talk and are like us. Her partner added that there is a lesson it teaches and lots of good versus bad.

As I circulated, I continued listening and asking questions to help students clarify the genre elements in literature they had read. Even though some students struggled with what makes a book historical or realistic fiction, I felt that when students helped me define the unique characteristics of the books they'd read, it helped everyone. The following list was created by the students and shows development of an understanding of each category:

➢ **Mystery**—has a detective, a mystery to be solved, clues, and sometimes a red herring where the author takes you off track to confuse you about who did it.

➢ **Historical Fiction**—is set in the past like colonial times. The characters are realistic for that time. You learn a lot about history from these books.

➢ **Realistic Fiction**—has plot that could happen today. Characters are like us with friends and family and problems like we have.

➢ **Folk or Fairy Tale**—has magic-like animals that can talk and feel like us. The hero can be an animal, a person, or a royal person like a prince or princess. There's good and evil and a lesson it teaches.

Focus Standard 4

> Assess how purpose or point of view shapes the style and content of a text.

The skills and strategies that follow are crucial for students to master in order to achieve proficiency with this standard.

Strategy	Intervention Timeframe	Resource Page(s)
Author's Purpose: Literature (page 147)	5 minutes	*The Gold Cadillac* by Mildred Taylor
Identifying Point of View: Literature (page 148)	10–15 minutes	*Personal Pronouns and Point of View* (page 249)

Author's Purpose: Literature

Overview

In this intervention, the materials point the student to events, words, and decisions in the book that reveal the author's purpose.

Materials

➡ *The Gold Cadillac* by Mildred Taylor

➡ text on racism/prejudice (*optional*)

Procedures

1. Read aloud the first 10 pages of the story. Model how the text reveals the author's purpose to show the excitement and pride the father, children, and relatives feel about an African American family owning a Cadillac. Explain that another purpose is to set up the conflict that the purchase of the Cadillac causes between the mom and dad.

2. Have the student determine the author's purpose using the section of the story that takes place in Memphis, TN. Possible student response: The sign "WHITE ONLY, COLORED NOT ALLOWED" helped me determine the purpose. This section of the story also shows how the whites in Memphis thought the Cadillac was stolen because they thought that no black person could afford one. The author's purpose was to show prejudice in the South.

3. If the student struggles, pair him or her with a peer partner for more practice the next time the rest of the class works on author's purpose.

Scaffolding Suggestions

➢ Explain to students that literature (fiction) can have these purposes: entertain, humor, create suspense, create adventure, create mystery, recreate a historical period, or create future worlds.

➢ Explain that events and situations the characters find themselves in can shed light on the author's purposes.

➢ Show students how to use the title, cover illustration, and first chapter to determine the author's purpose. Then, have students use the title, cover illustration, and first chapter to determine the purpose of a different text.

➢ Ask students to monitor how the author's purpose shifts based on where you are in the text.

➢ Tune students in to the author's word choice and model how you use word choice to figure out author's purpose. Point students to a chapter or section of text and have them select words that reveal the author's purpose.

➢ Explain that literature can have more than one purpose. For example, a book can be funny and have suspense or parts of a book about an historical period can have adventure and mystery.

➢ Ask students to stop after each chunk of text and think about author's purpose to see if they have discovered a purpose that differs from the purpose they had established.

10- to 15-Minute Intervention

Identifying Point of View: Literature

Overview

In this intervention, students examine pronouns in a text to help them determine the point of view.

Materials

➡ *Personal Pronouns and Point of View* (page 251)

➡ a variety of picture books

➡ document camera (*optional*)

Procedures

1. Distribute copies of the *Personal Pronouns and Point of View* resource sheet to students. Review each point of view and their respective pronouns.

2. Have each student select a picture book. Ask students to skim their picture books and look for the pronouns that signal point of view. With first person, students should notice that sometimes the text uses *we* and *me*.

3. Explain that the narrator is telling what other characters say and do. This may be confusing to students, so ask them to find passages where the author uses a pronoun that differs from the story's point of view. Have students read these passages out loud or project the passages in the book with a document camera and discuss each passage as a group.

4. Follow up with a 2 to 3-minute intervention during independent reading. Have students tell you the point of view and show you the passages that helped them determine this.

Scaffolding Suggestions

➤ Use your read-aloud texts to help students understand first, second, and third-person point of view.

➤ Help students understand the different kinds of narrators in literature: omniscient and limited.

➤ Organize students into pairs and have partners use their instructional-level texts to figure out the author's point of view.

➤ Have students offer evidence from the text that supports their conclusions about the point of view.

➤ Provide students who require extra practice with opportunities to work with you and/or a peer expert.

Teacher TIP

Here are some great books that demonstrate point of view:

Abuelo by Arthur Dorros (first person)

Dona Flor by Pat Mora (third person)

If You Decide to Go to the Moon by Faith McNulty (second person)

My Grandfather's Coat by Jim Aylesworth (third person)

Sweet, Sweet Memory by Jacqueline Woodson (first person)

Swift by Robert J. Blake (first person)

Reteaching Lessons for Fiction

If the text and/or instructional approach used during your interventions is not helping students improve, then it's time to reteach using a different instructional approach and a more accessible text (Fisher and Frey 2013; Howard 2009). You can present these reteaching lessons for one student, a pair of students, or a small group. It is possible that there will be times when the entire class or most of the class will benefit from a reteaching lesson. These lessons will support them, too. **Note:** Document each reteaching lesson with the *Reteaching Lesson Form* on page 239. Documenting each lesson will enable you to make decisions about future interventions.

Each text can be used to reteach any of the fiction standards addressed in Chapter 4. For example, I use *A Change of Heart* to explore theme, but the story can also be used to explain what causes changes in a character, to teach making inferences, to answer text-dependent questions, and to make predictions.

When to Move On:

➤ There will be students who don't absorb the process. Sometimes, it's helpful to move on to other skills and strategies and return to the skill or strategy after a few weeks have passed.

➤ Remember, some students might not become independent with a specific strategy during the year you have them. Keep practicing and planting seeds of understanding because eventually, the students will be able to move to independence.

Writing in Notebooks

Before students complete their notebook writing, have them plan by recording two to four points they want to include. Check these points *before* students write to make sure they are detailed. If their notes are too general, ask students to add specific details and let you see their plans again. Then, they can write using their plans as guides.

The following reteaching lessons are provided in this chapter.

Lesson Title	Resource Page(s)
Making Logical Inferences (pages 150–151)	*Best Night of the Year* (bestnight.pdf)
Finding Themes and a Central Theme (pages 152–154)	*A Change of Heart* (heart.pdf)
	Composing a Theme (page 248)
Skim to Answer Text-Dependent Questions (pages 155–156)	*Finding Kip* (kip.pdf)
Infer Character's Feelings and Personality Traits (pages 157–158)	*Walkabout* (walkabout.pdf)
	Adjectives That Describe Personality Traits (page 223)
Identify Antagonist and Protagonist (pages 159–160)	*Choices* (choices.pdf)

Making Logical Inferences

Materials

➤ Best *Night of the Year* (bestnight.pdf)

➤ Students' instructional reading books

Goal

To use dialogue and plot events to infer.

Teaching the Lesson

Day 1

1. Review with students that an inference is not stated in the text and that to infer you can study dialogue, plot events, characters' decisions, actions, and interactions.

2. Distribute copies of *Best Night of the Year* and have students read the text independently.

3. Ask students to turn and talk to a peer and infer what the best day of the year is, providing evidence from the text. Possible student inferences: Halloween and going out trick-or-treating is the best night of the year. Evidence is the breakfast labels: scary scrambled eggs, mutant muffins, petrified pancakes. Luis wears a black cape, slicks back his hair, smears red blood across his chin, and fills a pillowcase with candy that will last until Christmas.

4. Say, "Let me show you how I infer Luis's feelings using what he says and does. Luis is excited about getting to school early. In fact, that's all he can think of in the morning. There's evidence to support this inference: 'Luis skips breakfast at home, tells his mom he'll get breakfast at school, and runs out the door before his mother can stop him.'"

5. Ask the students to turn and talk and make one more inference about Luis using words and actions from the story as support. Possible student inference: Luis can't wait for school to end and trick-or-treating to begin. He says, "I hope the day goes fast." You learn that this is the one night he can eat as much junk food as he wants, he can dress up and be someone else, and he can be on the street in his neighborhood after dark by himself.

6. Ask students to use details to infer what Luis's mom is like. Possible student inferences: One inference is that Luis's mom is concerned that he ran out of the apartment before breakfast. Evidence is that she questioned Luis about this after school. It's possible to infer that Luis's mom thought he did something wrong and was being punished. Another inference about his mom is that she's proud of her son's costume. Evidence in the text is she says, "Let me take a picture!"

Day 2

1. Show students how to organize their inferences in a T-chart in their reader's notebooks. Below is a sample.

Inference	Text Evidence
Luis can't wait for school to end and for trick-or-treating to begin.	➤ Says, "I hope the day goes fast."
Luis's mom is concerned about his leaving the apartment before breakfast.	➤ This is the one night he can stay out late in the neighborhood, eat junk food, and dress up as someone else.
She thinks that he's being punished for doing something wrong.	➤ She questions Luis about this when he comes home from school.
Luis's mom is proud of her son's costume.	➤ She says, "Let me take a picture."

2. Explain to students that they can use the format of this chart as a planning guide in preparation for the journal response.

3. Allow students time to create a T-chart based on the instructional reading book of their choice.

Journal Response

Ask students to make an inference using a section from their instructional reading book. Ask them to set up their notebook page just as you did for *Best Night of the Year*.

Assessment Tips

➤ Decide who can infer and work independently or with a partner and which students need scaffolding or another reteaching lesson.

➤ Use a different story to prepare a reteaching lesson. Use *Best Night of the Year* to scaffold for students who are near independence.

Chapter 5

Finding Themes and a Central Theme

Materials

➤ *A Change of Heart* (heart.pdf)

➤ *Composing a Theme* (page 248)

➤ chart paper (*optional*)

Goal

To help students understand that a short text can have more then one theme but only one central theme.

Teaching the Lesson

Day 1

1. Distribute copies of *A Change of Heart* to students.

2. Allow students time to read the text and discuss the protagonist, problem, antagonists, and what causes changes in the protagonist.

3. Distribute copies of *Composing a Theme*. Review the steps from the resource sheet for stating a theme.

4. Have students record brief notes in their journals with their initial thoughts on what the theme(s) might be.

Day 2

1. Organize students into pairs.

2. Display the questions that follow on the board or chart paper and have pairs discuss them, citing details from the text. Circulate around the room to listen in on students' discussions and redirect/ question students as needed.

   ➤ What does Jay learn about Logan?

   ➤ Why does Jay agree to put green dough in the new kid's hair?

   ➤ How does Jay feel about following Logan's orders?

   ➤ Why does Jay change?

3. Share the following think-aloud with students: "You did an excellent job citing text evidence to answer these questions. These questions and answers can lead you to discovering themes. Let me show you how I figured out a theme and then used the guidelines to state the theme. In the first paragraph when Jay asks himself, 'Did he really want to make life miserable for the new kid?' and then says, 'he was happy to be part of something at school,' I saw two themes: One has to do with peer pressure and wanting to fit in. The second is that making someone you don't even know miserable can cause guilt. Now, I need to state the theme without using any character's names. Two themes from this section: 1) Peer pressure can cause you to do things that you know are wrong. 2) Sometimes we cave to peer pressure because we want to fit in and be seen as tough."

4. Have students reread the text to determine one more theme about bullying, and allow students to share their ideas.

5. As a class, determine the central theme of the text.

6. Provide time for students to share what they learned about finding themes and central themes.

Journal Response

Have students choose one or two themes and provide the text evidence that enabled them to pinpoint the theme.

Assessment Tips

➤ If some students continue to have difficulty finding themes in fiction, work with them in a different text.

➤ Prompt students with questions about the main character, problems, and conflicts to help them identify themes.

➤ Pair struggling students with those who understand theme and have them work together using their instructional texts.

Classroom Snapshot: Questioning to Understand Theme

The following is a dialogue between me and several students that occurred during the teaching of this lesson. This dialogue picks up after my think aloud.

Student 1: You make finding themes seem easy, but it's not.

Robb: I'll help you by having you reread a section and use the *Composing a Theme* chart to figure out the theme that shows what kind of person Logan is. Reread from "After school, in detention..." to "were silent the rest of detention."

Student 2: He's a bully.

Robb: Okay, now what does the story say about bullies that could be a theme? (Give students time to read, think, and discuss.)

Student 3: Bullies like giving orders, but they watch and let someone else do the dirty work.

Robb: Great observation of Logan's behavior! Now, reread from "Jay raced home..." to "And Logan didn't even like the one thing that Jay was really into: video games." Then, tell me what theme you think could be learned from that part of the text.

(Give students time to read, think, and discuss.)

Student 1: When you see how another person feels about bullying, it can make you think about what you did and change.

Robb: I noticed how you used the text to develop that theme statement. Did anyone have a different theme?

Student 4: Caving in to a bully's orders gets you in trouble more than the bully.

Student 2: Being bullied by someone can cause you to bully others.

Robb: You observed that Jay was becoming a bully like Logan by always doing what Logan said. I see so much progress! Now, reread to the end of the story and try to identify the one theme that's part of the entire story— that's the central theme.

(Give students time to read, think, and discuss.)

Students discussed the fact that bullying was part of the entire story and that bullying had to be part of the central theme. Here are questions I posed to help them move deeper in the text and find the central theme:

➤ What has Jay learned about himself?

➤ Who's in charge at the end of the story? What does this show?

These questions supported students' thinking and here's what a few said:

➤ When you can make your own decisions and show a bully that you're in charge, you become independent and won't follow the bully anymore.

➤ Following a bully's orders can turn you into a bully until you act on your own.

Finally, we reviewed what students learned about themes and central themes. Here's what students said:

➤ Reread chunks of the story and try to find a theme in the chunk.

➤ Ask questions 'cause these help you understand more.

➤ Think of the whole story and what the main character learns to help you find a central theme.

The students pinpointed the key areas so well that I decided to post their suggestions for the entire class.

Skim to Answer Text-Dependent Questions

Materials

➤ *Finding Kip* (kip.pdf)

➤ chart paper (*optional*)

➤ document camera (*optional*)

Goal

To show students how to use words in questions to skim a section and locate details in the text to answer the questions.

Teaching the Lesson

Day 1

1. Have students read *Finding Kip*.

2. Discuss the gist or main point the author makes.

Day 2

1. Organize students into pairs.

2. Share the following think-aloud: "Today we're going to identify key words in a question and use the words to skim the text to find the section that has details that answer a question. Here are questions for *Finding Kip*. Some questions will ask you to cite details from the text and other questions will ask you to use text details to infer. Remember, an inference is an unstated meaning. You won't find the inference in the text, but you will find details that help you infer."

3. Display the following questions/prompts on chart paper or by using a document camera:

➤ How does the narrator know she's in trouble when she walks in the door?

➤ Why does the narrator feel concerned when she calls Kip and the dog doesn't come?

➤ Why does the narrator feel happy at the end of the story?

➤ Why is fall the narrator's favorite time of year?

➤ Infer the narrator's feelings when she can't find Kip.

➤ How does Mrs. Hart help the narrator?

➤ Why does the narrator's dad comment on raking leaves?

4. Continue the think-aloud: "Let me model how I use key words in a question to find the part in the text that has evidence for the answer. The key words for the fourth question are *fall* and *favorite time of year*. I skim the text for these words and find them in the third paragraph. I skim the text and find my answer: In the fall there are football games, Halloween, and warm sweaters."

5. Depending on the number of students in your group, invite pairs to work on one or two questions, skim the text to locate the answers, and discuss.

5. Demonstrate for students how to write this response in their reader's notebook. First, write the question from the board, and then write the answer under the question.

Journal Response

Have students write the assigned question(s) and response(s) in their notebooks. Then, have pairs share their process and findings with the group.

Assessment Tips

➤ Make sure that students can use key words in questions to skim a text for details. Once students can do this, have them work with partners and then on their own.

➤ If some students require additional practice, use any short text, create text-dependent questions, and have students use key words in the questions to skim the text and locate the section(s) that contain answers.

➤ Teach students to pose text-dependent questions by giving them these verbs—*compare*, *contrast*, *evaluate*, and *connect*. Ask partners to compose questions for a specific story. Then, have pairs trade stories and questions, and answer one another's questions using the process practiced in the reteaching lesson.

Reteaching Lesson 4

Infer a Character's Feelings and Personality Traits

Materials

➢ *Walkabout* (walkabout.pdf)

➢ *Adjectives That Describe Personality Traits* (page 223)

Goal

To help students use a character's words, actions, and interactions to make inferences about the character's personality traits.

Teaching the Lesson

Day 1

1. Distribute copies of *Walkabout,* and have students read the text.

2. In pairs or as a group, discuss the character's feelings about summer camp.

3. Review personality traits. Help students understand that a personality trait describes what a person is like, such as assertive, helpful, jealous, angry, worried, anxious, etc.

4. Explain that in a story you can study what a character says and does, and the way the character interacts with other characters to determine his or her personality traits. You can also study a character's reactions to others and their inner thoughts to explore the emotions they are feeling. Provide examples from your read-aloud text or the instructional text students are reading.

Day 2

1. Provide students with time to reread the text *Walkabout* in pairs.

2. Share the following think-aloud with students: "Today, we will go through the story and study words, actions, and interactions to discover Tim's personality traits. For example, when Tim says, 'Please, please don't make me go!' I know he feels anxious and worried about going to camp for four weeks. When Tim slams the door, he shows his anger and frustration over his parents making a decision about his life."

3. Prompt students with questions that get them thinking about the words, actions, or interactions they are exploring. You can use these questions when students discuss and think about the second paragraph. How do the camp's activities make Tim feel? Why does Tim want to stay home? How does Tim feel about the fact that no phones or electronics are allowed?

4. Distribute copies of *Adjectives That Describe Personality Traits*. Then, have pairs reread the paragraph that starts with "rolling onto her bed" and ends with "four whole weeks."

5. Allow pairs to discuss what they learned about Tim's feelings and personality. Encourage them to use the *Adjectives That Describe Personality Traits* resource sheet to support their discussion. Here are possible student responses:

➢ Tim was pessimistic because his parents decided on and paid for four weeks of camp.

➤ Tim was clever about technology but disliked the outdoor sports featured at camp.

➤ Tim felt resentful because he could not take his iPhone or any other electronic devices.

➤ Tim felt angry and bitter that his parents didn't consult him.

6. Have students reread the conversation between Tim and Sam. Ask questions about feelings and personality traits such as, What does Tim saying "Sure" tell you about his feelings? Why does Sam call Tim's reply not enthusiastic? What do words like "stupid, sleep out in a tent, won't know anyone, stink" reveal? Why does Tim say he'll get the yogurt when he returns? Possible student responses:

➤ Tim feels disgusted about camp because he uses words and phrases like *stupid*, *stink*, and *sleep in a tent*.

➤ Saying "Sure" to Sam shows that Tim is not enthusiastic about anything since he learned about camp.

➤ Tim wants independence during the summer—he wants to stay home, go to movies, text friends, and play Xbox.

➤ Tim is a techno-geek, not an outdoors type.

7. Point out how students used the questions to help them before inferring. Have students use the last section and the first paragraph to draw conclusions about Tim's parents.

Journal Response

Have students make a T-Chart. Label the left side *Feeling or Trait*. Label the right side *Text Evidence*. Have students use any short text to complete the T-chart by adding three feelings and/or traits. Share the model that follows with them by writing it on the board or chart paper.

Title: Walkabout	
Feeling or Trait	Text Evidence
Tim was pessimistic.	His parents had made the decision about four weeks at camp and had paid for the camp. Tim knew he couldn't change their minds.

Assessment Tips

➤ Determine who needs additional help using text details to infer emotions and personality traits. Review words that describe emotions. Allow students to use the *Adjectives That Describe Personality Traits* reference sheet, and model how the list can support identifying a character's personality traits.

➤ Reteach the lesson using a different story for students who would benefit from experiencing the process again.

➤ Use your interactive read-aloud to model inferring personality traits and emotions, and provide students with the multiple modeling they need.

Identify Antagonist and Protagonist

Materials

➤ any read-aloud texts with antagonists

➤ *Choices* (choices.pdf)

Goal

To help students identify antagonists and understand that antagonists work against the protagonist to create problems and conflicts.

Teaching the Lesson

Day 1

1. Distribute copies of *Choices* to students. Have students read the text independently or in pairs and discuss the choices Yuki has.

2. Review the concept of an antagonist. To help students understand this literary element, show them the antagonists in any read-aloud text and how they create problems and conflicts.

3. Explain that antagonists can be the main character's inner thoughts or feelings, friends, physical traits, nature, other characters, or settings.

Day 2

1. As a group, discuss how antagonists work against the protagonist or main character and often can cause problems and conflicts for the protagonist.

2. Instruct students to reread the first paragraph of *Choices* and find the main antagonistic force. (Yuki's eyes are turning blue.)

3. Have students reread the second paragraph. Then, instruct pairs to discuss the problems Yuki faces. Possible student response: Now that Yuki has blue eyes, her life changes from good to bad. She can't vote or hold public office, she has to do awful work like wash diapers, she gets little pay for her work, and she can't finish school and be with her friends—she has to go to a school for blue eyes.

4. Have students skim/reread the rest of the story and discuss in pairs the problem that Yuki's dad sets up—the problem that creates a conflict within Yuki. Possible student responses:

➤ She can have an operation to change her eyes to brown—but it's dangerous and she could die.

➤ Yuki's grandma had blue eyes. She headed a group that fought for blue-eyed rights.

5. Have students discuss the conflicts Yuki has and the choices she must make. Prompt them to also think about why the author called this story *Choices*. Allow time for students to share their ideas with the class/group.

Journal Response

In your notebooks, write the choice you believe that Yuki will make and explain why you believe that she will make the choice.

Assessment Tips

➤ Identify students who have difficulty pinpointing antagonists and determining the problems and conflicts they cause.

➤ Have students discuss the antagonists in their lives and the problems these raise to enable them to better understand this literary element.

➤ Invite students to use a different story or their instructional book to find antagonists similar to theirs.

➤ Continue to use the interactive read-aloud to model antagonists and explain how these forces can lead to problems and conflicts.

➤ Prepare a scaffolding lesson about antagonists with a story that students read for a different purpose. Continue to scaffold until students can work independently.

Continue the Conversation

Discuss these prompts and questions with your team or a peer partner. Reflecting on what you learn, what you know, and your students' performance can support your decision-making process regarding the kind of intervention plan you will develop.

1. Share an example of how you used genre and/or literary elements to scaffold students' work.

2. Share a reteaching lesson you led. Discuss the lesson, why you decided to reteach, and the student outcomes of reteaching.

3. Share an example of an intervention lesson used with two students. Help your colleagues understand what you did to enable students to experience success and move forward.

4. Discuss the *Ten Tips for Reading Fiction That Work!* handout. What examples can you share about how some of the tips played out in your classroom?

Chapter 6

Learning From Students' Writing about Reading

In their landmark study, **Writing to Read:** *Evidence for How Writing Can Improve Reading*, Steve Graham and Michael Hebert (2010) make a compelling case to increase the amount of writing time students have for Writer's Workshop and writing about reading. Writing about reading includes short responses to what teachers have read aloud as well as brief responses to instructional-level and independent reading. The meta-analysis that Graham and Hebert provide at the end of their study makes the case for more writing time during the school day. In addition to improving students' comprehension, Graham and Hebert also found that writing about reading improves reading fluency and decoding.

Talk Before Writing about Reading

Talk creates oral texts that can clarify students' hunches about reading and deepen their understanding of structure, characters, and themes (Alvermann 2000; Gambrell 1996). Talking about reading includes a quick turn and talk to a partner, an in-the-head conversation with self, and a small- or whole-group discussion. These discussions are meaningful when they use details and facts to identify things like theme, big ideas, and inferences.

Whether the discussion is brief or long, developing readers, English language learners, and special education students benefit from opportunities to hear the thinking of others. Heterogeneous pairings and groupings also permit students to observe peers' thought processes (NMSA 1999; Tomlinson and Allan 2000; Tomlinson 2014). For example, two fourth-grade boys were discussing a picture book their teacher had read aloud: *Saturdays and Teacakes* by Lester Laminack. The teacher asked partners to share a memory from the story and explain why it was important. One boy, Alejandro, came to the U.S. from Ecuador two years prior, and his partner was from Virginia. I listened as each boy shared a memory from the story. The following shows part of their discussion transcribed from my notes:

Alejandro: Memories keep the boy and his grandma together. My grandmother is still in Ecuador.

Michael: What do you remember about her? (Michael takes Alejandro away from the text, but his instincts are perfect.)

Alejandro: My grandma, she took care of me until I was seven. I only knew her. My parents (in U.S.) adopted me.

Michael: What's your best memory about your grandma?

Alejandro: She take me when she worked in the fields. She let me help her make rice pudding. And eat it! I miss her.

Michael: You can write a letter to her about the book (*Saturdays and Teacakes*) and tell her about how teacakes made you remember rice pudding and missing her.

I could hardly breathe during this conversation. I did not want to step in and return the boys to text-dependent evidence. I had no idea where this discussion would go. What is remarkable about the exchange is the pairing of Michael, a sensitive and excellent reader with Alejandro, who is still refining his knowledge of English. Michael showed Alejandro that books often strengthen bonds between separated families. The discussion transcended Laminack's story by linking it to Alejandro's past, and that is what books and reading do. It's those personal connections to stories that bond readers to books and are equally important as text evidence-based discussions.

Teach Students Questions That Foster Discussion

It's helpful for students to observe you modeling prompts and questions that can keep a discussion moving forward. Even more beneficial to students is providing them with a reference sheet, such as *Questions That Help Discussions* (Figure 6.1) that they can use as they engage in small-group and partner discussions on their own. The reference sheet also supports the development of self-questioning by individual students. Practice enables them to pose questions during reading and while reflecting on their own after reading. The more students practice using these questions and prompts during discussions, the faster they will absorb them and use them as in-the-head discussion stimulators during silent reading and when writing.

Figure 6.1 Questions That Help Discussions

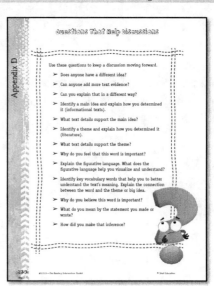

Writing about Reading

Researchers and teachers know that students can only write what they understand. Moreover, writing is an important tool for students because it helps them see what they know and understand and gives them opportunities to clarify and refine their thoughts. The emphasis in upper grades and middle school is often on reading. Writing, a tool that can improve comprehension, is often overlooked or omitted because teachers feel they don't have time in a 42-minute class period. The research is clear: students in middle and high school need to spend more time writing to learn (Applebee and Langer 2011; Kellogg and Whiteford 2009).

Ten Tips to Help Students Write about Reading

You can help students improve the quality of their written responses to reading by integrating the following into your daily practice:

➤ Present a mini-lesson that shows students how each tip works and reserve time for them to practice and ask questions.

➤ Show students how to organize or set up their readers' notebooks.

➤ Offer practical tips for writing responses such as specifically asking for the number of reasons you expect in a response.

1. **Get organized with a reader's notebook.** Having a reader's notebook allows students to document their thinking for the school year. Notebooks remain at school because if you send them home, several won't come back. Homework can be completed on separate paper and then pasted into the notebook.

2. **Complete prior knowledge notes.** Once students have previewed a text and discussed what they've learned from the preview with a partner or with their in-the-head voice, ask them to write Prior Knowledge Notes in their readers' notebooks. Students can use the handout *Activate Prior Knowledge and Set Purposes for Reading* (Figure 6.2) as a guide to write notes and use their notes to set purposes for reading.

3. **Cite evidence by paraphrasing or quoting from the text.** Offer students practice with citing text evidence by having them paraphrase the text or by quoting words from the text. Inferences, because they are unstated, need to be in the student's own words. Since some state tests require that students select a quote from a text as evidence, it's wise to have students practice this skill.

4. **Experience the benefits of reading their written responses out loud.** Reading their writing aloud invites students to slow down and listen carefully to the content and organization of the response. While students read their writing out loud, they can also pinpoint missing words, punctuation, and usage.

5. **Model the writing task.** Showing students how to write develops students' mental model of what you are asking them to do. Without a mental model of the type of response and your expectations, many students might miss the mark.

6. **Make the writing task clear and focused.** On the board, state and write the type of writing, its purpose, and a rubric that lists your expectations. For brief responses, keep the task tightly focused. (e.g., Use *Unforgettable Natural Disasters* by Tamara Leigh Hollingsworth to explain why forming a Global Alert System is important. Include two reasons.)

7. **Scaffold the writing task.** Provide specific guidelines to help students think and write with ease. (e.g., After reading *Jane Goodall: The Early Years* by William B. Rice, explain in your own words why the policy of apartheid deeply troubled Jane Goodall. Include the following elements: 1) explain what apartheid is, 2) show why it was unfair and cruel.)

8. **Share student responses that worked.** Provide students with multiple models of what a written response looks like. Knowing that they will share responses with peers provides a reason for thinking deeply and writing clearly.

9. **Explain that drawing is writing.** Drawing can provide the student with details that enable him or her to transfer specific information to writing. Drawing, a form of writing that uses visuals, is a supportive strategy for English language learners, special education students, struggling writers, and students who understand better by first creating a picture.

10. **Include informal and formal interventions.** As students write about reading, support individuals whose challenges can be repaired quickly. While circulating, you'll also decide on the type of longer intervention a student needs to move to independence with a writing task.

Figure 6.2 is a student resource sheet that can help students independently activate their prior knowledge and set purposes for reading.

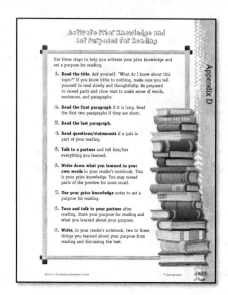

Figure 6.2 Activate Prior Knowledge and Set Purposes for Reading

More About Reader's Notebooks

I suggest that students write about reading in a reader's notebook. The school can purchase notebooks, or you can make them by placing composition paper between two sheets of colored construction paper. Staple in the upper left hand corner and ask students to print their names on the front cover and decorate it.

The notebooks remain at school. If you want students to complete an entry for homework, give them paper and have each student tape their homework into the notebook. If you plan to grade a homework assignment, let students know this. Notebooks are a record of students' thinking and progress with writing about reading for the entire year.

Benefits for Students

When teachers ask students to write about reading every day, students develop writing and thinking fluency. Over time, students find the writing easier because they automatically think deeply as they listen to a book read aloud or while they read instructional or independent reading materials. Take Maddie, who reads on a wide range of topics. After attending a play about Martin Luther King, Jr. at the local high school and listening to her teacher read books about Dr. King out loud, Maddie was able to write her own biography (Figure 6.3) that reveals her ability to remember details from listening. "It just poured out because I remembered a lot," she told me.

An overarching purpose of writing about reading is to build students' capacity to take a set of details and think with them. The bonus for teachers is that students' writing about reading reveals strengths and areas that can benefit from scaffolds and reteaching.

Share with colleagues how you integrate writing about reading into your curriculum, as well as what you are learning about students' reading ability through their writing.

Writing about Reading as an Assessment Tool

When students write short responses and paragraphs about their reading, you will learn about their use of writing conventions such as punctuation, spelling, and usage. Make note of these errors and address them in mini-lessons for the entire class or small groups of students. However, the focus of this book is intervention tools that can build students' reading strength so they can make solid gains in reading. Therefore, when you read what students write about reading, you can learn how they apply the strategies completed during guided practice and decide whether they need a short or long intervention (Knipper and Duggan 2006; Graham and Hebert 2010; Murray 1984). This type of writing is informal, and you can step inside a student's head and observe how he or she thinks about texts.

Figure 6.3 Maddie's Biography

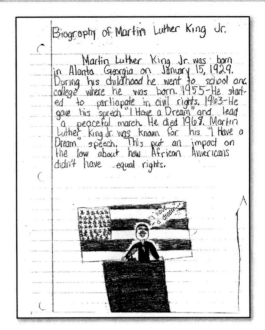

As you read students' writing, consider the task and your expectations. The list that follows shows what you can learn about comprehension and understanding of a text reading from their writing about reading. Students' writing reveals they can:

- ➢ recall information

- ➢ use text details to infer

- ➢ understand informational text features

- ➢ understand informational text structures

- ➢ understand literary elements

- ➢ demonstrate vocabulary strength: generating sets of words, multiple forms of words, using context to explain a word

- ➢ understand the meaning of a figure of speech and how it enhances the themes or big ideas of a text

- ➢ state ideas or positions clearly

- ➢ elaborate on an idea or position using text evidence

- ➢ support the answer to a question, an inference, or a prediction using text evidence

- ➢ include facts and inferences for text evidence

- ➢ connect ideas and text evidence to the question or prompt

- ➢ retell in sequence

- ➢ retell and include rich details

- identify key details

- follow directions

- organize ideas well

- build their prior knowledge

- use context clues to determine the meaning of unfamiliar words

- use prior knowledge to understand meaning

- only think literally about the text

- use a plan to summarize

- summarize by stating key points

- identify author's purpose

- identify author's point of view

- select words and phrases that illustrate mood

Teacher TIP

When students show you they need reteaching for planning and/or writing paragraphs about their reading, choose a different text, preferably an easier text so they can focus on the recall, thinking, and writing. By having students frequently plan and write paragraphs that explain an idea or argue for a claim, you are building writing fluency and stamina. Moreover, a paragraph is the building block of an essay and students will more easily make the transition to essay writing once they can plan and write organized, well-supported paragraphs.

Students' writing lets you into their thinking process because they can only write what they understand (Knipper and Duggan 2006; Murray 1984). Once you pinpoint strengths and needs, you will have to make decisions about the type of intervention(s) a student requires.

Often, a written notebook entry has more than one item that requires attention. My recommendation is that you select the item that will most improve reading comprehension. For example, the assignment for a group of fifth-grade students is to select two figures of speech from their guided reading book and explain how the figure of speech helps them understand the author's meaning. Three students have difficulty explaining each figure of speech and don't link it to meaning. Working on the author's meaning would be a top priority because students must be able to understand author's meaning in order to link meaning to figurative language.

As you make the rounds, read students' brief responses about their reading. On sticky notes, record notes about what students' writing teaches you about their reading comprehension. These notes, along with other formative assessments, can help you decide the topic and length of an intervention. For example, the notes in Figure 6.4 indicate that the student isn't reading, she dislikes the book, and she can't tell me about the two chapters she's read. To immediately support the student, I negotiate changing the book and offer her three different books to choose from. However, to explore why she feels this way, I set up a 5-minute exploratory intervention to try to pinpoint the issues. Figure 6.5 is a reminder and takes a few minutes of teacher modeling and student practice for the eighth grader who avoids skimming part of a text before answering text-dependent questions.

Figure 6.4 Sample Teacher Notes 1

> Student says: I hate this book. Little recall of any details in first 2 Chapters. Offered choice of new book—gave 3 books.
> 5 min. exploratory Conference

Figure 6.5 Sample Teacher Notes 2

> Answered question—very general ideas. Together, we locate page w/information. Student rereads + tells me details. She adjusts journal entry—see. Talk about the benefits of rereading. + Skimming

Chapter 6

Struggling Writers

This group of students often includes English language learners, special education students, and developing readers. When these students write daily and receive quick feedback from their teacher, they can improve their writing, recall of reading, and analytical thinking. Daily writing tasks should be short. The students' focus should be on content and finding the words to express thinking and ideas. By increasing the amount of writing about reading this group does, you can improve writing fluency and build their vocabulary and comprehension (Graham and Hebert 2010; Robb 2014; Snow and Biancarosa 2004).

Let's look at the writing of three students who struggle expressing their ideas on paper.

Classroom Snapshot: Carlita

Carlita is a seventh-grade English language learner. Her responses to the book I was reading aloud—*Testing the Ice*, by Sharon Robinson—reveal her personal concerns about school and her ability to infer. When I chatted with Carlita, she said that learning new things was hard and made her "scared." The cover of the picture book did not show school; it showed Jackie Robinson, surrounded by children standing on ice. To make her prediction about the contents of the book, Carlita used the words in the title and excluded the illustration. I pointed out how her prediction was personal, raising her awareness of feelings toward learning, and that her honesty was helpful to herself and her teachers (Figure 6.6).

Figure 6.6 Carlita's Notebook Entry

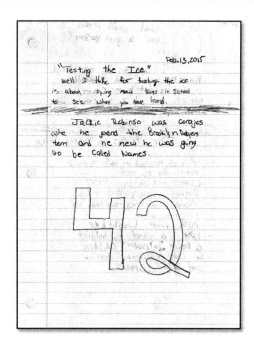

We also discussed the value of then writing a prediction that included all available text evidence. I praised Carlita for her excellent use of story details to infer why Robinson was courageous and asked her to discuss the cover of *Testing the Ice* with Kayla, Carlita's reading partner.

Without these brief interactions and written responses, I would have no idea what Carlita or other students were thinking and would not gain insight into her reading process in order to decide whether she needed to practice with me or with a peer partner.

Classroom Snapshot: Mira and Ali

The second student, Mira, who is close to the end of third-grade and reading at a second-grade level, illustrates writing about the reading of new information. Mira experiences success writing about Narwhal whales because her teacher scaffolds the writing process with headings that help Mira organize her ideas and know what to write (Figure 6.7). In contrast, Mira's classmate Ali, who is instructionally on a fifth-grade level, writes with confidence and a strong creative voice about Beluga whales (Figure 6.8). The point is that with continued opportunities to write about reading, Mira will require less scaffolding, improve her comprehension and recall, and refine her writing skill.

Types of Writing about Reading

Teachers often feel that they need to read and grade all students' writing. This is a myth that causes great pressure and often results in reducing the amount of writing students complete. If you spot check students' short responses while making the rounds, you can substantially reduce the amount of reading and grading. Moreover, decide what types of writing about reading you will grade. I grade plans, paragraphs, and short essays. Quick, daily responses in notebooks are to develop analytical thinking and writing fluency.

Whenever possible, have students organize notebook entries into a T-chart. T-charts are simple graphic organizers that help students organize their thoughts and plan their writing. Students can

Figure 6.7 Mira Organizes Her Ideas

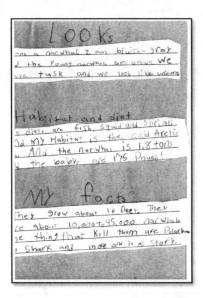

Figure 6.8 Ali's Writing About Beluga Whales

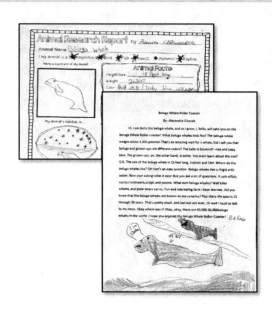

complete these and paste them in their notebooks, or you can project the T-chart onto a whiteboard and have students copy the format into their notebooks.

There are many different ways that students can write in response to reading. The following represent my suggestions and include sample T-charts wherever applicable.

Brief Responses

A quick pair-share precedes written responses as this activates ideas, and students can learn from and observe a peer's thinking process. Writing responses in notebooks should take from one to four minutes. Quick thinking can train students' minds to generate hunches and ideas about daily read-alouds, instructional-level materials, and independent reading. As students read more of a text, you can ask them to reread and adjust a previous entry.

Quick Writes

Quick writes are a type of brief response that has a set amount of time in which to respond, usually no more than five minutes for students to pour out their thoughts. Quick writes develop fluency and rapid thinking as students write without stopping or lifting their pencils from paper (Rief 2003). Using quick writes, also called free writes, is an effective writing strategy when asking students to activate prior knowledge about a genre or topic or to reflect on a theme, the protagonist and his or her problem, antagonists, or a word or concept. Quick writes can also be used to explain an idea in a text or to flesh out what students know about a topic/concept or a historical period.

Metacognitive Writing

This type of writing invites students to note what they do and do not understand in a text. Students can use the INSERT notation to quickly identify their level of comprehension. Then, students closely read parts of the text using what they know and have learned to construct meaning. You can also require that students write, in their notebooks, a brief summary of what they did to improve comprehension as well as explain their improved understandings. Figure 6.9 shows how students can use a T-chart to organize information for this type of writing.

Figure 6.9 Metacognitive Writing T-Chart

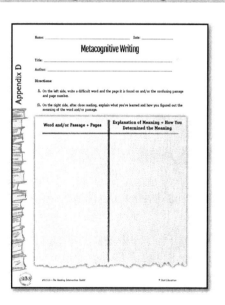

Predictions

Ask students to use evidence from the text to support predicting what will happen next. Students can use text details, inferences, text features, and photos and illustrations to support their predictions. The more text students have read, the closer their predictions are likely to be to the author's outcomes. Figure 6.10 shows how a T-chart can be used with this type of writing.

Vocabulary

This type of writing includes discussing a word's meaning, figurative language, or a concept the word implies and then showing (in writing) how it connects to the text's meaning. Writing about a text's vocabulary can also include multiple forms of a word, synonyms, and antonyms. Figure 6.11 shows how a T-chart can be used with this type of writing.

Figure 6.10 Predictions T-Chart

Figure 6.11 Vocabulary T-Chart

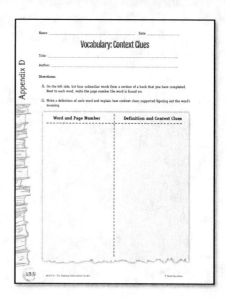

Four Words

This is a strategy that asks students to think of four words that come to mind after listening to the teacher read a text aloud or after reading a text on their own. Students select one word and in their notebooks link the word to the text by citing specific text evidence. Figure 6.12 shows a T-chart to support this strategy.

Writing about Emotions

Emotions are stirred by texts students read. Invite them to write the dominant emotion they felt and then cite text evidence to show the origin of that feeling. In addition to text details, students can make a personal connection that the text inspired. Figure 6.13 shows how a T-chart can be used to organize emotions about reading.

Writing to Evaluate

Evaluation writing invites students to judge a character's decision, the outcome of a conflict, interactions with other characters, and reactions to settings. Figure 6.14 represents a T-chart that can be used to organize evaluations about a character.

Figure 6.12 Four Words T-Chart

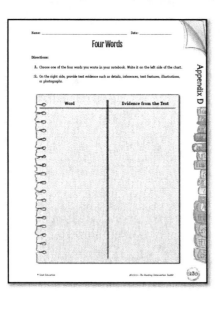

Figure 6.13 Writing about Emotions T-Chart

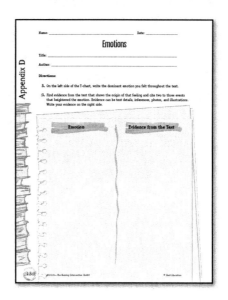

Making Inferences

To infer asks students to find an unstated or implied meaning in a text and offer textual details to support their inference. Students can infer big or main ideas, themes, characters' personalities, how setting affects characters' decisions or solutions to problems, and author's point of view. Figures 6.15 and 6.16 show T-charts that students can use to make inferences.

Draw and Write

Draw and Write works well for writers who struggle, English language learners, and students who are visual and use drawing as a path to writing. Students can draw and write about literary elements or information in texts. Drawing and writing can also include creating a labeled diagram, a chart, and a bar or pie graph.

Lists

Lists can generate a wealth of ideas relating to literary elements, a stream of synonyms and antonyms for specific words, a range of emotions, or a list of words related to a topic.

Paragraphs and Essays

Paragraphs and essays are more intentional and require that students plan in order to gather text evidence to argue, explain, or analyze. Though students resist planning, they need to think before writing so that they present the best text evidence as well as consider a title, introduction, and conclusion.

Figure 6.14 Evaluation T-Chart

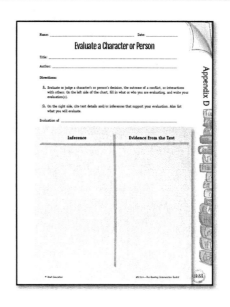

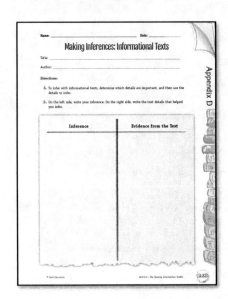

There are many types of paragraphs and essays that students can write. The most common types used in the classroom are argument, explanation, and writing about pivotal events.

➤ **Argument** asks students to read deeply, understand big ideas or themes, and then develop a claim. Students find text evidence to argue for their claim. To assess argument writing, see Figure 6.17.

➤ **Explanation** invites students to provide an explanation of how something works. In addition, students can explain why an event occurred, the meaning of a concept, or an outcome in fiction or nonfiction. To assess explanatory writing, see Figure 6.18.

➤ **Pivotal Event** asks students to select and briefly describe a significant or pivotal event in literature. The main part of this writing is to analyze the event and how it impacts plot, setting, characters, decisions, conflicts, or problems.

For additional information see my books on writing:

➤ *Teaching Middle School Writers: What Every English Teacher Should Know.* Heinemann, 2010.

➤ *SMART WRITING: Practical Units for Teaching Middle School Writers.* Heinemann, 2012.

➤ *Teaching Nonfiction Writing: A Practical Guide.* Scholastic, 2004.

Assessing Students' Needs and Planning Interventions

Students who have completed worksheets that ask them to write about reading by filling in the blanks or answering multiple-choice questions can experience difficulty writing a response that they develop. When the written response calls for analytical thinking and finding inferences to support a position or describe a character's personality, students often view the task as challenging and write very little. As you circulate and listen to pairs talk and then write, you will be able to determine which students you can support with an informal conversation, and those who require longer interventions. When anxiety and fear invade a student's mind, the writing task can seem insurmountable. Your interventions can show students that they can successfully complete the work.

Using Rubrics to Assess Writing

Give students the rubric for an explanatory paragraph or for a paragraph that argues for a claim before they begin to plan. The rubric, which you can adjust for the population you teach, lets students know your expectations for a "writing about reading" task. When students can revise their plans using the rubric, they often have more success writing a quality paragraph. In addition, students can use the rubric to self-evaluate first drafts and make sure they've included the required elements.

I don't read first drafts. But I do circulate and support students while they draft. If students are to become independent writers, they need to practice using a rubric to revise the content of their first drafts and make them better. Then, you can read an improved second draft and offer feedback.

Figure 6.17 Argument Paragraph Rubric

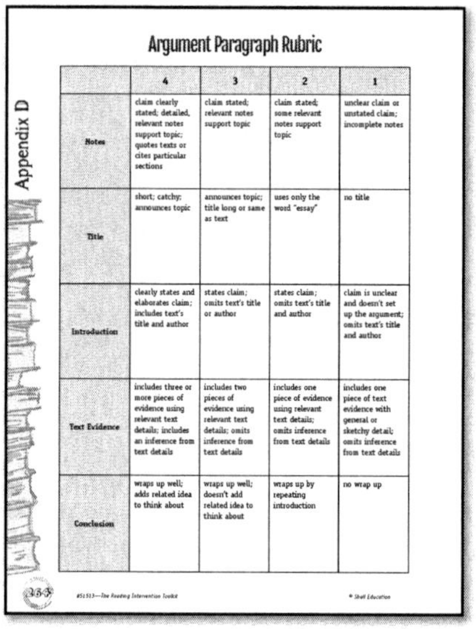

Appendix D

Argument Paragraph Rubric

	4	3	2	1
Notes	claim clearly stated; detailed, relevant notes support topic; quotes texts or cites particular sections	claim stated; relevant notes support topic	claim stated; some relevant notes support topic	unclear claim or unstated claim; incomplete notes
Title	short; catchy; announces topic	announces topic; title long or same as text	uses only the word "essay"	no title
Introduction	clearly states and elaborates claim; includes text's title and author	states claim; omits text's title or author	states claim; omits text's title and author	claim is unclear and doesn't set up the argument; omits text's title and author
Text Evidence	includes three or more pieces of evidence using relevant text details; includes an inference from text details	includes two pieces of evidence using relevant text details; omits inference from text details	includes one piece of evidence using relevant text details; omits inference from text details	includes one piece of text evidence with general or sketchy detail; omits inference from text details
Conclusion	wraps up well; adds related idea to think about	wraps up well; doesn't add related idea to think about	wraps up by repeating introduction	no wrap up

364 #51513—The Reading Intervention Toolkit © Shell Education

Figure 6.18 Explanatory Paragraph Rubric

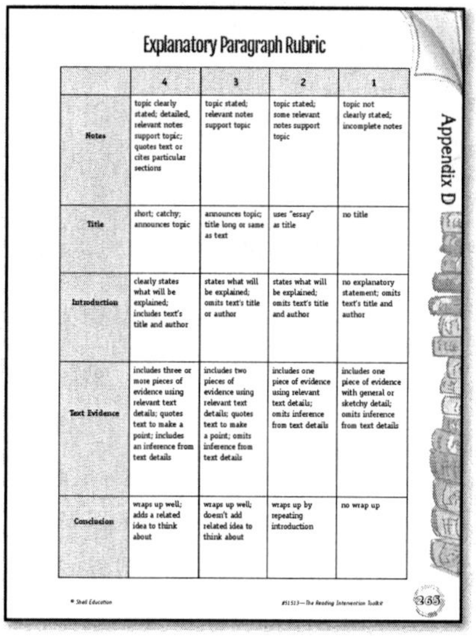

Explanatory Paragraph Rubric

Appendix D

	4	3	2	1
Notes	topic clearly stated; detailed, relevant notes support topic; quotes text or cites particular sections	topic stated; relevant notes support topic	topic stated; some relevant notes support topic	topic not clearly stated; incomplete notes
Title	short; catchy; announces topic	announces topic; title long or same as text	uses "essay" as title	no title
Introduction	clearly states what will be explained; includes text's title and author	states what will be explained; omits text's title or author	states what will be explained; omits text's title and author	no explanatory statement; omits text's title and author
Text Evidence	includes three or more pieces of evidence using relevant text details; quotes text to make a point; includes an inference from text details	includes two pieces of evidence using relevant text details; quotes text to make a point; omits inference from text details	includes one piece of evidence using relevant text details; omits inference from text details	includes one piece of evidence with general or sketchy detail; omits inference from text details
Conclusion	wraps up well; adds a related idea to think about	wraps up well; doesn't add related idea to think about	wraps up by repeating introduction	no wrap up

© Shell Education #51513—The Reading Intervention Toolkit 365

Writing Standards and Interventions for Writing about Reading

The interventions in this chapter follow the key focus standards for writing. They were selected based on analysis of a variety of current standards. Additionally, I've selected writing elements that enable students to focus on content. Content becomes primary because what students write can assist you in deciding whether they need help with developing a claim or topic sentence, finding text evidence for a paragraph or short response, or planning and thinking through ideas before writing.

For each strategy, one of these interventions will be provided: a quick, 2 to 3-minute intervention, a 5-minute intervention, a 10- to 15-minute intervention, or a 30 to 40-minute intervention. To help break the process down into steps that can ultimately support students' progress, a menu of scaffolding tips is included so you can decide which ideas might help a student move to independence with the task. If one suggestion doesn't support the student, try another one.

You can assess students' performance and determine the kind of intervention you'll try first by observing them while they plan and write as you make the rounds or in a conference that you document. Look for these "red flags":

Teacher TIP

When you make the rounds, you will be able to decide which students can benefit from a 2- to 3-minute intervention. You can determine which level of intervention other students require, by scheduling a five-minute investigative conference to observe how students manage and complete a task.

➤ The student doesn't talk during pair-shares.

➤ The student is completing no writing or very little writing.

➤ The writing support doesn't relate to the claim or topic sentence.

➤ The student says, "I can't do this."

➤ The student shows anger toward writing about reading.

➤ The student refuses to plan or plans have little detail.

➤ The student doodles or draws cartoons.

➤ The student's head is on the desk.

Focus Standards

Write explanatory texts to convey ideas and information clearly and accurately through the effective selection, organization, and analysis of content.

Write arguments to support claims from the analysis of selected topics or texts using valid reasoning and relevant and sufficient evidence.

Develop and strengthen writing as needed by planning, revising, editing, and/or rewriting.

Produce clear and coherent writing in which the development, organization, and style are appropriate to task, purpose, and audience.

The skills and strategies that follow are crucial to master in order to achieve proficiency in writing about reading.

Strategy	Intervention Timeframe	Resource Page(s)
Writing Short Responses (pages 176–177)	2–3 minutes	*Activities that Describe Personality Traits* (page 223)
Writing an Explanatory Paragraph (pages 178–180)	15 minutes	N/A
Developing a Claim (pages 181–182)	5 minutes	N/A
Planning Writing (pages 183–184)	15 minutes	*Writing Plan* (page 264)
Writing a Topic Sentence (pages 185–187)	5 minutes	N/A
Writing Endings (page 188)	2–3 minutes	N/A
Vocabulary (pages 189–190)	30–40 minutes	N/A

Writing Short Responses

Chapter 6

Overview

In this intervention, students use a T-chart to examine a character's personality traits and provide supporting text evidence. Then, they write a short response.

Materials

➡ *Adjectives That Describe Personality Traits* (page 223)

➡ any instructional-level text

Procedures

1. Distribute copies of *Adjectives That Describe Personality Traits*. Instruct students to review the chart and then discuss what a personality trait is.

2. Have students give you examples of personality traits for a family member or a friend.

3. Using the selected instructional text, review and discuss any features found in the text and the information that they provide.

4. Select a character (or the narrator) from the text. Ask students to use what the character/narrator says and does, as well as any text features to determine one personality trait.

5. Help students set up the T-chart. Have the students write the personality trait on the left side and offer text evidence on the right side.

6. Have students add to their T-charts based on other events, actions, or information from the text. Once they have completed this, have students write a short response to summarize the character/narrator's personality.

7. Based on what students do, decide whether they can work alone or if you need to set up any additional interventions.

Teacher TIP

When students have difficulty writing about their reading, check to make sure that they can explain orally how they infer or analyze an event or information. Expressing orally an understanding of applying higher-level thinking to a text precedes writing. However, when students understand but avoid writing, show them that their ideas are valid by starting the writing for them and then asking them to complete the task. This strategy permits the student to observe you writing their words and is an effective way to build self-confidence and the ability to risk putting their thoughts on paper.

Writing Short Responses *(cont.)*

Scaffolding Suggestions

➢ Make sure each student understands the directions.

➢ Model by writing a response and thinking aloud to reveal your process.

➢ Make sure that the student can infer and analyze.

➢ Ask students to tell you what they discussed with their partner. Take the student's pencil and write in his or her notebook as he or she speaks.

➢ Compliment the student's recall and thinking, and return the writing responsibility back to the student: "What you said showed me you can infer and analyze this character (or whatever the response is). I know you can make one more inference and show your support. Raise your hand when you're done, and I'll come back and read it."

Classroom Snapshot: Jane Goodall

A group of sixth-grade students has completed reading pages 20 and 21 in *Jane Goodall: The Early Years* by William B. Rice. Students set up a T-chart and write *Jane's Personality Traits* at the top of the left column and *Text Evidence* at the top of the right column. I ask students to discuss two things they learned about Jane's personality by using the text and text features and then completing the T-chart on their own.

While circulating, I hear a pair saying that they learned chimps like bananas, and I pause to redirect their thinking with a question: What can you learn about Jane's personality from the fact that chimps like bananas? Students giggle, but one says that she's a good observer because she noticed the chimp wanted the banana inside the tent. "Good use of inferring," I say. "Write that on your T-chart and find a second trait."

As I continue to make the rounds I notice a pair of students who aren't talking or writing. Both admit they are unsure about what I mean by personality traits. They say that they learned that Jane likes chimps. I schedule a 5-minute intervention with students that day, during independent reading and discover that to help these students understand personality traits they would benefit from a 15-minute intervention followed by a few 5-minute interventions.

Writing an Explanatory Paragraph

Chapter 6

Overview

In this intervention, students use their notes to write an explanatory paragraph.

Materials

➤➤ any instructional-level text

➤➤ chart paper (*optional*)

Procedures

Prior to this intervention, select a topic based on information presented in the selected instructional text. Have students record notes and text evidence in their readers' notebooks that support the topic.

1. Provide students time to review their notes on the selected topic. Explain to students that they will be writing a short paragraph about the topic using their notes.

2. Invite students to suggest text evidence that supports the topic. Record these ideas on chart paper or the board.

3. Have students collaborate to suggest possible titles for the short paragraph they will write in response to the topic. Record these on the chart paper or board, as well.

4. Think aloud and show how to use the topic and the notes to create your own title.

5. Organize students into pairs and ask them to discuss and suggest topic sentences. Write these on the chart paper or board. Or you can have students write them in their notebooks.

6. Have students choose two points from their notes to include in their paragraphs and put a checkmark next to each one.

7. Provide students time to select or compose their own title, select or compose their own topic sentence, and use their notes to write complete supporting sentences.

8. Circulate and start the writing of the support section of the paragraph for students who appear reluctant to do this. Schedule a series of five-minute conferences for students who require additional scaffolding.

Scaffolding Suggestions

➤ Plan and compose an explanatory paragraph with the class to build students' mental model of the process.

➤ Have students collaborate to develop notes for the paragraph and write these on chart paper or display them on the board.

➤ Ask students to suggest two or more titles and topic sentences.

➤ Continue to scaffold the process with students' input and gradually move them to independence with titles, topic sentences, and notes for supporting details.

Writing an Explanatory Paragraph *(cont.)*

Classroom Snapshot: Sharing the Pencil

A group of seventh-grade English language learners read three years below grade level. Other than worksheets with short texts and fill-in-the-blank questions, these students have not constructed an entire response to their reading. Students have completed reading and discussing *Roberto Clemente* by Dona and William Rice.

To prepare them for writing a short paragraph that explains why people called Clemente "the pride of Puerto Rico," I ask students to suggest possible titles and topic sentences.

I record three titles and two topic sentences that students suggest on chart paper. Students have already discussed and taken notes that offer reasons why Clemente was the pride of Puerto Rico.

I tell the group to choose a title and topic sentence or write their own. Then, I ask them to support the topic sentence by selecting three pieces of support from their notes and put them into sentences.

As I circulate, I notice that Kayla is tapping her pencil on the table while staring out the window. What follows is a transcription from my notes of the conversation between Kayla and me.

Robb: I notice that you chose a title from the board.

Kayla: Yeah. Couldn't think of another (title).

Robb: Would you like to use one of the topic sentences on the board or try writing your own?

Kayla: I can't do this. I never wrote a paragraph. I don't know what to do.

Robb: Do you remember that we worked together yesterday to write a paragraph?

Kayla: It's too hard for me.

Robb: Choose a topic sentence from the board, and I'll write it for you.
(Next I show Kayla the list of notes she had in her notebook and asked her to reread these.)

Kayla: What do I do with these? I can't do this.

Robb: Pick one and in your head put the details into a sentence.

Kayla: (She says the sentence.) I can't write it. (Tears well up in Kayla's eyes.)

15-Minute Intervention

Writing an Explanatory Paragraph *(cont.)*

Chapter 6

Robb: I repeat Kayla's sentence and write: "He played." (Kayla grabs the pencil and finishes the sentence!)

Kayla: I did it!

Robb: You did, and I know that you can add two more supporting sentences by using your notes. You understand that having notes supports writing.

Once Kayla realized that her notes would support her thinking and ability to compose sentences, her anxiety diminished. Completing the remainder of the paragraph raised her self-confidence and taught her the value of planning writing.

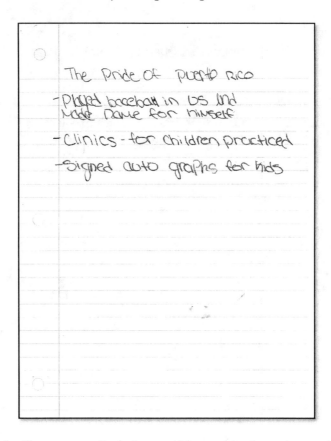

Moving forward, I will encourage Kayla to use titles and topic sentences the group generated for her next paragraph. Then, I will schedule a 15-minute intervention to help Kayla develop a title and topic sentence. The last element we will work on is how to wrap-up a paragraph with a closing sentence.

Developing a Claim

Overview

In this intervention, students use theme statements from an instructional-level text to develop claims.

Materials

➤ any instructional-level text

➤ chart paper (*optional*)

Procedure

Prior to this intervention, make sure that students understand theme and can compose theme statements.

1. Think aloud to show students that a theme statement is general, but a claim can be text-specific because the evidence comes from the text. Have students share possible theme statements from the selected instructional text and record those on the board or chart paper.

2. Explain that a claim has a positive and negative point of view. The side students choose has to be supported by text evidence.

3. Choose one of the theme statements from Step 1. Explain that having a theme statement enables you to develop a claim. Model how to create a claim based on the selected theme statement.

4. Divide students into pairs. Have pairs choose a theme statement and use it to write a claim.

5. Allow pairs to continue to practice developing a claim from a theme statement. Circulate around the room and support students as necessary.

6. Schedule additional 5-minute interventions for students who require more support.

Scaffolding Suggestions

➤ Remind students that themes are general statements. Therefore, theme statements don't mention specific information related to the text.

➤ Show students that having themes can enable them to develop claims that relate to a specific text or texts.

➤ Make sure students understand that a claim can be stated positively or negatively.

➤ Have students select a claim statement based on available text evidence.

➤ Have students use a different book at their instructional reading level to find themes and create claims for a paragraph.

Developing a Claim (cont.)

Classroom Snapshot: Making Claim Statements

A large group of seventh-grade students works with me to develop claim statements. Students have observed me model how I change themes into claim statements using the read-aloud text *Galen: My Life in Imperial Rome* by Marissa Moss.

Students have just read *Rome* by Christine Dugan. I organize students into partners and ask pairs to chose two theme statements and turn them into claim statements. I remind students that a claim has a yes and no, or positive and negative, point of view. I invite students to test each claim statement to see if it has two perspectives and to make sure the general themes are claims that relate to the book *Rome*. Themes students identified are as follows:

➤ A system of paved roads makes a country strong.

➤ A well-trained army can protect a country.

➤ Ancient architects have influenced modern buildings.

➤ City people could buy everything they needed in markets.

➤ A classed society creates rich, who have rights, and poor with few rights.

➤ People enjoy leisure activities and games.

➤ Many words in our language come from Latin.

➤ Persecution can harm people.

As pairs work, I circulate. One pair says that the theme is already a claim because it can be stated positively or negatively. I agree, but I remind students that the claim should relate to ancient Rome, and I think aloud to show them. I say, "Since ancient Rome has a system of well-paved roads, it made travel for people and soldiers easy."

I ask students to notice how I linked the theme statement to a claim statement about ancient Rome. I ask the pair to try changing another theme into a claim and show me their work when they've finished.

For the students who still have difficulty developing a claim statement, I set up a series of 5-minute interventions to support them.

Planning Writing

Overview

In this intervention, students use a planning guide to gather claims, text evidence, and supporting details in preparation for writing about their reading.

Materials

➡ any read-aloud text

➡ any instructional-level texts

➡ *Writing Plan* (page 264)

➡ projector or document camera

Procedures

1. Display a copy of the *Writing Plan* using a project or document camera. Use your read-aloud text to model how you plan a piece of writing, filling in each section of the form. As much as possible, involve the students in helping you complete the plan. Emphasize that supporting details need to be specific and that students might have to reread a section of the text to refresh their memories about details.

2. Distribute copies of the *Writing Plan* to students. Have them use their selected instructional-level texts to plan in class. Set aside part of two class periods for planning.

3. Tell students to raise their hands when their plans are complete. Check the student's plan: If it's solid and detailed, initial the plan; if it needs more specific details, write your suggestions on a sticky note for the student, have him or her revise in class, and then show you the completed plan.

4. Instruct students to use their plans to draft their paragraphs. Have students explain the benefits of using a plan to draft the paragraph.

5. For students who struggle, schedule another 15-minute intervention to help them plan a different paragraph. If students show progress, have them work independently on a third paragraph. However, monitor them as you make the rounds.

Scaffolding Suggestions

➢ Be specific and tell students what you expect in a plan for a paragraph. See the *Writing Plan Form* on page 264 for headings. Feel free to adjust the form to your students' needs. Explain that a "working title" is one you use in the plan, but that it could change at the drafting stage.

➢ Collaborate with students and complete a plan (or two to three plans) for an explanatory paragraph or a paragraph that argues for a claim.

➢ Have students plan during class and not for homework. Check plans as students complete them and initial the plan if it has enough details. Otherwise, jot what the student needs to do on a sticky note and give it to the student as a reminder. Once you check the initial plans, students can draft the paragraph.

➢ Help students locate sections of text that have supporting details. Ask them to reread the information and then put it in their own words on the plan.

➢ Support students with taking notes for the wrap-up sentence. Think aloud to show students ideas you might include in the wrap-up and have students choose one or develop their own ideas.

➢ If students resist planning or struggle with the process, meet with the students and provide the support that guarantees a successful experience.

Planning Writing *(cont.)*

Classroom Snapshot: Getting It "Out of Their Heads"

An eighth-grade student refuses to plan; he tells me the ideas are "in his head." Most of the time, this kind of statement shows a desire to avoid the extra work of planning or that writing ideas on a plan is difficult for the student because he or she has no idea what to write.

To support this student, I plan two 15-minute interventions. The student uses *Amazon Rainforest* by William B. Rice to explain why the Amazon Rainforest is important to the entire world. I schedule two 15-minute interventions so the student wouldn't feel overwhelmed with completing drafting and planning on the same day.

During the first meeting, I think aloud and show the student how writing a topic sentence (or claim statement) helps me think of a title that prepares the reader for the content of the paragraph. Next, the student and I discuss text evidence, and I invite him to reread specific sections. I have the student write details on the plan and step in only if the evidence needs additional details. Together, we discuss a wrap-up sentence, and the student says he will include that we depend on the rainforest for water and unusual animals and insects.

During the second meeting, I monitor the student as he uses the plan to draft the paragraph. Then, I ask the student how the plan helped the writing. He explains that with notes, he only had to turn his thoughts into sentences. I praise the student for completing the thinking part of writing before drafting. For the next plan and paragraph, I will support the student with 5-minute interventions. If he feels secure with the process, I'll pair him with a peer, and they can support one another.

Writing a Topic Sentence

Overview

This is a series of two interventions where students watch movie trailers to learn how to create compelling topic sentences.

Materials

➤➤ any movie trailer for a grade-appropriate film

➤➤ any read-aloud text

Procedure

Day 1

1. Explain to students that a topic sentence introduces a topic.

2. Show students a movie trailer and discuss how the trailer introduces what the movie will be about. Link the trailer to the job of a topic sentence.

3. Model for students how to write a topic sentence based on a section of the selected read-aloud text. Think aloud to show your process; have students ask questions.

Day 2

1. Organize students into pairs and select (or have partners choose) a section of a text students have read and discussed that's at their instructional reading level.

2. Invite pairs to compose a topic sentence for the section. You can also give students titles, have them think of what information would be in a paragraph with a specific title, and then compose a topic sentence.

3. Ask students to share what they wrote.

4. Support students who need more help by scheduling another 5-minute intervention or by having the student work with a peer partner.

Teacher TIP

Resist the urge to tell students the information needed to plan, draft, or write a topic sentence or ending. Instead, pose a series of questions and ask students to think about and discuss the questions, take some notes based on their discussion, and complete the writing about the reading task. Hopefully, the modeling you do using questions to gather details will provide the mental model students need to ask their own questions while reading and to support writing about reading.

Writing a Topic Sentence *(cont.)*

Chapter 6

Scaffolding Suggestions

➤ Explain that a topic sentence introduces what the paragraph will be about.

➤ Use your informational text read-aloud to pinpoint a topic sentence and discuss the supporting details that follow. If you have a document camera, show the written text to students.

➤ Have students locate topic sentences in informational books or in a science or social studies textbook. Discuss the relationship of the topic sentence to information in the paragraph.

➤ Model how you develop topic sentences for your read-aloud texts. Show students how knowing information you plan to explain helps you frame the topic sentence.

➤ Ask a series of questions that can push students to think deeply about the task.

➤ Assign pages in students' instructional-level reading books for them to reread. Have pairs or small groups find the main point or idea and compose a topic sentence.

Classroom Snapshot: Crafting a Topic Sentence

Most fourth-grade students start their first paragraph with *I'm going to tell you about...* My goal is to help students understand what makes a topic sentence interesting as well as how to compose one.

To help students understand that a topic sentence lets readers know what information will be in a paragraph, I show them trailers from two movies and share headlines from the local newspaper. My purpose is to help students understand that a topic sentence is like a sneak preview—it prepares you for what's to come.

I think aloud using the topic sentence from *Unforgettable Natural Disasters*: "*Terrible things can happen when there is too much water, but not having enough water can be just as deadly.*"

I say, "The heading is 'Famine and Drought.' If I combine that with the topic sentence, I think the paragraph will contain details about why a drought is deadly and harmful." Then, I offer partners practice using different sections of the book. Students noticed that not one topic sentence began with "I'm going to tell you about...."

To practice writing a topic sentence, I ask pairs to choose a title, think about what they would include in a paragraph, and write a topic sentence. Here are a few of the titles I gave students:

➤ Gusty Winds and Fire

➤ Hurricanes Damage and Destroy

➤ Snow Closes a City

➤ Dangerous Thunder and Lightning

As partners compose their topic sentences I circulate to answer questions and provide support. Two pairs need additional support; they can't figure out the focus of the paragraph and their topic sentences aren't effective. One pair writes: "Lots of snow is dangerous"; the second pair writes: "Gusty winds are annoying." I set up a 5-minute intervention for each pair and use the questioning technique. Students and I meet when the rest of the class is completing a writing task.

Questions for *Gusty Winds and Fire*: Can you describe gusty winds? How strong can wind gusts be? What could strong wind gusts do to a fire? Why would gusty winds make it hard for firemen to fight the fire?

Questions for *Snow Closes a City*: How much snow do you think must fall to close a city? What do you think "closes a city" means? How does closing a city affect the people who live there?

Pairs use the questions to take notes and then use their notes to write a revised topic sentence. Revised topic sentences:

➤ Gusty winds made the fire spread from one house to other houses on the street.

➤ Four feet of snow fell and everything closed because people couldn't get around.

2- to 3-Minute Intervention

Writing Endings

Overview

In this intervention, students practice writing wrap-up sentences using their notes from the reading on an instructional-level text.

Materials

➨ any instructional-level text

Procedure

1. Make sure that students understand that the wrap-up sentence or ending does much more than repeat the topic sentence or claim. Explain that the wrap-up includes an idea related to the support but not explicitly stated in the support.

2. Create a plan for a paragraph using your read-aloud text and think aloud to show students how you use questions to figure out ideas to include in the end.

3. Demonstrate how posing questions about the text can help them find details.

4. Have partners practice using questions to find related ideas for their wrap-up sentence.

5. Schedule a series of five-minute conferences for students who need more one-on-one support.

Classroom Snapshot: Wrapping Up

Sixth-grade students are planning explanatory paragraphs based on their guided reading books. Students have completed all of their plans on the *Writing Plan* except the notes for a wrap-up sentence. One student chose to write a paragraph explaining why a volcano erupts using *Unforgettable Natural Disasters*.

Here are questions that the student and I discussed for the wrap-up sentence: Why are warnings about a potential volcanic eruption important? What needs to happen to improve warning systems? Besides warnings, what other help do people need?

The student said that people needed time to escape. He also said that there needed to be a plan for ways to leave a city and be safe and improve warning systems to save lives.

Vocabulary

Overview

In this intervention, students use context clues to determine the meaning of selected vocabulary words.

Materials

➤ any text right at or slightly below instructional level

Procedure

1. Review where in the text you can typically find context clues (e.g., in the sentence or in sentences that came before or after the sentence with the word; in text features such as photographs, captions, charts, or diagrams).

2. Think aloud and model how you use context clues to determine a word's meaning.

3. Choose a word from the selected instructional text. Organize students into pairs and have pairs figure out the word's meaning using context clues.

4. Ask students to share their thinking with the group (or class).

5. Have pairs continue to practice finding the meaning of selected words using context and sharing their understandings with the group.

6. Ask students to work on their own to identify context clues that enabled them to figure out a word's meaning. If students can do this, they can work independently.

7. Schedule a shorter intervention (10–15 minutes) with pairs or individuals who need additional practice with you.

Scaffolding Suggestions

➤ Make sure students understand the task and directions for completing the task.

➤ Think aloud to show how you use context clues to figure out unfamiliar words. Use a read-aloud text or students' instructional-level text.

➤ Explain that often the sentence contains the clue to a word's meaning. However, in addition to reading sentences that came before and after the word, sometimes students will have to use photographs, captions, and other text features.

➤ Model how to substitute the definition you develop for the unfamiliar word to see if it makes sense.

➤ Have students practice using context clues with you and then with a partner until they can work independently.

➤ Have students use an online or print dictionary if there are no context clues to determine a word's meaning. Help students find the dictionary meaning that offers insight into the way the word is used in the text.

➤ Review how to set up a T-chart to show the context clues and how they help define a word.

Vocabulary *(cont.)*

Classroom Snapshot: 30- to 40-Minute Intervention

A group of eighth-grade students is reading close to a mid-fourth-grade instructional level. I've decided to stretch them by using the biography *Nelson Mandela* by Tamara Leigh Hollingsworth. Some of the vocabulary will challenge students, but the goal is to show them how to use context clues to help them quickly determine a word's meaning.

First, I read aloud the following passage:

Signs of a Leader

*Once in college, Mandela joined the Students' Representative Council. But Mandela and the council soon learned that they had little power to improve student life. The school refused many of their requests. In response, Mandela **boycotted** council elections. The school told Mandela and Oliver Tambo, his friend and fellow activist, to leave.*

I say, "The boycott was a reaction to the council's refusal to improve student life. What Mandela boycotted was elections to the council. Boycott must be serious because the school told Mandela to leave. Boycotted must mean that he didn't vote in the election and maybe stopped others from voting."

Next, I organize students into pairs and have them read, "Confronting Apartheid" and find all the details that explain *apartheid*. Partners continue to practice using boldface words, and the phrase *Indian Inspiration*. Pairs take turns sharing their use of context clues.

I schedule a 15-minute intervention to show students how to record their use of context clues on a T-chart. Based on observations, some students might work with me in a series of 5-minute interventions while others can continue to work with a partner.

Continue the Conversation

Discuss these prompts and questions with your team or a peer partner. Reflecting on what you learn, what you know, and your students' performance can support your decision-making process regarding the kind of intervention plan you will develop.

1. Bring one to two pieces of student writing to a department or team meeting and discuss what you learn about the student's reading from the writing.

2. Why is it important to have students write about your read-alouds in addition to instructional-level texts? What can you learn about students' listening capacity?

3. Why is it important for students to discuss their reading before writing about it? Share some ways you use discussions in your class.

4. Discuss planning paragraphs and how it helps students. Bring in plans for paragraphs that show a range of detail and share with colleagues interventions you tried that helped students.

Chapter 7

Closing Thoughts on Responsive Teaching and Interventions

In Chapter 1, I stated that research indicates that 80% of the students in a class could make adequate yearly progress with excellent Tier 1 instruction. In 2008, William Brozo, Gerry Shiel, and Keith Topping published a seminal article, "Engagement in Reading: Lessons Learned From Three PISA Countries." After studying the results of the PISA (Program for International Student Achievement) for these countries—the United States, the Republic of Ireland and the United Kingdom (England, Wales, Scotland, Northern Ireland)—the researchers formed conclusions about reading engagement and outlined the implications and findings for policy and classroom practice. The PISA test measures students' ability to analyze, reason, and explain their interpretations of problems and diverse situations using knowledge gained from reading selections.

The study described three elements of reading that reflected students' engagement and motivation (307).

➢ Diversity of reading: Students reported reading six types of texts: magazines, comics, fiction and nonfiction books, email, and webpages.

➢ Independent reading: The study called this "leisure reading," and students reported how much leisure or independent reading they did each day. Mean reading scores correlated with the amount of independent reading students completed each day. Scores for students who spent 60 minutes per day on independent reading were much higher than students who read 30 minutes or less per day. Krashen (2004) and Allington (2009 and 2011) find these same correlations.

➢ Attitude toward reading: Students responded to statements such as "I only read if I have to," "Reading is one of my favorite hobbies," or "I can't sit still and read for more than a few minutes." It's obvious that students who love to read develop positive feelings and attitudes toward reading while students who struggle develop negative feelings and attitudes.

Students who scored highest on the PISA test were called diversified readers because they read a variety of long texts. They read the entire book not just a chapter or short selection that are in many basal and RTI programs. Practicing skills without reading complete books can result in a backward slide (Allington and McGill-Frazen 2003).

Brozo, Shiel, and Topping (2008) offer conclusions based on their study of PISA test results and feedback from students who took the tests that impact teaching reading in Tier 1 instruction:

➢ Socio-economic status did not affect student engagement.

➢ An increase of time for students to read self-selected books is needed. The authors call this personalized reading because choice links to students' personal interests. Allocating time in and outside of schools for independent reading needs to occur, and the authors recommend that teachers develop ways to monitor whether students are learning from their independent reading.

➢ In early and middle-school years, students need to read and make progress on a range of text types. In the early years, students benefit from extensive practice reading leveled texts (Fountas and Pinnell 2006), engaging in relevant and meaningful reading activities, having opportunities to self-select diverse materials for independent reading, and having opportunities to learn, practice, and apply reading strategies in meaningful contexts.

Access to Books

Access to books is critical to developing engaged and motivated readers of all ages (Allington and Johnston 2000; Brozo, Shiel, and Topping 2008; Krashen 2004; Miller 2010 and 2013; Robb 2010 and 2013). Developing exemplary teachers who can support students with a wide range of instructional reading levels is also a key factor in improving students' reading expertise (Allington and Johnston 2000). The 2008 article by Brozo, Shiel, and Topping as well as research of other respected educators (Allington 2009, 2010 and 2011; Allington and Gabriel 2001; Allison 2009; Bomer 2011; Robb 2000b) highlight three needs that can improve students' reading, writing, vocabulary, and thinking:

1. **Organize ongoing professional study at the building level.** When professional study occurs each week throughout the year, teachers have opportunities to use research to develop and adjust their theory of learning and improve their teaching practices and students' learning. Schools have a wide range of inexpensive choices for professional study that includes reading and discussing professional articles and books, watching and discussing educational videos on TeacherTube and YouTube, and sharing and discussing lessons and interventions. In addition, I recommend that during these meetings teachers reserve time with colleagues for discussing students who aren't making progress in reading and writing about reading in order to collect ideas that can help them move students forward.

Suggestions for organizing ongoing professional study:

➢ Have grade-level teams or department members meet weekly during a common planning period. School administrators can rotate through these meetings to learn with their staff and stay abreast of changes and adjustments in instruction and materials needed for students. Librarians and media specialists attend a different meeting each week.

➢ Assemble the faculty and administrators bi-monthly during scheduled full-faculty meetings. Teachers and administrators can organize themselves into smaller groups that meet on specific topics that the group agrees to investigate. To make this possible the principal or another school administrator emails teachers schedule changes and upcoming events a few days prior to a full-faculty meeting.

➢ Use online collaboration tools, such as Google Docs, to facilitate online professional study conversations. Evan Robb, principal of Johnson Williams Middle School in Berryville, Virginia, uses Google Docs to post articles to the entire faculty or to specific departments or groups. Doing this permits Mr. Robb to start the conversation by posting his comments and inviting teachers to read the materials and join the conversation. The principal and teachers can read each other's comments and continually extend the conversation. This type of professional study is especially effective for schools with large faculties that do not have regular full-faculty meetings or common planning times.

➤ Invite an educator/consultant to your school to lead professional study on a topic that interests all teachers. Continue the professional study with bi-monthly or monthly Skype or Google Plus sessions between the educator and teachers so the effects of one inspirational day continue to boost teachers' and administrators' learning throughout the school year. However, teachers and administrators need to meet in small groups on a regular basis.

2. **Have access to classroom libraries, school libraries, and leveled book rooms** that meet the diverse instructional reading levels of students in every class. For students to make solid gains in reading that include building prior knowledge, vocabulary, and improving fluency they need to learn from materials at their instructional reading levels and develop a rich, independent reading life (Allington 2009 and 2011; Allington and Gabriel 2012; Allison 2009; Atwell 2014; Brozo, Shiel, and Topping 2008; Fountas and Pinnell 2013; Krashen 2004; Rasinski and Griffith 2011; Robb 2010 and 2013).

Investing in classroom and school libraries enables schools to have the reading materials that can motivate disengaged readers because students can self-select books and/or ebooks on a wide range of topics and reading levels (Allington 2009 and 2011; Brozo, Shiel, and Topping 2008; Krashen 2004). A key part of Tier 1 instruction to develop advanced readers means that students have access to books in their classroom libraries as well as their school libraries. Moreover, self-selection should always be part of independent reading and, as much as possible, a part of the instruction students receive.

Leveled book rooms contain multiple copies of fiction and nonfiction books from Levels A to Z to meet the diverse instructional reading levels of a class of students (Fountas and Pinnell 2005). It's best for teachers to collaborate and make recommendations for titles to fill their book rooms so that the materials reflect the cultural and reading needs of their school community. Teachers can also find leveled books by searching on the Internet for resources such as Scholastic Book Wizard or Teacher Created Materials Leveled Readers.

3. **Schedule longer teaching periods.** It's challenging to plan in-depth reading lessons in a 42–45-minute class period. In these short classes, it's difficult to schedule guided reading groups, teach vocabulary, schedule independent reading time, and conduct intervention lessons. Having 60 minutes per day to teach reading is more ideal to enable readers to improve enough to meet grade-level standards during Tier 1 instruction. See Chapter 1 for planning suggestions with 45- and 60-minute class periods.

Instruction to Improve Reading Achievement

In today's global economy driven by technology and literacy skill, we need to prepare students for a continually changing job market (Gunderson, Jones, and Scanland 2004). In *Revolutionary Wealth* (2007) Alvin and Heidi Toffler discuss the impact the technology and communication revolution has on education, wealth, and jobs. Alvin Toffler's definition of literacy highlights the importance of teaching students *how* to learn in order to be a productive member of the 21st century and beyond. Toffler says that in the future, persons identified as illiterate will be those who don't know how to learn, not those who can't read. When you teach students how to analyze information and use it to think and solve problems instead of memorizing information and definitions, you are preparing them to be literate in the 21st century and beyond.

Using interventions to respond to learners who struggle is only part of the teaching and learning canvas. It's important to avoid buying into the belief that if a student receives intervention from you and/or a reading specialist, that is enough to accelerate progress. Besides targeted interventions, for you to respond to the wide range of students' needs in culturally and literacy diverse classes, you need to teach every student how to read, think, and learn every day of the school year—that is the heart and soul of Tier 1 instruction and a huge challenge (Allington 2006; Ford and Opitz 2015; Howard 2009).

High-quality Tier 1 classroom instruction is for all students and invites teachers to differentiate and respond to the diverse needs of each learner. Effective, responsive teachers use research-tested best practices to meet the diverse instructional reading levels of students. Teachers can improve the reading achievement of all students every day during whole- and small-group instruction (Allington 2006; Ford and Opitz 2015; Tomlinson 2014; Wormeli 2007). To help you maximize instruction every day of the school year, explore the suggestions that follow for whole and small groups—suggestions that can strengthen all students' learning. These include practices that support the diversity of learners in your classes (Allington 2011; Ford and Opitz 2015; Robb 2010 and 2013; Routman 2014).

Whole-Group Instruction

The mini-lesson, a 10- to 15-minute explicit lesson, enables you to build students' vocabulary and background knowledge before they read and write (Wilhelm 2002). Called *frontloading* by Jeff Wilhelm, the goal is to assist and reach all readers. Well-thought-out frontloading activities can help inform teachers because based on students' responses, the teacher can determine whether students have enough background knowledge to start a unit. If not, set aside time to work with all students or a small group to increase prior knowledge. Effective uses of whole-group instruction are as follows:

➤ **Prepare students to read and learn.** This includes building prior knowledge of a genre such as historical fiction, a topic such as natural disasters, or a concept such as devastation. Depending on the purpose for reading, building students' prior knowledge may also include pre-teaching vocabulary that they need to learn from a text. Therefore, pre-teach word meanings that relate to how the word is used in the text.

➤ **Help students set purposes for reading and discussing** so you focus their thinking on themes, main ideas, big ideas, or any literary element such as setting, a character's problems, decision, or conflicts.

➤ **Use interactive read-alouds** to think aloud and show students how you analyze a text and apply a strategy such as making logical inferences. After you model and think aloud, have students practice the strategy with a partner so you can determine whether their answers reflect understanding. If not, repeat the lesson the next day using a different text.

➤ **Pre-teach vocabulary** that is part of a unit, such as words needed to study ecosystems or to understand the Civil War. Introduce around four to five new and challenging words a week and help students build a set of related words for each word. For example, for a unit on the Amazon Rainforest students might generate a set of related words such as *trees, shade, canopy, roof, sunshade, covering, fresh water supply, deforestation,* and *shield.*

➤ **Create enthusiasm** for a unit of study by introducing students to a theme that links to the unit and having them create discussion questions. You can also build interest by showing and discussing a video clip, or by reading an article, poem, or short text that relates to the unit.

➤ **Write specific directions for students.** If you want the entire class to practice what you've modeled, display the directions on the board or by using a document camera to diffuse confusion and enable students to work independently.

➤ **Encourage independent reading.** If students complete their class work early, they can read a self-selected independent reading book. Students who read 40 or more books a year can accelerate their reading achievement (Cullinan 2000; Krashen 2004; Miller 2010 and 2013; Robb 2010 and 2013; Wilhelm and Smith 2013).

Small-Group Instruction

Groups of four to five students can discuss reading materials, share what they've written about reading, or work on using context clues to determine the meaning of a set of words. Teachers make the rounds to listen to groups at work and support small confusions with 2- to 3-minute interventions and identify students who require additional support. While students read or write independently, teachers can meet with those who require longer interventions. Small-group instruction can be used in the following ways:

➤ **Help students understand directions.** Directions include what each group will work on, reminders to bring their materials including notebooks, and prompts for discussions and writing about reading. Clear directions enable students to complete their work without continually asking questions.

➤ **Review a whole-group lesson** if you feel groups need to hear the lesson again. Taking the time to refresh a frontloading lesson in students' minds can enable them to succeed with group work.

➤ **Have students read at their instructional levels.** Offer students books they can learn from which means that they can read the text and have basic comprehension or recall of details. Students reading below grade level should apply grade-level strategies and skills to their texts.

➤ **Monitor students' time on task.** Circulate while students read or write and help students who are off task get back on track. You can gently redirect students back to the task and watch them work for a few minutes, offering positive feedback when students re-focus on a task. Another way to redirect students to a task is to have them work with a partner who can focus and concentrate.

➤ **Monitor groups as they work.** Circulate among groups to listen and observe carefully as students discuss and write about their reading. Doing this enables you to identify students who might benefit from targeted interventions.

➤ **Pair a student with a peer expert.** When your observations let you know that a student is close to grasping the nuances of a task, pair them with a peer expert. Check on the pair's progress and end the partnership when you observe that the student who needed extra support can work independently.

Reading Stamina

Students who struggle with reading and avoid reading frequently lack stamina and are unable to focus on a text for a few minutes without asking to get a drink, change books, or go to the bathroom. Reading stamina is having the energy and the concentration to read for at least 30 minutes. For students who lack stamina, reading is a frustrating and unpleasant experience, and they read as little as possible. However, today, reading is a life skill needed for college and career as well as for the joy that a personal reading life brings. The good news is that teachers can help students boost their reading stamina at school and at home by having them self-select books and creating the motivation to read (Allington 2011; Allington and Gabriel 2012; Miller 2010; Krashen 2004).

Teach students to self-select a "just right" book for independent reading by showing them the two-finger method. Students read a page in a text and if there are more than two words they can't pronounce or can't figure out meaning from context, then ask them to save the book for another time. Teaching students to choose books that are accessible and enjoyable will also motivate them to read at home.

To build stamina start small. During independent reading, have students who lack stamina concentrate for five minutes, then 10 minutes, and slowly increase the reading time and focus to 30, then 40 minutes. Remind students that developing reading stamina is like training to run a mile in less than eight minutes. Both require continual practice to increase physical energy and concentration.

Schedule independent reading at least three times a week so you can observe students and identify those who lack stamina. Try some of these suggestions:

> Minimize distractions during independent reading so students can concentrate.

> Avoid having students read at their desks; instead, encourage them to find a comfortable space.

> Have students who are trying to increase their stamina complete the checklist that follows (Figure 7.1) twice a semester, and until they have reached their goal.

Celebrate small but consistent improvement. Keep in mind that all students will not improve their reading stamina at the same rate and some might need more than one school year to be able to read for long periods of time. That's okay. Coordinate your efforts with other teachers, celebrate progress, and give students the gift of time.

Figure 7.1 Checklist for Evaluating Reading Stamina

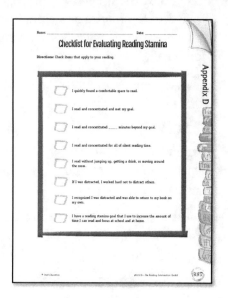

Reflections about Interventions

I often hear teachers referring to students as "He's a Tier 2, and she's a Tier 3." Actually, the tiers refer to the kind of instruction a student receives and not to the student. As a school year unfolds, students improve as readers and their needs change. The kind of interventions students require should be fluid, meaning that sometimes a brief two to three minutes will suffice and at another time the same student needs a 15-minute intervention. It's important to avoid putting a student into a box; it's beneficial to be flexible and know that students' growth patterns in reading differ, as will the interventions you provide. For example, a sixth-grade student, an excellent reader and writer, struggled with a book about Vietnam because she was uninterested in wars and had no background knowledge. She benefitted from three consecutive 5-minute interventions. During those meetings she looked at photographs, read captions, and watched video clips. She also recognized that she would have to reread sections that seemed confusing. I've observed students reading below grade level develop an independent reading life, make great progress in reading, and require fewer long interventions.

Frequent assessment of students' writing about reading can support your monitoring of their progress and enable you to make decisions about the kind of intervention they need. One sure path to reading improvement is to have students read whole books for instruction and independent reading so students develop the stamina to concentrate, and build background knowledge and vocabulary. (Allington 2009 and 2011; Allington and McGill-Franzen 2003 and 2013; Brozo, Shiel, and Topping 2008; Krashen 2004; Miller 2010 and 2013; Robb 2010 and 2013).

In this book, I've purposely created interventions that have students use short and complete texts because to improve, students must read every day at school and at home. My hope is that by using the interventions in this book and modifying them with new texts to meet the needs of your students, you will help them enjoy a rich, independent reading life; they will be able to make expected reading gains; and eventually develop the reading expertise needed to comprehend grade-level and above materials.

Continue the Conversation

Discuss these prompts and questions with your team or a peer partner. Reflecting on what you learn, what you know, and your students' performance can support your decision-making process regarding the kind of intervention plan you will develop.

1. Discuss ways you can improve ongoing professional study at your school.

2. Set up a format for discussing students who aren't making progress with colleagues. Here are some guidelines that you can use and adjust to fit your needs:

   ➢ Name the problem.

   ➢ Explain the kinds of interventions students have received.

   ➢ Share students' work, your conference forms that chronicle interventions, and goal-setting or data review forms.

   ➢ Ask for suggestions and feedback and try a different approach.

   ➢ Discuss the same students in two weeks to check back on progress.

3. What Tier 1 instructional practices do you use to support whole-group lessons? Are you getting the results you expected? Why or why not?

4. What Tier 1 instructional practices do you use to support small-group work? Are you getting the results you expected? Why or why not?

Chapter 7

Appendices
Table of Contents

References Cited

Adler, Mary and Eija Rougle. 2005. *Building Literacy Through Classroom Discussion*. New York, NY: Scholastic.

Afflerbach, Peter. 2012. *Understanding and Using Reading Assessment, K–12*. Newark, DE: The International Reading Association.

Afflerbach, Peter, P. David Pearson and Scott G. Paris. 2008. "Clarifying Differences Between Reading Skills and Reading Strategies." *The Reading Teacher* 61 (5): 366–373.

Allington, Richard L. 2006. "Interventions All Day Long: New Hope for Struggling Readers." *Voices From the Middle* 14 (4): 7–14.

———. 2006. "Research and the Three Tier Model." *Reading Today* 23(5): 20.

———. 2009. "If they don't read much...30 years later." In *Reading More Reading Better* , edited by Elfrieda Hiebert, 30–54. New York, NY: Guilford.

———. 2010. *Essential Readings on Struggling Learners*. Newark, DE: International Reading Association.

———.2011. *What Really Matters for Struggling Readers: Designing Research-based Programs*. Boston, MA: Allyn & Bacon.

Allington, Richard L. and Rachael E. Gabriel. 2012. "Every Child, Every Day." *Educational Leadership* 69 (6): 10–15.

Allington, Richard L. and Peter H. Johnston. 2000. "What Do We Know About Effective Fourth Grade Teachers and Their Classrooms?" *Learning to Teach Reading: Setting the Research Agenda*, 150–165. Newark, DE: International Reading Association.

Allington, Richard L. and Anne McGill-Franzen. 2003. "The Impact of Summer Setback on the Summer Reading Achievement Gap." *Phi Delta Kappan* 85 (1): 68–75.

———. 2013. "One Equally Effective Lower-Cost Option to Summer School." In *Literacy Daily*, accessed January 18, 2016, http://www.literacyworldwide.org/blog/literacy-daily/2013/03/21/one-equally-effective-but-lower-cost-option-to-summer-school.

Allison, Nancy. 2009. *Middle School Readers: Helping Them Read Widely, Helping Them Read Well*. Portsmouth, NH: Heinemann.

Alvermann, Donna E. 2000. "Classroom Talk About Texts: Is It Dear, Cheap, or a Bargain At Any Price?" *Reading for Meaning: Fostering Comprehension in the Middle Grades*, edited by Barbara M. Taylor, Michael F. Graves, and Paul Van Den Broek. Newark, DE: International Reading Association.

Anderson, Carl. 2000. *How's it Going?* Portsmouth, NH: Heinemann.

Applebee, Arthur and Judith Langer. 2011. T*he National Study of Writing Instruction: Methods and Procedures*. Albany, NY: Center on English Learning & Achievement, 2011. Retrieved from http://www.albany.edu/cela/reports/NSWI_2011_ methods_procedures.pdf.

Atwell, Nancie. 1991. *Side by Side*. Portsmouth, NH: Heinemann.

———.2014. *In the Middle: A Lifetime of Learning About Writing, Reading, and Adolescents*, 3rd ed. Portsmouth, NH: Heinemann.

Baker, Scott K., Deborah C. Simmons, and Edward J. Kame'enui. 1998. "Vocabulary Acquisition: Research Bases." In *What Reading Research Tells Us About Children With Diverse Learning Needs: Bases and Basics,* edited by Deborah C. Simmons and Edward J. Kame'enui 183–217. Mahwah, NJ: Erlbaum.

Baumann, James R., Leah A. Jones, and Nancy Seifert Kessell. 1993. "Using Think Alouds to Enhance Children's Comprehension Monitoring Abilities." *The Reading Teacher* 47 (3): 184–193.

Bear, Donald R., Marcia Invernizzi, Francine Johnston, and Shane Templeton. 2011. *Words Their Way: Word Study for Phonics, Vocabulary, and Spelling Instruction*. Boston, MA: Allyn & Bacon.

Beck, Isabel L., Margaret G. McKeown, and Linda Kucan. 2013. *Bringing Words to Life: Robust Vocabulary Instruction*, 2nd ed. New York, NY: The Guilford Press.

Beers, Kylene. 2002. *When Kids Can't Read, What Teachers Can Do; A Guide for Grades 6–8*. Portsmouth, NH: Heinemann.

Benjamin, Steve. 2014. "Shifting from Data to Evidence for Decision Making." *Phi Delta Kappan* 95 (7): 45–49.

Bomer, Randy. 2011. *Building Adolescent Literacy in Today's English Classrooms*. Portsmouth, NH: Heinemann.

Boss, Suzie and Jane Krauss. 2007. *Reinventing Project-Based Learning: Your Field Guide to Real-World Projects in the Digital Age*, 2nd ed. Washington, D.C.: International Society for Technology Education.

Brown, Tara. 2014. "Getting to the Heart of Teaching and Learning." *AMLE Magazine* 2 (3): 10–13.

Brown-Chidsey, R., Louise Bronaugh, and Kelly McGraw. 2009. *RTI in the Classroom: Guidelines and Recipes for Success*. New York, NY: The Guilford Press.

Brozo, William G., Gerry Shiel, and Keith Topping. 2007. "Engagement in Reading: Lessons Learned From Three PISA Countries." *Journal of Adolescent and Adult Literacy* 51 (14): 304–315.

———. 2008. "Engagement in Reading: Lessons Learned from Three PISA Countries." *Journal of Adolescent and Adult Literacy* 31(4): 304–305.

Buehl, Doug. 2005. "Scaffolding." *Reading Room*. Retrieved November 11, 2006 from www.weac.org/News/2005-06/sept05/readingroomoct05.htm.

Buffum, Austin, Mike Mattos, and Chris Weber. 2009. *Pyramid Response to Intervention: RTI, Professional Learning Communities, and How to Respond When Students Don't Learn*. Bloomington, IN: Solution Tree.

———. 2010. "The Why Behind RTI." *Educational Leadership* 68 (2): 10–16. Alexandria, VA: ASCD.

Burke, Jim. 2010. *What's the Big Idea? Question Driven Units to Motivate Reading, Writing, and Thinking*. Portsmouth, NH: Heinemann.

Calkins, Lucy M. 1994. *The Art of Teaching Writing*. Portsmouth, NH: Heinemann.

Chingo, Matthew M. and Russ J. Grover. 2011. "Class Size: What Research Says and What it Means for State Policy." Accessed January 18, 2016 http://www.brookings.edu/research/papers/2011/05/11-class-size-whitehurst-chingos.

Coles, Robert. 1990. *The Call of Stories*. Boston, MA: Houghton Mifflin.

Cooter, Robert B., E. Sutton Flynt, and Kathleen Spencer. 2014. Cooter *Flynt/Cooter Comprehensive Reading Inventory-2: The Assessment of K–12 Reading Skills in English and Spanish*. New York, NY: Pearson.

Cullinan, Bernice. 2000. *Read to Me: Raising Kids Who Love to Read*. New York, NY: Cartwheel.

Delpit, Lisa. 2006. *Other People's Children: Cultural Conflict in the Classroom*. New York: NY: The New Press.

Duckworth, Angela, L. and Lauren Eskreis-Winkler. 2013. "True Grit." *Observer* 26 (4).

Duke, Nell K. 2000. "3.6 Minutes Per Day: The Scarcity of Informational Texts in The First Grade." *Reading Research Quarterly* 35 (1): 202–224.

———. 2003. *Reading & Writing Informational Text in the Primary Grades*. New York, NY: Scholastic.

———. 2014. *Inside Information: Developing Powerful Readers and Writers of Informational Text through Project-Based Instruction*. New York, NY: Scholastic.

Duke, Nell K., and David P. Pearson. 2002. "Effective Practices for Developing Reading Comprehension." *What Research Has to Say About Reading Instruction*, edited by Alan E. Farstrup and S. Jay Samuels, 205–242. Newark, DE: International Reading Association.

Farstrup, Alan E. and S. Jay Samuels. 2011a. "The Critical Importance of Teacher Quality." *What Research Has to Say About Reading Instruction* (1): 1–3. Newark, DE: International Reading Association.

———. 2011b. "Research on Reading/Learning Disability Interventions." *What Research Has to Say About Reading Instruction*, 4th ed., 236–265. Newark, DE: The International Reading Association.

Fisher, Douglas. 2008. "Effective Use of the Gradual Release of Responsibility Model." Accessed January 18, 2016 https://www.mheonline.com/_treasures/pdf/douglas_fisher.pdf.

Fisher, Douglas and Nancy Frey. 2003. "Writing Instruction for Struggling Adolescent Readers: A Gradual Release Model." *Journal of Adolescent and Adult Literacy 46* (1): 396–407.

———. 2013. *Better Learning Through Structured Teaching: A Framework for the Gradual Release of Responsibility*, 2nd ed. Alexandria, VA: ASCD.

Ford, Michael P. and Michael Opitz. 2015. "Classroom Catalysts: Accelerating the Growth Of ALL Readers: Differentiated Literacy Instruction." *Colorado Reading Journal (1)*: 6–12.

Fountas, Irene C. and Gay Su Pinnell. 1996. *Guided Reading: Good First Teaching for All Children*. Portsmouth, NH: Heinemann.

———. 2000. *Guiding Readers and Writers (Grades 3–6): Teaching Comprehension, Genre, and Content*. Portsmouth, NH: Heinemann.

———.2005. *Leveled Books, K–8: Matching Texts to Readers for Effective Teaching.* Portsmouth, NH: Heinemann.

———.2006. *Teaching for Comprehension and Fluency: Thinking, Talking, and Writing About Reading*, K–8. Portsmouth, NH: Heinemann.

———. 2009. *Benchmark Assessment System.* Portsmouth, NH: Heinemann.

———.2012. "Guided Reading: The Romance and the Reality." *The Reading Teacher* 66 (4): 268–284.

———.2013. *Comprehension Clubs: Bringing Deep Reading, Deep Thinking and Deep Discussion to the Whole Class, 6–8.* New York, NY: Scholastic.

Francois, Chantal. 2015. "An Urban School Shapes Young Adolescents' Motivation to Read." *Voices From the Middle* 23 (1): 68–72.

Gambrell, Linda B. 1996. "What Research Reveals About Discussion." In *Lively Discussions! Fostering Engaged Reading*, edited by Linda B. Gambrell and Joan F. Almasi 25–38. Newark, DE: International Reading Association.

Ganske, Kathy. 2013. *Word Journeys: Assessment-Guided Phonics, Spelling, and Vocabulary Instruction*, 2nd ed. New York, NY: Guilford Press.

Gay, Geneva. 2000. *Culturally Responsive Teaching: Theory, Research, Practice.* New York, NY: Teachers College Press.

Gillespie, Amy and Steve Graham. 2015. "Evidence-based practices for teaching writing." *Better: Evidence-based Education Magazine*. Accessed January 18, 2016 http://education.jhu.edu/PD/newhorizons/Better/articles/Winter2011.html.

Graham, Steve and Michael A. Hebert. 2010. *Writing to Read: Evidence for How Writing Can Improve Reading.* New York, NY: Carnegie Corporation.

Graves, Donald. 1983. *Writing: Teachers and Children at Work.* Portsmouth, NH: Heinemann.

Gunderson, Stephan, Robert Jones, and Scanland, Kathryn. 2004. *The Jobs Revolution: Changing how America Works*, 2nd ed. Baltimore, MD: Copywriters Inc..

Guthrie, John T. 2004. "Teaching for Literacy Engagement." *Journal of Literacy Research* 36 (1): 1–30.

Guthrie, John T. and Allan Wigfield. 2000. "Engagement and Motivation in Reading." *Handbook of Reading Research*, edited by Michael L. Kamil, Peter B. Mosenthal, David P. Pearson and Rebecca Barr, 403–422. Mahwah, NJ: Lawrence Erlbaum.

Hart, Betty and Todd R. Risley. 1995. *Meaningful Differences in the Everyday Experience of Young American Children.* Baltimore, MD: Brookes Publishing.

———. 2003. "The Early Catastrophe: The 30 Million Word Gap." *American Educator* 27 (1), 4–9.

Hawkins, Beth. 2012. "Culturally Responsive Teaching: It's Something You Do Every Day." *Minnpost*. Accessed January 18, 2016 http://www.minnpost.com/learning-curve/2012/05/culturally-responsive-teaching-its-something-you-do-every-day.

Hiebert, Elfrieda. H. 2013. "Growing Students' Capacity With Complex Texts: Information, Exposure, Engagement." Text Project & University of California, Santa Cruz. http://textproject.org/assets/library/powerpoints/Hiebert-webinar-Growing-Students-Capacity-with-Complex-Text-Information-Exposure-Engagement-2013-02-18.pdf.

Howard, Mary. 2009. *RTI From All Sides: What Every Teacher Needs to Know*. Portsmouth, NH: Heinemann.

Hoyt, Linda. 2013a. *Interactive Read-Alouds Lesson Matrix for Grades 4–5*. Portsmouth, NH: Heinemann.

———.2013b. *Interactive Read-Alouds Lesson Matrix for Grades 6-7*. Portsmouth, NH: Heinemann.

Johnston, Peter. 2004. *Choice Words: How Our Language Affects Children's Learning*. York, ME: Stenhouse.

Keene, Ellin. O. 2008. *To Understand: New Horizons in Reading Comprehension*. Portsmouth, NH: Heinemann.

Kellogg, Ronald T. and Alison P. Whiteford. 2009. "Training Advanced Writing Skills: The Case for Deliberate Practice." *Educational Psychologies* 44 (4): 250–266.

Knipper, Kathy J. and Timothy J. Duggan. 2006. "Writing to Learn Across the Curriculum: Tools for Comprehension in Content Area Classes." *The Reading Teacher* 59 (5): 462–470. Newark, DE: International Reading Association.

Krashen, Steven. 2004. *The Power of Reading: Insights from Research,* 2nd ed. Englewood, CO: Libraries Unlimited.

Lent, ReLeah. 2007. *Literacy Learning Communities: A Guide for Creating Sustainable Change in Secondary Schools*. Portsmouth, NH: Heinemann.

Magrath, Douglas. 2016. "How Cultural Differences Can Affect Learning." *Multibriefs Exclusive*. Accessed January 18, 2016 http://exclusive.multibriefs.com/content/how-cultural-differences-can-affect-learning.

Marzano, Robert J. 2009a. "The Art and Science of Teaching: Six Steps to Better Vocabulary Instruction." *Educational Leadership,*\ 67 (1): 83–84.

———. 2009b. "The Art and Science of Teaching: When Students Track Their Own Progress." *Educational Leadership* 67 (4): 86–87.

Marzano, Robert J., Debra Pickering, and Jane E. Pollock. 2004. *Classroom Instruction That Works: Research-Based Strategies for Increasing Student Achievement*. Upper Saddle River, NJ: Prentice Hall.

Miller, Donalyn. 2009. *The Book Whisperer*. San Francisco, CA: Jossey-Bass.

———. 2010. "Becoming a Classroom of Readers." *Educational Leadership* 67 (8):30–35.

———. 2013. *Reading in the Wild*. San Francisco, CA: Jossey-Bass.

Murray, Donald M. 1984. *Write to Learn*. New York, NY: Holt.

Nagy, William E. 2005. "Why Vocabulary Instruction Needs to be Long-term and Comprehensive." *Teaching and Learning Vocabulary: Bringing Research to Practice*, edited by Elfrieda H. Hiebert and Michael L. Kamil 27–44. Mahwah, NY: Erlbaum.

Nagy, William E., Patricia A. Herman. and Richard C. Anderson. 1985. "Learning Words From Context." *Reading Research Quarterly* 20 (1): 233–253.

National Assessment of Educational Progress (NAEP). 2012. *Reading Report Card for the Nation and the States.* Washington, DC. U.S. Department of Education Office of Educational Research and Improvement.

National Association of State Directors of Special Education (NASDSE). 2006. "Response to Intervention: NASDSE and CASE White Paper on RTI." Accessed January 18, 2016 http://www.betterhighschools. org/docs/NASDSE_RtI_AnAdministratorsPerspective_1-06.pdf.

National Middle School Association, NMSA. 1999. "NMSA Research Summary #6 Heterogeneous Grouping." Accessed January 18, 2016 http://www.ncmle.org/research%20 summaries/ressum6.html.

Nilsson, Nina L. 2008. "A Critical Analysis of Eight Informal Reading Inventories." *The Reading Teacher* 6 (17): 526–536.

Oster, Leslie. 2001. "Using the Think-Aloud for Reading Instruction." *The Reading Teacher*, 55 (1): 64–69.

Owocki, Gretchen. 2010. *The RTI Daily Planning Book, K–6.* Portsmouth, NH: Heinemann.

Owocki, Gretchen and Yetta Goodman. 2002. *Kidwatching: Documenting Children's Literacy Development.* Portsmouth, NH: Heinemann.

Padak, Nancy and Timothy V. Rasinski. 2005. *3-minute Assessments, 1–4.* New York, NY: Scholastic.

———. 2005. *3-Minute Assessments, 5–8.* New York, NY: Scholastic.

Paterson, Katherine. 2012. "Katherine Paterson Quotes" *Goodreads.* Accessed January 18, 2016 http:// www.goodreads.com/author/quotes/1949.Katherine_Paterson.

Pinnell, Gay S. and Irene C. Fountas. 2003. "Teaching Comprehension." *The California Reader* 36 (4): 7–14.

Rasinski, Timothy V. 2003. *The Fluent Reader.* New York, NY: Scholastic.

———. 2004. "Creating Fluent Readers." *Educational Leadership* 61 (6): 46–51.

Rasinski, Timothy V. and Lorraine Griffith. 2011. *Fluency Through Practice and Performance.* Huntington Beach, CA: Shell Education.

Richardson, Jan. 2009. *The Next Steps in Guided Reading.* New York, NY: Scholastic.

Rief, Linda. 2003. *100 Quickwrites: Fast and Effective Freewriting Exercises that Build Students' Confidence, Develop Their Fluency, and Bring Out the Writer in Every Student.* New York, NY: Scholastic.

Rip, Pernille. 2016. "When We Harm Rather than Help–Some Thoughts on Reading Interventions." *Pernille Rip* (blog), February 6, 2016, http://pernillesripp.com/2016/02/06/when-we-harm-rather-than-help-some-thoughts-on-reading-interventions/.

Robb, Laura. 2000a. *Redefining Staff Development: A Collaborative Model for Teachers and Administrators*. Portsmouth, NH: Heinemann.

———. 2000b. *Teaching Reading in Middle School*. New York, NY: Scholastic.

———. 2004. *Teaching Nonfiction Writing: A Practical Guide*. New York, NY: Scholastic.

———. 2008. *Differentiating Reading Instruction: How to Teach Reading to Meet the Needs of Each Student*. New York, NY: Scholastic.

———. 2010. *Teaching Reading in Middle School*, 2nd ed. New York, NY: Scholastic.

———. 2012. "Getting Started: Strengthening Student Partnerships." *SMART WRITING: Practical Units for Teaching Middle School Writers* (1):76–79. Portsmouth, NH: Heinemann.

———. 2013. *Unlocking Complex Texts; A Systematic Framework for Building Adolescents' Comprehension*. New York, NY: Scholastic.

———. 2014. *Vocabulary Is Comprehension: Getting to the Root of Text Complexity*. Thousand Oaks, CA: Corwin.

Rosenblatt, Louise. 1993. *The Reader, The Text, The Poem: The Transactional Theory of The Literary Work*. Carbondale, IL: Southern Illinois University Press.

Routman, Regie. 2014. *Read, Write, Lead: Breakthrough Strategies for Schoolwide Literacy*. Alexandria, VA: ASCD.

Rowe, Meredith L. 2008. "Child-directed Speech: Relation to Socioeconomic Status, Knowledge of Child Development, and Child Vocabulary Skill." *Journal of Child Language* 35 (1): 185–205.

———. 2012. "A Longitudinal Investigation of the Role of Quantity and Quality of Child-directed Speech in Vocabulary Development." *Child Development* 83 (5): 1762–1774.

Ryan, Allison M. and Gary W. Ladd. 2012. *Peer Relationships and Adjustment at School*. New York, NY: Scholastic.

———. 2013. *The Literacy Teacher's Playbook, 3 to 6*. Portsmouth, NH: Heinemann.

Scanlon, Donna M., Kimberly, L. Anderson, and Joan M. Sweeney. 2010. *Early Intervention for Reading Difficulties: The Interactive Strategies Approach*. New York, NY: Guilford Press.

Schunk, Dale. 2009. "Goal Setting." *School and Education*. Accessed January 18, 2016 http://www.education.com/reference/article/goal-setting/.

Serafini, Frank. 2010. *Classroom Reading Assessments: More Efficient Ways to View and Evaluate Your Readers*. Portsmouth, NH: Heinemann.

Serravallo, Jennifer. 2010. *Teaching Reading in Small Groups: Differentiated Instruction for Building Strategic, Independent Learners*. Portsmouth, NH: Heinemann.

Smith, Michael and Jeffrey Wilhelm. 2007. *Going With the Flow: How to Engage Boys (and girls) in Their Literacy Learning*. Portsmouth, NH: Heinemann.

Snow, Catherine and Gina Biancarosa. 2004. *Reading Next: A Vision for Action and Research in Middle and High School Literacy*. New York, NY: Carnegie Corporation.

Sparks, Sarah D. 2015. "Study: RTI Practice Falls Short of Promise." *Education Week* 35(12): 1–12.

Tankersley, Karen. 2005. *Literacy Strategies for Grades 4–12: Reinforcing the Threads of Reading*. Alexandria, VA: ASCD.

Toffler, Alvin. 2015. "Quotes by Alvin Toffler." *BrainyQuotes*. Accessed January 18, 2016 http://www.brainyquote.com/quotes/authors/a/alvin_toffler.html.

Toffler, Alvin and Heidi Toffler. 2007. *Revolutionary Wealth: How It Will Be Created and How It Will Change Our Lives.* New York, NY: Crown Business.

Tomlinson, Carol A. 2007. "Learning to Love Assessment." *Educational Leadership* 65 (4): 8–13.

———. 2014. *The Differentiated Classroom: Responding to the Needs of All Learners,* 2nd ed. Alexandria, VA: ASCD.

Tomlinson, Carol A. and Susan D. Allan. 2000. *Leadership for Differentiating Schools and Classrooms*. Alexandria, VA: ASCD.

Valencia, Sheila W. 2011. "Using Assessment to Improve Teaching and Learning." *What Research Has to Say About Reading Instruction*, edited by S. Jay Samuels and Alan E. Farstrup 379–405. Newark, DE: International Reading Association.

Verhoeven, Ludo and Charles A. Perfetti. 2011. "Vocabulary Growth and Reading Skill." *Scientific Studies of Reading* 15 (1): 1–7.

Vygotsky, Lev. 1978. *Mind in Society: The Development of Higher Psychological Processes*. Cambridge, MA: Harvard University Press.

Wells, Gordon. 1985. *The Meaning Makers: Children Learning Language and Using Language to Learn*, 1st ed. Portsmouth, NH: Heinemann.

Wilhelm, Jeffrey. 2002. *Action Strategies for Deepening Comprehension: Role Plays, Text Structure, Tableaux, Talking Statues, and Other Enactment Techniques That Engage Students With Text*. New York, NY: Scholastic.

———. 2013. *Improving Comprehension With Think-Aloud Strategies: Modeling What Good Readers Do*, 2nd ed. New York, NY: Scholastic.

Wilhelm, Jeffrey and Michael Smith. 2013. *Reading Unbound: Why Kids Need to Read What They Want—and Why We Should Let Them*. New York, NY: Scholastic.

Woods, Mary L. and Alden J. Moe. 2015. *Analytical Reading Inventory With Readers' Passages*, 10th ed. Boston, MA: Allyn & Bacon.

Wormeli, Rick. 2007. *Differentiation: From Planning to Practice, Grades 6–12*. Portland, OR: Stenhouse.

Zemelman,Steven, Harvey "Smokey" Daniels, and Arthur Hyde. 2012. *Best Practice: Bringing Standards to Life in America's Classrooms*. Portsmouth, NH: Heinemann.

Zimmerman, Barry J. 2000. "Attaining Self-Regulation: A Social Cognitive Perspective." *Handbook of Self-Regulation*, edited by Monique Boekaerts, Paul R. Pintrich, and Moshe Zeidner 13–39. San Diego, CA: Academic Press.

Zimmerman, Barry J. and Anastasia Kitsantas. 1999. "Acquiring Writing Revision Skill: Shifting From Process to Outcome Self-Regulatory Goals." *Journal of Educational Psychology* 91 (1): 241–250.

Zubrzycki, Jaclyn. 2012. "Research Links Responsive Teaching to Academic Gains." *Education Week*. Accessed January 18, 2016 http://www.edweek.org/ew/articles/2012/09/13/04responsive.h32.html.

Literature Cited

Adler, David A. 2004. *Enemies of Slavery*. New York, NY: Scholastic.

Adler, David A. and Gordon C. James. 2007. *Campy: The Story of Roy Campanella*. New York, NY: Viking.

Avi. 2010. *Nothing But The Truth*. New York, NY: Scholastic Paperbacks.

Aylesworth, Jim and Barbara McClintock. 2004. *My Grandfather's Coat*. New York, NY: Scholastic.

Blake, Robert. J. 2007. *Swift*. New York, NY: Philomel.

Bogacki, Tomek. 2009. *The Champion of CHILDREN: The Story of Januz Korczak*. New York, NY: Farrar, Straus, and Giroux.

Boyne, John. 2007. *The Boy in the Striped Pajamas*. New York, NY: Random House Children's Books.

Bradley, Timothy J. 2013. *Bug Builders*. Huntington Beach, CA: Teacher Created Materials.

Bruchac, Joseph and S.D. Nelson. 2002. *Crazy Horse's Vision*. New York, NY: Lee & Low Books.

Coles, Robert and George Ford. 2010. *The Story of Ruby Bridges*. New York, NY: Scholastic.

Collier, John L. 2005. *My Brother Sam Is Dead*. New York, NY: Scholastic.

Covert, Ralph, Mills G. Riley, and Giselle Potter. 2007. *Sawdust and Spangles: The Amazing Life of W.C. Coup*. New York, NY: Abrams Books.

Deans, Karen and Elbrite Brown. 2007. *Playing to Win: The Story of Althea Gibson*. New York, NY: Holiday House.

DiCamillo, Kate. 2009. *Because of Winn Dixie*. Cambridge, MA: Candlewick.

Dorros, Arthur. 2014. *Abuelo*. New York, NY: HarperCollins.

Dugan, Christine. 2007. *Rome*. Huntington Beach, CA: Teacher Created Materials.

Ehrlich, Amy and Wendell Minor. 2008. *Rachel: The Story of Rachel Carson*. Boston, MA: HMH Books for Young Readers.

Elliott, Laura M. 2003. *Under a War-Torn Sky*. New York, NY: Disney-Hyperion.

Gardiner, John. R. 2010. *Stone Fox*. New York, NY: HarperCollins.

Giblin, James C. 1997. *When Plague Strikes: The Black Death, Smallpox, AIDS*. New York, NY: HarperCollins.

Giovanni, Nikki and Bryan Collier. 2007. *Rosa*. New York, NY: Square Fish.

Harness, Cheryl. 2003. *Rabble Rousers: Twenty Women Who Made a Difference*. New York, NY: Dutton.

Herweck, Diana. 2013. *On the Scene: A CSI's Life*. Huntington Beach, CA: Teacher Created Materials.

Hinton, S.E. 1982. *The Outsiders*. New York, NY: Viking.

Hollingsworth, Tamara L. 2013. *Nelson Mandela: Leading the Way*. Huntington Beach, CA: Teacher Created Materials.

———. 2013. *Unforgettable Natural Disasters*. Huntington Beach, CA: Teacher Created Materials.

———. 2013. *Unforgettable News Reports*. Huntington Beach, CA: Teacher Created Materials.

Jordan, Shirley. 2007. *Egypt: World Cultures Through Time*. Huntington Beach, CA: Teacher Created Materials.

Kerley, Barbara and Edwin Fotheringham. 2014. *A Home for Mr. Emerson*. New York, NY: Scholastic.

Kline Suzy. 2008. *Horrible Harry and the Triple Revenge*. New York, NY: Puffin Books.

Korman, Gordon. 2001. *Island Book I: Shipwreck*. New York, NY: Scholastic.

———. 2001. *Island Book II: Survival*. New York, NY: Scholastic,.

———. 2001. *Island Book III: Escape*. New York, NY: Scholastic.

Krull, Kathleen. 2000. *Wilma Unlimited: How Wilma Rudolph Became the World's Fastest Woman*. Boston, MA: HMH Books for Young Children.

———. 2003. *Harvesting Hope: The Story of Cesar Chavez*. Boston, MA: HMH Books for Young Children.

———. 2008. *Leonardo DaVinci*. New York, NY: Puffin Books.

Laminack, Lester L. and Chris Soentpiet. 2004. *Saturdays and Teacakes*. Atlanta, GA: Peachtree Publishers.

Laminack. Lester L. and Henry Cole. 2011. *Three Hens and a Peacock*. Atlanta, GA: Peachtree Publishers.

Lauber, Patricia. 1991. *Summer of Fire: Yellowstone 1988*. New York, NY: Scholastic.

Levy, Elizabeth and Mordecai Gerstein. 2002. *The Principal's on the Roof*. New York, NY: Aladdin Books.

McCann, Michelle R. and Amelie Welden. 2012. *Girls Who Rocked the World: Heroines From Joan of Arc to Mother Teresa*. New York, NY: Aladdin Books.

McGill, Alice and Chris K. Soentpiet. 2009. *Molly Bannaky*. Boston, MA: HMH Books for Young People.

McGovern, Ann. 1990. *The Secret Soldier: The Story of Deborah Sampson*. New York, NY: Scholastic.

———. 1978. *Adventures of Shark Lady: Eugenie Clark Around the World*. New York, NY: Scholastic.

McKissack, Patricia. C. and Frederick McKissack. 1994. *Sojourner Truth: Ain't I a Woman?* New York, NY: Scholastic.

McNulty, Faith and Steven Kellogg. 2005. *If You Decide to Go to the Moon*. New York, NY: Scholastic.

Mora, Pat and Raul Colon. 2005. *Dona Flor*. New York, NY: Knopf.

Morpurgo, Michael. 2010. *War Horse*. New York, NY: Scholastic.

Moss, Marissa. 2002. *Galen: My Life in Imperial Rome*. New York, NY: Silver Whistle Books.

Munoz Ryan, Pam. 2005. *Becoming Naomi Leon*. New York, NY: Scholastic.

Murphy, Jim. *The Great Fire*. New York, NY: Scholastic, 1995.

———. 2010. *The Crossing: How George Washington Saved the American Revolution*. New York, NY: Scholastic.

Myers, Walter D. and Leonard Jenkins. 2003. *Malcolm X: A Fire Burning Brightly*. New York, NY: HarperCollins.

———. 2004. *I've Seen the Promised Land: The Life of Dr. Martin Luther King, Jr*. New York, NY: HarperCollins.

Myers, Walter D. and Alix Delinois. 2009. *Muhammad Ali: The People's Champion*. New York, NY: HarperCollins.

Naylor, Phyllis R. 1991. *Shiloh*. New York, NY: Dell.

Norwich, Grace. 2013. *I Am Harriet Tubman*. New York, NY: Scholastic.

Osei, Leah, Reteller and Tracie Grimwod. 2014. *The Bremen Town Musicians: A Retelling of the Story by the Brothers Grimm*. Huntington Beach, CA: Teacher Created Materials.

Paterson, Katherine. 2004. *Bridge to Terabithia*. New York, NY: HarperTeen.

———. 2004. *The Great Gilly Hopkins*. New York, NY: HarperCollins.

Pinkney, Andrea D. 2013. *Let It Shine: Stories of Black Women Freedom Fighters*. Boston, MA: HMH Books for Children.

———. 2013. *Profiles #6: Peace Warriors*. New York, NY: Scholastic.

Pinkney, Andrea D. and Brian Pinkney. 2006. *Duke Ellington*. New York, NY: Hyperion.

———. 2012. *Hand in Hand: Ten Black Men Who Changed the World*. New York, NY: Disney-Hyperion.

Rappaport, Doreen. 2006. *United No More: Stories of the Civil War*. New York, NY: HarperCollins.

———. 2012. *Helen's Big World: The Life of Helen Keller*. New York, NY: Disney-Hyperion.

Ray, Deborah K. 2006. *To Go Singing Through the World: The Childhood of Pablo Neruda*. New York, NY: Farrar, Straus, and Giroux.

Rice, Dona and William B. Rice. 2012. *Roberto Clemente*. Huntington Beach, CA: Teacher Created Materials.

Rice, William B. 2012. *Amazon Rainforest*. Huntington Beach, CA: Teacher Created Materials.

———. 2012. *Jane Goodall: The Early Years*. Huntington Beach, CA: Teacher Created Materials.

Robinson, Sharon and Kadir Nelson. 2009. *Testing the Ice: A True Story About Jackie Robinson*. New York, NY: Scholastic.

Roop, Peter and Connie Roop. 2003. *Go Fly a Kite, Ben Franklin*. New York, NY: Scholastic.

Ryan, Pam M. 2000. *Esperanza Rising*. New York, NY: Scholastic.

Ryan, Pam M. and Brian Selznick. 2009. *When Marian Sang: The True Recital of Marian Anderson*. New York, NY: Scholastic.

Sachar, Louis. 2000. *Holes*. New York, NY: Yearling Books.

Simon, Seymour. 1999. *The Time Machine and Other Cases: Einstein Anderson: Science Detective*. New York, NY: Camelot.

———. 2000. *Bones: Our Skeletal System*. New York, NY: HarperCollins.

———. *Lightning*. 2006. New York, NY: HarperCollins.

Taylor, Mildred. 1998. *The Gold Cadillac*. New York, NY: Puffin Books.

Tevares, Matt. 2015. *There Goes Ted Williams: The Greatest Hitter That Ever Lived*. Cambridge, MA: Candlewick.

Tolstoy, Leo. 1972. *Fables and Fairy Tales*. Indiana University: New American Library.

Towle, Wendy and Will Clay. 1993. *The Real McCoy: The Life of an African-American Inventor*. New York, NY: Scholastic.

Vernick, Audrey and Don Tate. 2010. *She Loved Baseball: The Effa Manley Story*. New York, NY: HarperCollins.

Watkins, Yoko K. 2008. *So Far From the Bamboo Grove*. New York, NY: HarperCollins.

Weatherford, Carole B. and Eric Velasquez. 2007. *I, Matthew Henson, Polar Explorer*. New York, NY: Walker Children's Books.

Winter, Jeanette. 2006. *The Librarian of Basra: A True Story From Iraq*. Boston, MA: HMH Books for Young Readers.

Woodson, Jacqueline. 2010. *Miracle's Boys*. New York, NY: Speak.

Woodson, Jacqueline and Floyd Cooper. 2000. *Sweet, Sweet Memory*. New York, NY: Hyperion.

Yoo, Paula and Dom Lee. 2005. *Sixteen Years in Sixteen Seconds: The Story of Sammy Lee*. New York, NY: Lee & Low Books.

Recommended Nonfiction Books

These are challenging books intended for students who can read complex, grade-evel materials. They also make superb read-alouds. You can read a section or several paragraphs.

Freeman, Russell. 1989. *Kids at Work: Lewis Hine and the Crusade Against Child Labor*. Boston, MA: HMH Books for Young Readers.

——. 1989. *Lincoln: A Photobiography*. Boston, MA: Houghton Mifflin Harcourt.

——. 1994. *The Wright Brothers: How They Invented the Airplane*. New York, NY: Holiday House.

——. 1999. *Out of Darkness; The Story of Louis Braille*. Boston, MA: Houghton Mifflin Harcourt.

George, Jean Craighead. 1996. *One Day in the Desert*. New York, NY: HarperCollins.

——. 1996. *One Day in the Prairie*. New York, NY: HarperCollins.

——. 1995. *One Day in the Tropical Rainforest*. New York, NY: HarperCollins.

——. 1997. *There's a Tarantula in My Purse: and 172 Other Wild Pets*. New York, NY: HarperCollins.

Giblin, James. 2005. *Good Brother, Bad Brother: The Story of Edwin Booth and John Wilkes Booth*. Boston, MA: Clarion Books.

——. 1993. *The Riddle of the Rosetta Stone: Key to Ancient Egypt*. New York, NY: HarperCollins.

——. 2009. *The Rise and Fall of Senator Joe McCarthy*. Boston, MA: Clarion Books.

——. 1997. *When Plague Strikes: The Black Death, Smallpox, AIDS*. New York, NY: HarperCollins.

Krull, Kathleen. 2010. *Charles Darwin (Giants of Science)*. New York, NY: Viking Books for Young Readers.

——. 2008. *Isaac Newton (Giants of Science)*. New York, NY: Puffin Books.

——. 2009. *Marie Curie (Giants of Science)*. New York, NY: Puffin Books.

——. 2014. *The Boy Who Invented TV: The Story of Philo Farnsworth*. New York, NY: Dragonfly.

Marrin, Albert. 2002. *Dr. Jenner and the Speckled Monster: The Discovery of the Smallpox Vaccine*. New York, NY: Dutton Juvenile.

——. 2015. *FDR and the American Crisis*. New York, NY: Knopf Books for Young Readers.

——. 2015. *Flesh & Blood So Cheap: The Triangle Fire and Its Legacy*. New York, NY: Yearling.

——. 2014. *Oh, Rats!*. New York, NY: Puffin Books.

Meltzer, Milton. 2001. *Case Closed: The Real Scoop on Detective Work*. London, England: Orchard.

——. 2005. *Emily Dickinson: A Biography*: Minneapolis, MN: Twenty-First Century Books.

———. 2005. *Hear That Train Whistle Blow! How the Railroad Changed the World*. New York, NY: Random House.

———. 2012. *Hunted Like a Wolf*. Sarasota, FL: Pineapple Press.

Murphy, Jim. 2006. *Blizzard: The Storm That Changed America*. New York, NY: Scholastic.

———. 2010. *The Crossing: How George Washington Saved the American Revolution*. New York, NY: Scholastic.

———. 2013. *The Giant and How He Humbugged America*. New York, NY: Scholastic.

———. 2010. *The Great Fire*. New York, NY: Scholastic.

Sheinkin, Steve. 2012. *Bomb: The Race to Build—and Steal—the World's Most Dangerous Weapon*. New York, NY: Flash Point.

———. 2013. *Lincoln's Grave Robbers*. New York, NY: Scholastic.

———. 2014. *Port Chicago 50: Disaster, Mutiny, and the Fight For Civil Rights*. New York, NY: Roaring Brook Press.

———. 2013. *The Notorious Benedict Arnold: A True Story of Adventure, Heroism and Treachery*. New York, NY: Square Fish.

Simon, Seymour. 2012. *Animals Nobody Loves*. San Francisco, CA: Chronicle Books.

———. 2011. *Earthquakes*. New York, NY: HarperCollins.

———. 2015. *The Moon*. New York, NY: Simon & Schuster.

———. 2011. *Volcanoes*. New York, NY: HarperCollins.

Intervention Conference Form

Student Name: _____ Date: _____

Focus of the Conference: _____

Materials:

Student's Comments:

_____

_____

_____

_____

Teacher's Notes:

_____

_____

_____

_____

Goal:

_____

_____

_____

Check One:

❏ Works with a peer

❏ Works with the teacher

❏ Can work independently

Follow-up Conference Date: _____

Before-Reading Checklist

Directions: Check the strategies you've observed the student using. Jot notes to help you recall important observations and comments the student had after you discussed specific items.

Student Name: _____ Date: _____

Before Reading List of Strategies	Notes/Comments

Building Prior Knowledge

☐ Brainstorms a list

☐ Uses quick-writes

☐ Creates a web or cluster

☐ Raises questions

☐ Understands vocabulary and context

☐ Reads headings and predicts content

☐ Visualizes

☐ Uses photographs, charts, diagrams, illustrations

☐ Sets purposes

Additional Comments:

During-Reading Checklist

Directions: Check the strategies you've observed the student using. You can do this while making the rounds or in a five-minute conference. Have the student read one to two pages silently and retell them. Then discuss the strategies the student uses. Or, have the student read one to two pages out loud and note your observations. Jot notes to help you recall important observations and comments the student had after you discussed specific items.

Student Name: _____ Date: _____

During Reading List of Strategies	Notes/Comments

Becoming a Self-Monitoring Reader

❑ Sets and adjusts reading rate

❑ Predicts/Supports/Confirms/Adjusts

❑ Raises questions

❑ Self-corrects for meaning

❑ Self-monitors for recall

❑ Self-monitors for understanding

❑ Rereads

❑ Understands context clues and unfamiliar words

❑ Identifies text structure

❑ Jots notes

❑ Closely reads

Additional Comments:

After-Reading Checklist

Directions: Check the strategies you've observed the student using. Jot notes to help you recall important observations and comments the student had after you discussed specific items.

Student Name: _____ Date: _____

After Reading List of Strategies	Notes/Comments

Thinking, Talking, and Writing

- ❏ Confirms/Adjusts predictions
- ❏ Retells
- ❏ Summarizes
- ❏ Talks to develop ideas
- ❏ Talks to explore meanings
- ❏ Writes/draws to explain ideas

- ❏ Infers
- ❏ Discusses questions
- ❏ Skims to find text evidence
- ❏ Uses text evidence to support thinking
- ❏ Uses text structure to think
- ❏ Closely reads

Additional Comments:

Interpreting Assessments Form

Student Name: _____ Date: _____

Directions: Check the assessments you are using to evaluate the student. In the blank spaces add any assessments not on the list.

❑ notebook writing   ❑ conferences   ❑ tests

❑ student's data review ❑ student's goals   ❑ quizzes

❑ checklists   ❑ self-evaluations   ❑ fluency

❑ discussions   ❑ peer coaching note

Directions: Respond to the prompts that follow.

In a conference away from the class, ask the student a question about his or her goal:

_____

_____

_____

_____

_____

Read through the assessments and list everything the student does well.

_____

_____

_____

_____

_____

_____

Interpreting Assessments Form (cont.)

Think about your observations, discussions with the student, and specific assessments. Decide the area that needs support, then note it below.

_____

_____

_____

Intervention Plans

Directions: Check possible actions listed below and/or add what you'd like to try. Add supporting information in the space provided.

❑ Five-minute conference(s). What to scaffold _____

❑ Peer partner. Student name: _____

❑ Reteach. Topics needed: _____

❑ Have the student set a goal based on assessments and your discussions with him/her.

❑ Other _____

Goal:

_____

_____

_____

Teacher's notes based on support student receives:

_____

_____

_____

_____

_____

Name: _____ Date: _____

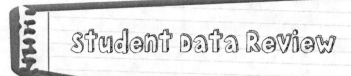

List of data I reviewed:

1.

2.

3.

4.

5.

6.

7.

8.

Learning Goal:

_____

_____

_____

_____

List of the specific things I will do to reach my learning goal:

_____

_____

_____

_____

Date I believe I can reach my goal: _____

Adjectives That Describe Personality Traits

adventurous	dutiful	joyful	sarcastic
aggressive	empathetic	kind	secretive
aloof	evil	knowledgeable	sensitive
ambitious	exacting	lazy	silly
anxious	excitable	lively	sincere
assertive	fearful	loving	snobby
bitter	fearless	loyal	sociable
bland	fierce	meek	spiteful
bloodthirsty	foolish	modest	stubborn
boisterous	friendly	moody	suspicious
bossy	fussy	morbid	timid
brave	gentle	mysterious	tolerant
brutal	grouchy	naughty	treacherous
calm	gullible	nosy	tyrannical
capable	harsh	obnoxious	unfaithful
careful	hasty	optimistic	ungrateful
careless	haughty	overbearing	unhappy
cheerful	helpful	patient	unique
clever	heroic	pessimistic	unpopular
conceited	hopeful	popular	unruly
confident	humane	practical	unsociable
confused	humble	proud	unwise
controlling	imaginative	pushy	vain
courageous	impatient	quick-tempered	villainous
cowardly	impish	rash	violent
cruel	impulsive	rational	vivacious
daring	innocent	realistic	weak
determined	insensitive	reasonable	willful
dignified	insincere	rebellious	wise
distrustful	intolerant	reckless	wishy-washy
domineering	inventive	rowdy	witty

Name: _____ Date: _____

Setting a Goal

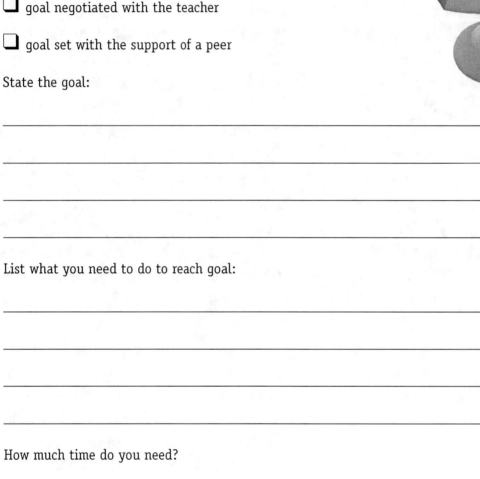

Directions: Set a learning goal by computing each section below.

Check one:

❏ goal set independently

❏ goal negotiated with the teacher

❏ goal set with the support of a peer

State the goal:

_____

_____

_____

_____

List what you need to do to reach goal:

_____

_____

_____

_____

How much time do you need?

_____

_____

Evidence used to show achievement of goal:

_____

_____

_____

Name: _____ Date: _____

Summarizing Fiction, Memoir, and Biography Form

Directions: Record notes about your text in each section below.

Title _____

Author _____

Somebody: Name an important character.

_____

_____

Wanted: State a problem faced.

_____

_____

_____

_____

But: Explain some forces that worked against the problem.

_____

_____

_____

_____

So: Show how the problem was resolved, without giving the ending away.

_____

_____

_____

_____

Summarizing Fiction, Memoir, and Biography Form (cont.)

Directions: Write a summary by turning your notes under each heading into a complete sentence. Include the title and author of your book in your first sentence.

Summary

_____

_____

_____

_____

_____

_____

_____

_____

_____

_____

_____

_____

_____

_____

_____

Retelling Checklist for Informational Texts

Student Name: _____ Date: _____

Title: _____

Author: _____

Page(s) student rereads: _____

Directions: Ask the student to reread one to two pages silently. Have the student retell all the recalled details. Jot notes on the checklist as you listen to the student retell.

Elements to Note in Student's Retelling	Teacher's Notes
❑ Stated the title and/or topic.	
❑ Included many facts and details.	
❑ Explained a main point.	
❑ Paraphrased, put information in own words.	
❑ Made comments on information.	
❑ Connected to another text.	
❑ Connected to what he or she knows.	

Speaking Patterns	Teacher's Notes
❑ Showed enthusiasm.	
❑ Spoke clearly and in complete sentences.	
❑ Hesitated often.	
❑ Made comments like, "I can't remember" or "I'm not sure."	
❑ Sequenced information when appropriate.	

Additional Teacher Notes:

_____

_____

Ten Tips to Comprehending Informational Texts

Review these 10 reading and thinking tips, use them to improve your recall of information, and then use the information to analyze the material.

1. **Do a Quick Text Preview Before Reading.**

   Before you start reading, do a quick preview that can build your background knowledge of a topic. Read the title, the first and last paragraphs of a short text, or the first chapter and last page of a book. Study text features such as bold vocabulary, photographs, and captions. Have an in-the-head conversation that reviews what information you learned from the preview. Now you have background information that can support recall and understanding.

2. **Study Text Features.**

   Read and think about text features, such as boldface headings and vocabulary, photographs and captions, maps, diagrams, charts, snippets of letters or diary entries, and boxed sets of facts related to the topic. Doing this introduces you to information in the text and enlarges prior knowledge about the topic.

3. **Set a Reading Purpose.**

   Make your purpose to read to discover why the author used this title. You can also use what you learned from the preview to set a reading purpose.

4. **Raise Questions.**

   Before reading use text features to raise a few questions that along with your purpose drive the reading and enable you to focus on important details.

5. **Use Context.**

   Try to determine the meaning of a word that is unfamiliar by looking for clues in the sentence that contains the word, by reading a few sentences that come before the word and sentences that come after the word. Sometimes the author defines the word immediately after using it by separating the word and definition with a comma or with "or."

6. Consider Informational Text Structure.

Informational text writers use these text structures: description, sequence, question/answer, problem/solution, compare/contrast, cause/effect. Usually, writers mix structures so that a paragraph might be descriptive but also include comparisons and contrasts. Your knowledge of text structure can assist comprehension because you know what to expect as you read and think about why the author chose sequence or why she compared and contrasted, etc. Reflecting on structure can focus you on the way the writer organizes information as well as help you consider how the organization improves understanding of the author's purpose, the themes of the piece, and how details connect.

7. Stop, Check Recall, Assess, Reread or Read On.

To ensure that you can paraphrase information you've read, it's helpful to pause at the end of a section or page to see how much information can be recalled. If you recall little information, then reread and test yourself again. As you reread, pause to evaluate recall, to better comprehend information in a sentence or section, and to deepen your knowledge of a text. Rereading is an excellent repair strategy.

8. Skim to Find Important Details.

It's helpful to understand that skimming to locate key details under text headings is an excellent review strategy that highlights important details. Skimming can also help you pinpoint information that answers text-dependent questions.

9. Discuss Text-Dependent Questions.

It's important to return to specific parts of the text to answer questions. You might use several passages to answer a question. To demonstrate understanding, paraphrase text details—put the ideas into your own words to show comprehension of facts and also use the facts to draw inferences. When you read a text with layers of meaning, there will be diverse interpretations among classmates.

10. Closely Read.

Close reading is a useful tool to figure out the meanings of unfamiliar words and to unpack meaning from sentences and passages that are confusing. It is a repair strategy that helps you unpack meaning from challenging parts of texts.

Close Reading Guidelines for Informational Text

When you're reading a text, assume that every word and phrase carries meaning. If you're unsure of what something means, do a close reading.

If it's a difficult word...

> Look carefully at the word. Are there any prefixes, suffixes, or roots you recognize?

> Reread the sentences before and after the one containing the difficult word. Do they contain any clues to what the word means?

> Is there a glossary you can consult? Are there any text features, such as charts or illustrations, that provide clues to the word?

> Have you seen or heard the word or phrase? In what situation? Can you recall what the word or phrase meant in the specific situation?

Dig Deeper

> Can you connect the word or phrase to information that came before it? To what you know and have learned from the preview?

> Why do you think the writer uses this particular word or phrase?

> How does this word or phrase relate to the tone, mood, or theme of the text?

> What is the connection between this word or phrase and others within the text?

> What is the significance of this word or phrase in relation to other ideas in the sentence or paragraph?

Close Reading Guidelines for Informational Text *(cont.)*

If it's a difficult sentence, paragraph, or section...

➤ Read each sentence word-by-word, chunking phrases and making sure you know what each one means. If a particular word gives you trouble, use the strategies above to figure it out.

➤ Paraphrase each sentence by saying it in your own words.

➤ Continue rereading and paraphrasing each sentence. When you get to the end of a paragraph, retell it for yourself. If you can't retell several details, then reread the paragraph.

➤ Continue rereading and retelling paragraphs. When you get to the end of a section, retell it for yourself.

Dig Deeper

➤ Consider the themes of the text. How does the sentence, paragraph, or section relate to them?

➤ Why did the writer include this sentence, paragraph, or section in the text?

➤ How does this sentence, paragraph, or section connect to the title?

➤ How does this sentence, paragraph, or section connect to other parts of the text?

➤ What inferences can you make from this sentence, paragraph, or section?

Scaffolding Conference Form

Student Name: _____ Date: _____

Focused Topic: _____

Teacher's Preparation Notes and Observations:

_____

_____

_____

Materials used with student:

_____

_____

Student's comments:

_____

_____

_____

Teacher records outcomes:

_____

_____

_____

Negotiated goal:

_____

_____

Check one:

❏ schedule another conference

❏ have student work with a peer

❏ student can work independently

Six Kinds of Context Clues

1. **Definitions and Synonyms.** A definition is given or a similar word is used immediately after or close to the unfamiliar word. A definition or synonym follows a comma, a dash, or words, such as *or, is called, that is*, and *in other words*.

    Example: Amazon water is **fresh water**. That means it does not have much salt in it.

2. **Concrete Examples.** An example is provided that helps you figure out the word's meaning. Examples can be found in the sentence, in a new sentence, or following these words/phrases: f*or example, such as*, and *especially*.

    Example: While Roberto was one of the best players, he was never asked by any company to **endorse** its products in commercials or advertisements.

3. **Restated Meanings:** The word is defined by restating its meaning in simpler terms. Often commas set off the word from the meaning. You'll also find the meaning of a word stated after words and phrases such as: *or, that is,* and *in other words*.

    Example: Sericulture is the practice of raising silkworms to make silk.

4. **Comparison:** The author uses a comparison to help you understand a tough word.

    Example: Her dress was as **flamboyant** as a peacock's feathers.

5. **Words or phrases that modify.** Modifiers such as adjectives, adverbs, or relative clauses can have clues to a word's meaning. A relative clause begins with *who, which, that, whose,* or *whom* and often explains or extends an idea or word in the main part of the sentence.

    Example: It [the Amazon River] is <u>so big</u> (adverb, adjective) that it breaks into many **stems**.

6. **Conjunctions that show relationships and link ideas.** Coordinating and subordinating conjunctions show relationships and help you link unknown words and ideas to known words and ideas. *And, but, or, not, for,* and *yet* are coordinating conjunctions. Common subordinating conjunctions are *when, if, since, whenever,* and *because*.

    Example: An **epidemic** occurs <u>when</u> a disease spreads through a wide area.

Name: _____   Date: _____

5 Ws Organizer for Summarizing

Title: _____

Author: _____

Directions: Read the explanation of each of the *Ws*. Then, take detailed notes under each heading.

WHO or *WHAT* is this about?

_____

_____

WHAT did the person do? Or *WHAT* happened?

_____

_____

WHEN refers to time. *WHEN* did this happen?

_____

_____

WHERE refers to the place or places. *WHERE* did this happen?

_____

_____

WHY asks for causes behind what happened and connections to community and world issues.

_____

_____

5 Ws Organizer for Summarizing (cont.)

Write a summary of your text in the space below.

Informational Text Features

Sidebars: These are boxes containing information on a page of a book or magazine article that didn't quite fit into the next text but that the author wanted to include. Sidebars can contain a list of fascinating facts, quotes, part of an interview, a newspaper clipping, or a letter.

Boldface Type: This is the **darker type** used for titles and headings. Some vocabulary can also be in boldface type. This feature calls the reader's attention to words or phrases and indicates they are important.

Photographs and Captions: These supply an image of an object or person and can give you extra information about the topic. Captions are one or two sentences that explain the photograph.

Quotes and Interviews: These features can be in sidebars or on a section of the page separate from the story. Quotes and interviews give the exact words of a person.

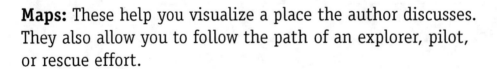

Maps: These help you visualize a place the author discusses. They also allow you to follow the path of an explorer, pilot, or rescue effort.

Introduction: This part of a text can explain how the author conceived of the idea as well as recognize others who helped the author gather information.

Table of Contents: This provides chapter titles and page numbers. It's also an overview of what you'll find in the text.

Informational Text Features (cont.)

Glossary: This alphabetical list of important terms explains tough or unusual words found in the text. It usually comes near the end of the book. Sometimes a glossary entry also includes guidelines for pronouncing the word.

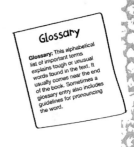

Afterword: Information about a person or event that occurs after the end of the book.

Index: This alphabetical list of key words, topics, and names of people and places in the text comes at the end of the book. Next to each item is a page number or several page numbers, referring the reader to the places in the book where the idea or person is mentioned. The more page numbers an index entry has, the more details you'll find about that topic.

Timeline: This feature can include key dates in a person's life. It can also cover the dates of key events in a historical period such as the Middle Ages, the Renaissance, or a major war like World War II. Timelines can have photographs, illustrations, and short write-ups under each date.

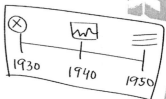

Bibliography: This list at the end of the book cites the books and magazines the author used to write his or her book.

Authors of informational texts use structures that relate to an idea they are trying to communicate. Text structure can help you comprehend a text as well as help you skim and locate information. Review these structures and the meanings each can develop.

> **Description:** helps you visualize or picture what a place, an event, a setting, a person or character looks like. When you can visualize something you read, it shows that you understand it.

> **Sequence:** when the author writes about something in the order it happened. Sequence helps you see and understand connections among events.

> **Compare/Contrast:** shows how two things are alike and how they differ. This can be persons or characters, settings, problems, information, and events.

> **Cause/Effect:** the cause comes before the effect or effects and shows how words, nature, decisions, problems, actions, and events can cause other things to happen.

> **Problem/Solution:** shows you a problem and then helps you understand one or more solutions.

> **Question/Answer:** sometimes a paragraph opens with a question or there's a question within the paragraph, and the author offers answers.

> **Main Idea/Details:** sometimes a paragraph opens or ends with the main idea. However, there are times when you will have to use details in one or more paragraphs to determine the main idea.

Reteaching Lesson Form

Title of Lesson: _____ Date: _____

Names of Students:

1. _____

2. _____

3. _____

4. _____

5. _____

Teacher's Observations:

_____

_____

_____

Name of student(s) who require scaffolding:

_____

Name of student(s) and scaffolding plan:

_____

_____

_____

Name of student(s) who require more reteaching:

_____

_____

Name of student(s) and needs to focus on during the lesson:

_____

_____

Appendix D

Close Reading Guidelines for Fiction

When you're reading fiction, assume that every word and phrase carries meaning. If you're unsure of what something means, do a close reading.

If it's a difficult word...

> Look carefully at the word. Are there any prefixes, suffixes, or roots you recognize?

> Reread the sentences before and after the one containing the difficult word. Do they contain any clues to what the word means?

> Have you seen or heard the word or phrase? In what situation? Can you recall what the word or phrase meant in the specific situation? Can you visualize or picture the situation?

Dig Deeper

> Can you connect the word or phrase to something a character said or an action the character took to what you have learned up to this point in the book?

> Why do you think the writer uses this particular word or phrase?

> How does this word or phrase relate to the tone, mood, problems, conflicts, interactions between characters, antagonists, or theme of the text?

> What is the connection between this word or phrase and others within the text?

> What is the significance of this word or phrase in relation to other ideas in the sentence or paragraph?

Close Reading Guidelines for Fiction (cont.)

If it's a difficult sentence, paragraph, or section...

➤ Read each sentence word-by-word, chunking phrases and making sure you know what each one means. If a particular word gives you trouble, use the strategies above to figure it out.

➤ Paraphrase each sentence by saying it in your own words.

➤ Continue rereading and paraphrasing each sentence. When you finish a few pages or a short chapter, retell it for yourself. If you can't retell several plot details, then reread the paragraph.

➤ Continue rereading and retelling and try to create mental pictures of the characters and plot details.

Dig Deeper

➤ Consider the characters, their problems, and decisions. How does the sentence, paragraph, or section relate to these elements? Consider antagonists and how they relate to the paragraph or sections.

➤ Why did the writer include this sentence, paragraph, or section in the text?

➤ How does this sentence, paragraph, or section connect to the title of the chapter (if it has a title) and of the book?

➤ How does this sentence, paragraph, or section connect to specific conversations between or among characters, settings, antagonists, problems, conflicts, decisions, and outcomes?

➤ What inferences can you make from this sentence, paragraph, or section?

➤ What do the inferences let you know about a character, a setting, a solution to a problem?

1. **Do a Preview Before Reading.** This includes reflecting on the cover illustration, the title of the book, and first chapter. Read the first chapter and think about what you have learned. In your reader's notebook, record what you recall about the setting, the protagonist, problems and conflicts, and other characters. Skim and reread sections to collect specific details. You can turn and talk to a partner and try to connect the book and chapter's title to what you have learned from the preview. Titles provide clues that focus you on themes and what's important.

2. **Set Reading Purposes.** Having a purpose for reading can make the process motivating and engaging. With fictional texts, a first purpose for reading can come from a text preview or you can use the title and read to discover why the author used that title. Purposes can change while you continue reading and can include predictions about plot, characters' decisions and interactions, and how setting changes will affect the plot and characters. It's helpful to adjust your reading purpose before starting a new chunk of text.

3. **Check Out Chapter Titles and Themes.** Since chapter titles usually point out a key theme in the chapter, the title can help you identify that theme and locate the details that support it. Here's how to state a theme: the statement is general and does not mention a character or specific event. The theme applies to the book you are reading but also can apply to other books. Themes are also statements about life, relationships with others and self, decisions, events, problems, and reactions to settings. To figure out themes of books that don't have chapter titles or to find multiple themes in a chapter, you can use these questions:

> ➤ How do characters' actions and words lead to themes?

> ➤ What decisions have characters made that can support themes?

> ➤ What relationships in the book can lead to discovering themes?

> ➤ Do characters have rich inner lives that can lead to themes?

> ➤ How does setting contribute to theme?

Next, use the chart that follows to pinpoint general topics. These common topics can be transformed into themes.

Common Topics That Can Become Themes

abuse	freedom	love	self-reliance
childhood	friendship	loyalty	stereotyping
courage	growing up	nature	success
death	hate	patience	trust
devastation	hope	patriotism	truth
dreams	identity	prejudice	unhappiness
faith	independence	race relations	violence
family	justice	self-improvement	war

4. **Use Context.** There are six different types of context clues: definitions and synonyms, concrete examples, restated meanings, comparison, words or phrases that modify, and conjunctions that show relationships and link ideas. Use these to find examples from your instructional and independent reading. You can avoid letting an unfamiliar word stump you by asking a peer partner for help. The more often you "meet" a word in your reading, the better you'll understand how it works in different situations or contexts.

5. **Consider Literary Elements or Narrative Structure.** Knowing literary elements means that you have the tools for understanding literature or narrative texts. An important goal is to know the definition of each element and demonstrate your understanding by identifying from a specific text the protagonist, antagonist(s), conflict, or problems, and offering evidence from the text that supports your understanding of a specific element.

6. **Stop to Check Recall and Make Predictions.** Stopping to think and reflect on one or two chapters in a fictional text enables you to check recall of events and to keep track of characters. Stopping to think at the end of one long chapter or two short chapters also enables you to decide if you have recalled enough details or whether you need to reread. This self-monitoring strategy supports independence while reading and enables you to savor the story, word choice, and literary elements.

7. **Make Inferences.** With fictional texts you can infer using a wide range of elements: dialogue, interactions between characters and with various settings, reactions to problems, antagonists, what other characters say, decisions characters make, their motivation for actions, resolving or not resolving conflicts or problems, and their inner thoughts.

Appendix D

8. **Discuss Text-Dependent Questions.** Discussing text-dependent questions can deepen your knowledge of the narrative as well as literary elements or text structure. Use the skimming technique for locating details that answer questions by identifying key words in a question and skimming a text to find those words. In addition, you can use chapter titles to locate information and skim a character's name or a specific setting to locate details that answer a question.

   You can create your own text-dependent questions by using verbs that create interpretive, open-ended questions: *why, how, evaluate, explain, compare/contrast, defend,* etc. For you to be able to create your own open-ended questions, you need a solid knowledge of the plot and characters. You can determine whether your questions are interpretive by testing each one to see if it has two or more different possible responses.

9. **Think about Relationships.** A work of fiction contains characters, and as the plot unfolds relationships between and among characters develop. Reflecting on relationships and how these affect decisions the protagonist makes can enrich your reading of literature. In addition, relationships can lead to determining themes as well as help you understand how relationships affect conflicts and the protagonist's ability to solve problems. It's also beneficial for you to pinpoint antagonistic or adversarial relationships and consider how these affect the plot, problems, decisions, and conflicts.

10. **Closely Read.** A close read can help you make sense of confusing passages and to deepen your understanding of figurative language and connotations. Close reading asks you to reread and analyze a passage phrase-by-phrase and sentence-by-sentence in order to link ideas and improve your comprehension. Keep your copy of the handout *Close Reading Guidelines for Fiction* close by and use it as a resource and reminder to help you comprehend tough passages.

Retelling Checklist for Narrative Texts

Student's Name: _____ Date: _____

Title: _____

Author: _____

Chapter(s) or specific pages: _____

Directions:

➤ Ask the student to read the selection silently.

➤ Have the student retell all of the recalled details.

➤ Encourage the student to include literary elements.

➤ Jot notes on the checklist as you listen to the student retell.

Elements to Note in Student's Retelling	Teacher's Notes
❏ Stated title	
❏ Included setting: time and place	
❏ Identified the protagonist and why he/she is the main character	
❏ Explained a problem the protagonist faced	
❏ Named other characters and their relationship to the protagonist	
❏ Included plot details	
❏ Made inferences about characters	
❏ Made connections to other texts and issues	

Retelling Checklist for Narrative Texts *(cont.)*

Student's Speaking Patterns: Check box, if "yes." Give examples when helpful.

❑ Spoke in complete sentences.

❑ Told details in sequence.

❑ Added details when asked for more.

Additional Notes and Comments:

_____

_____

_____

_____

© Shell Education

Appendix D

Composing a Theme

Compose a theme statement by using the four steps that follow:

1. **Make a point.**
   A theme makes a point about people, friendship, families, relationships, and life. State your theme in a complete sentence.

2. **Be precise and exact.**
   Avoid using vague words such as *good*, *bad*, *nice*, and *cool*.

3. **Don't use characters' names.**
   A good theme statement applies to people in general and not just to specific characters.

4. **Check your theme statement.**
   A theme statement applies to your text, but it can also apply to other texts.

Literary Elements and Text Meaning

Setting: includes time and place. A short text can focus on one setting while longer texts have multiple settings. How characters function in and react to a setting can deepen readers' understanding of characters' motivation and personality traits.

Protagonist: the main character in a text with problems to solve. Observing how the protagonist interacts with others, makes decisions, and tries to solve problems offers insight into this character's personality and motivations.

Antagonists: forces that work against the protagonist and create tension in a literary text. Antagonists can be nature, other characters, decisions, actions, and within the character's mind and emotions. Understanding how the protagonist copes with antagonists can offer insight into his or her personality as well as the theme.

Other Characters: observing how other characters relate to, dialogue with, and interact with the protagonist can deepen our knowledge of all their personalities as well as the themes in a book.

Plot: events that occur in a text and enable readers to observe characters in diverse situations. Plot supports an understanding of theme and characters' personalities.

Conflicts: struggles or differences between opposing forces such as man and nature, two characters, internal between the character and self, man and a specific event or situation. Some conflicts become problems. For example, the inner conflict of deciding whether to drive in a snowstorm becomes a problem when the person's car is stuck in a snowdrift on a desolate road. Observing how characters deal with inner conflicts and conflicts with other characters and/or setting can reveal much about their personalities and themes.

Problem: something that requires solving or thinking about a resolution such as to risk diving from the high board when you're a weak swimmer or lying to parents about where you've been and coping with guilt. Problems ask characters to figure out solutions such as having no money for food, or what to do after a twister or fire destroyed their home. How characters tackle problems and cope with their inability to resolve some can provide readers with deep insights into personality and decision-making processes.

Climax: the moment or point of greatest intensity in the plot. Short stories usually have one climax, but novels can have small climaxes as the plot unfolds. The major climax is near the end. The climax, the highest point of the action, can deepen comprehension of plot details and also offer insights into themes.

Denouement: events that resolve the climax in a novel, short story, or drama; often referred to as the outcome. Understanding the outcomes of a narrative can lead to figuring out main and central themes, and deepen readers' understanding of how the plot brought them to this specific outcome.

Personal Pronouns and Point of View

First-Person Narrator
The reader hears the narrator's thoughts and sees everything through the narrator's eyes.

Pronouns

me   my
mine   we
ours

Second-Person Narrator
This point of view is not used very often because it makes the reader a participant in the story.

Pronouns

you   your
yours

Third-Person Narrator
This is the point of view that authors frequently use. The writer may choose third-person omniscient, the all-knowing narrator, so that the thoughts of every character are available to readers. Or the writer may select third-person limited and can only enter one character's mind. Third-person point of view means you hear the author's voice and not the character's voice as in first person point of view.

Pronouns

he   his
him   she

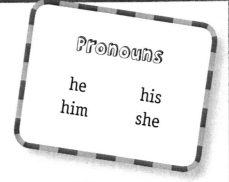

© Shell Education

Questions That Help Discussions

Use these prompts to keep a discussion moving forward.

➤ Does anyone have a different idea?

➤ Can anyone add more text evidence?

➤ Can you explain that in a different way?

➤ Identify a main idea and explain how you determined it (informational texts).

➤ What text details support the main idea?

➤ Identify a theme and explain how you determined it (literature).

➤ What text details support the theme?

➤ Explain the figurative language. What does the figurative language help you visualize and understand?

➤ Identify key vocabulary words that help you to better understand the text's meaning. Explain the connection between the word and the theme or big idea.

➤ Why do you believe this word is important?

➤ What do you mean by the statement you made or wrote?

➤ How did you make that inference?

Activate Prior Knowledge and Set Purposes for Reading

Use these steps to help you activate your prior knowledge and set a purpose for reading.

1. **Read the title.** Ask yourself, "What do I know about this topic?" If you know little to nothing, make sure you tell yourself to read slowly and thoughtfully. Be prepared to reread parts and close read to make sense of words, sentences, and paragraphs.

2. **Read the first paragraph** if it is long. Read the first two paragraphs if they are short.

3. **Read the last paragraph.**

4. **Read questions/statements** if a quiz is part of your reading.

5. **Talk to a partner** and tell him/her everything you learned.

6. **Write down what you learned in your own words** in your reader's notebook. This is your prior knowledge. You may reread parts of the preview for more recall.

7. **Use your prior knowledge** notes to set a purpose for reading.

8. **Turn and talk to your partner** after reading. State your purpose for reading and what you learned about your purpose.

9. **Write**, in your reader's notebook, two to three things you learned about your purpose from reading and discussing the text.

Name: _____ Date: _____

Metacognitive Writing

Title: _____

Author: _____

Directions:

1. On the left side, write a difficult word and the page it is found on and/or the confusing passage and page number.

2. On the right side, after close reading, explain what you've learned and how you figured out the meaning of the word and/or passage.

Word and/or Passage + Pages	Explanation of Meaning + How You Determined the Meaning

Name: _____ Date: _____

Predictions

Title: _____

Author: _____

Directions:

1. On the left side, write your prediction.

2. On the right side, provide text evidence to support your prediction. Evidence can include text details, inferences, text features, photos, and illustrations.

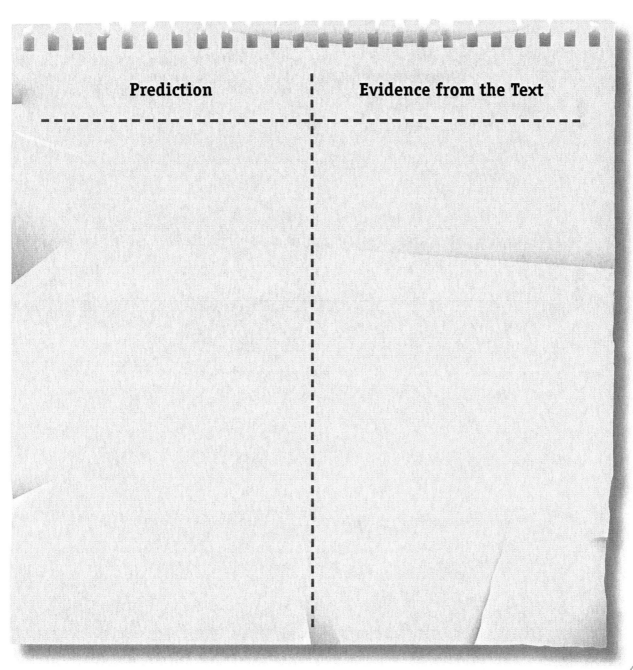

Prediction	Evidence from the Text

Name: _____ Date: _____

Vocabulary: Context Clues

Title: _____

Author: _____

Directions:

1. On the left side, list four unfamiliar words from a section of a book that you have completed. Next to each word, write the page number the word is found on.

2. Write a definition of each word and explain how context clues supported figuring out the word's meaning.

Word and Page Number	Definition and Context Clues

Name: _____ Date: _____

Four Words

Directions:

1. Choose one of the four words you wrote in your notebook. Write it on the left side of the chart.

2. On the right side, provide text evidence such as details, inferences, text features, illustrations, or photographs.

Word	Evidence from the Text

Name: _____   Date: _____

Emotions

Title: _____

Author: _____

Directions:

1. On the left side of the T-chart, write the dominant emotion you felt throughout the text.

2. Find evidence from the text that shows the origin of that feeling and cite two to three events that heightened the emotion. Evidence can be text details, inferences, photos, and illustrations. Write your evidence on the right side.

Emotion	Evidence from the Text

Name: _____ Date: _____

Evaluate a Character or Person

Title: _____

Author: _____

Directions:

1. Evaluate or judge a character's or person's decision, the outcome of a conflict, or interactions with others. On the left side of the chart, fill in what or who you are evaluating, and write your evaluation(s).

2. On the right side, cite text details and/or inferences that support your evaluation. Also list what you will evaluate.

Evaluation of _____

Inference	Evidence from the Text

Name: _____   Date: _____

Making Inferences: Literature (Fiction)

Title: _____

Author: _____

Directions:

1. Study a character's decisions, conversations, and interactions with other characters to infer personality traits.

2. List three personality traits and the evidence from the text that supports each choice. You can use the adjective chart to help you pinpoint traits.

Character's Name: _____

Inference	Evidence from the Text

Name: _____ Date: _____

Making Inferences: Informational Texts

Title: _____

Author: _____

Directions:

1. To infer with informational texts, determine which details are important, and then use the details to infer.

2. On the left side, write your inference. On the right side, write the text details that helped you infer.

Inference	Evidence from the Text

Argument Paragraph Rubric

Student Name: _____   Date: _____

	4	3	2	1	Score
Notes	claim clearly stated; detailed, relevant notes support topic; quotes texts or cites particular sections	claim stated; relevant notes support topic	claim stated; some relevant notes support topic	unclear claim or unstated claim; incomplete notes	
Title	short; catchy; announces topic	announces topic; title long or same as text	uses only the word "essay"	no title	
Introduction	clearly states and elaborates claim; includes text's title and author	states claim; omits text's title or author	states claim; omits text's title and author	claim is unclear and doesn't set up the argument; omits text's title and author	
Text Evidence	includes three or more pieces of evidence using relevant text details; includes an inference from text details	includes two pieces of evidence using relevant text details; omits inference from text details	includes one piece of evidence using relevant text details; omits inference from text details	includes one piece of text evidence with general or sketchy detail; omits inference from text details	
Conclusion	wraps up well; adds related idea to think about	wraps up well; doesn't add related idea to think about	wraps up by repeating introduction	no wrap up	

Explanatory Paragraph Rubric

Student Name: _____ Date: _____

	4	**3**	**2**	**1**	**Score**
Notes	topic clearly stated; detailed, relevant notes support topic; quotes text or cites particular sections	topic stated; relevant notes support topic	topic stated; some relevant notes support topic	topic not clearly stated; incomplete notes	
Title	short; catchy; announces topic	announces topic; title long or same as text	uses "essay" as title	no title	
Introduction	clearly states what will be explained; includes text's title and author	states what will be explained; omits text's title or author	states what will be explained; omits text's title and author	no explanatory statement; omits text's title and author	
Text Evidence	includes three or more pieces of evidence using relevant text details; quotes text to make a point; includes an inference from text details	includes two pieces of evidence using relevant text details; quotes text to make a point; omits inference from text details	includes one piece of evidence using relevant text details; omits inference from text details	includes one piece of evidence with general or sketchy detail; omits inference from text details	
Conclusion	wraps up well; adds a related idea to think about	wraps up well; doesn't add related idea to think about	wraps up by repeating introduction	no wrap up	

Appendix D

Name: _____ Date: _____

Writing Plan

Working Title: _____

Claim statement for an argument paragraph: _____

_____

_____

Topic sentence for an explanatory paragraph: _____

_____

_____

Evidence from the text (two to four specific details and/or inferences): _____

_____

_____

_____

Wrap-up sentence (details that will keep the reader thinking): _____

_____

_____

Name: _____ Date: _____

Checklist for Evaluating Reading Stamina

Directions: Check items that apply to your reading.

☐ I quickly found a comfortable space to read.

☐ I read and concentrated and met my goal.

☐ I read and concentrated _____ minutes beyond my goal.

☐ I read and concentrated for all of silent reading time.

☐ I read without jumping up, getting a drink, or moving around the room.

☐ If I was distracted, I worked hard not to distract others.

☐ I recognized I was distracted and was able to return to my book on my own.

☐ I have a reading stamina goal that I use to increase the amount of time I can read and focus at school and at home.

Contents of the Digital Resource CD

Excerpt Pages

Page Number	Title	Filename
Page 152	A Change of Heart	heart.pdf
Pages 75, 110	Amazon Rainforest	amazon.pdf
Page 150	Best Night of the Year	bestnight.pdf
Pages 126, 132, 141	The Bremen Town Musicians	bremen.pdf
Pages 72	Bug Builders	bug.pdf
Page 159	Choices	choices.pdf
Page 105, 114	Excerpt from Bug Builders	bugexcerpt.pdf
Page 155	Finding Kip	kip.pdf
Page 116	The Great City of Rome	greatrome.pdf
Page 96	Jane Goodall: The Early Years	goodall.pdf
Pages 134, 136	The King and the Shirt	king.pdf
Page 88	Nelson Mandela: Leading the Way	mandela.pdf
Page 108	Nelson Mandela: Political Prisoner	political.pdf
Page 107	On the Scene: A CSI's Life	scene.pdf
Pages 124, 130	The Raven and His Young	raven.pdf
Pages 79, 102, 116	Roberto Clemente	roberto.pdf
Pages 73, 81	Rome	rome.pdf
Pages 93, 101	Unforgettable Natural Disasters	disasters.pdf
Page 77	Unforgettable News Reports	news.pdf
Page 157	Walkabout	walkabout.pdf

Teacher and Student Resources

Page Number	Title	Filename
Page 216	Intervention Conference Form	intervention.pdf intervention.docx
Page 217	Before Reading Checklist	beforeread.pdf beforeread.docx
Page 218	During Reading Checklist	duringread.pdf duringread.docx
Page 219	After Reading Checklist	afterread.pdf afterread.docx

Appendix E

Contents of the Digital Resource CD *(cont.)*

Page Number	Title	Filename
Pages 220–221	Interpreting Assessments Form	interpreting.pdf interpreting.docx
Page 222	Student Data Review	data.pdf data.docx
Page 223	Adjectives That Describe Personality Traits	adjectives.pdf
Page 224	Setting a Goal	goal.pdf goal.docx
Pages 225–226	Summarizing Fiction, Memoir, and Biography Form	summarizing.pdf summarizing.docx
Page 227	Retelling Checklist for Informational Texts	retelling.pdf retelling.docx
Pages 228–229	Ten Tips to Comprehending Informational Texts	comprehending.pdf
Pages 230–231	Close Reading Guidelines for Informational Text	closeread.pdf
Page 232	Scaffolding Conference Form	scaffolding.pdf scaffolding.docx
Page 233	Six Kinds of Context Clues	context.pdf
Pages 234–235	5 Ws Organizer for Summarizing	5worganizer.pdf 5worganizer.docx
Pages 236-237	Informational Text Features	informtext.pdf
Page 238	Informational Text Structures and Text Meanings	textmean.pdf
Page 239	Reteaching Lesson Form	reteaching.pdf reteaching.docx
Pages 240–241	Close Reading Guidelines for Fiction	closeguide.pdf
Pages 242–245	Ten Tips for Reading Fiction That Work!	readfiction.pdf
Pages 246–247	Retelling Checklist for Narrative Texts	retellcheck.pdf retellcheck.docx
Page 248	Composing a Theme	composing.pdf
Pages 249–250	Literary Elements and Text Meaning	literary.pdf
Page 251	Personal Pronouns and Point of View	personalpro.pdf
Page 252	Questions That Help Discussions	questiondisc.pdf
Page 253	Activate Prior Knowledge and Set Purposes for Reading	activate.pdf
Page 254	Metacognitive Writing	metacognitive.pdf metacognitive.docx

Appendix E

Contents of the Digital Resource CD *(cont.)*

Page Number	Title	Filename
Page 255	Predictions	predictions.pdf predictions.docx
Page 256	Vocabulary: Context Clues	vocabulary.pdf vocabulary.docx
Page 257	Four Words	fourwords.pdf fourwords.docx
Page 258	Emotions	emotions.pdf emotions.docx
Page 259	Evaluate a Character or Person	evaluate.pdf evaluate.docx
Page 260	Making Inferences: Literature (Fiction)	inferenceslit.pdf inferenceslit.docx
Page 261	Making Inferences: Informational Texts	inferencesinform.pdf inferencesinform.docx
Page 262	Argument Paragraph Rubric	argument.pdf
Page 263	Explanatory Paragraph Rubric	explanatory.pdf
Page 264	Writing a Plan	plan.pdf plan.docx
Page 265	Checklist for Evaluating Reading Stamina	readstamina.pdf readstamina.docx

Appendix E

#51513—The Reading Intervention Toolkit

© *Shell Education*

Notes

Notes

Notes

Notes